The Four Zoas

by William Blake

The Four Zoas
by William Blake

*A Photographic Facsimile
of the Manuscript with
Commentary on the
Illuminations*

CETTINA TRAMONTANO MAGNO
DAVID V. ERDMAN

*LEWISBURG: BUCKNELL UNIVERSITY PRESS
LONDON AND TORONTO:
ASSOCIATED UNIVERSITY PRESSES*

Associated University Presses
440 Forsgate Drive
Cranbury, NJ 08512

Associated University Presses
25 Sicilian Avenue
London WC1A 2QH, England

Associated University Presses
2133 Royal Windsor Drive
Unit 1
Mississauga, Ontario
Canada L5J 1K5

Library of Congress Cataloging-in-Publication Data

Blake, William, 1757–1827.
  The Four zoas by William Blake.

  Bibliography: p.
  Includes indexes.
  1. Blake, William, 1757–1827—Manuscripts—
Facsimiles. 2. Manuscripts, English—Facsimiles.
3. Illumination of books and manuscripts, English.
I. Magno, Cettina Tramontano, 1924–
II. Erdman, David V. III. Title. IV. Title: 4 zoas by
William Blake. V. Title: Four zoas. VI. Title: 4 zoas.
PR4144.F68   1987   821'.7   84-45891
ISBN 0-8387-5083-4 (alk. paper)

Printed in the United States of America

Contents

Acknowledgments

FOR ASSISTANCE RANGING FROM PARTICULAR FAVORS TO general encouragement we are grateful to Martin Bailey, John Beer, David Bindman, Mark Bracher, Martin Butlin, Irene Chayes, Elio Chinol, Aileen Cloonan, Michael Crump, Jackie DiSalvo, Landon E. Dowdey, Morris Eaves, Martha Winburn England, Heidi and Wendy Erdman, Robert N. Essick, Claudio Gorlier, George Goyder, John and Mary Lynn Grant, Jean Howard Hagstrum, Robert Halsband, the late Sir Geoffrey Keynes, Agostino Lombardo, Marilan Lund, Giorgio Melchoiri, Karen Malhallen, William J. McClung, E. B. Murray, Sergio Perosa, Frank Prasil, the late Mario Praz, George and Susan Quasha, Edward J. Rose, Silvano Sabatini, Frank Scricco, Catherine F. Smith, Mark T. Smith, John Sutherland, Irene Tayler, Michael Tolley, Janet Warner, Rose Zimbardo, and Marilyn Zucker.

We are grateful to the staff of the Manuscript Room and Photograph Services of the British Library, and to Ian Willison and Hugh Cobbe, for enabling us to base this work on infrared and color photographs of the manuscript; to Philip Pulsiano and Salvatore Montano and Charles Webber for help with tracing and drawing and photography to recover hidden details in the designs; and to Julien and Thomas Yoseloff and Katharine Turok of Associated University Presses for rising to a difficult occasion.

Cettina Tramontano Magno wishes particularly to thank the helping friends she has found during her long stays at Stony Brook: the staff of the Library and English Department, especially Richard Levine and David Sheehan and their wives Felice and Lynda. Also Lord Lyndsay Alexander and his wife Lady Maud for their hospitality in London and assistance in her research at the British Library. For his loving and material assistance, she recalls with gratitude the memory of her dear father.

For sustaining comfort in the corporeal and mental warfare, David Erdman wishes to thank his wife Virginia.

Introduction

Introduction

THE MANUSCRIPT

WILLIAM BLAKE IN 1796 OR 1797 BEGAN THIS "DREAM OF NINE Nights" with the idea of producing an elegantly inscribed manuscript poem illuminated with large and small designs accompanying the text and separating the "Nights" or cantos. He had been preparing a vast series of 537 watercolor drawings to illuminate and surround the text of Edward Young's *Night Thoughts on Life, Death, and Immortality,* and had engraved 43 of these designs for publication in a volume presenting the first four of Young's nine "Nights" as a unit. This was printed in 1797 by a commercial firm; if it succeeded there would be six score or so further engravings to make for the three volumes that should follow. Blake obviously worked with tremendous rapidity of invention and execution to produce these hundreds of graphic interpretations of another poet's visions. But the engraving was laborious, and Blake's idea of "Rest before Labour" (the caption of his frontispiece) was to let his imagination dream and his fingers write and draw the web of his own visions on the sheets that make up the present manuscript. Meanwhile, he happily accepted a commission from his good friends John and Ann Flaxman to make a similar series of 116 watercolor designs—not to be engraved—for the poems of Thomas Gray. And he ultimately finished all of his Young watercolors to make a fine two-volume set of illuminations for the publisher's own library.

We do not know whether he had a purchaser in mind when he began to make the illuminated manuscript which he first called "Vala." Its title page is confidently dated "1797," but it did not find a patron until about 25 years later when the aging Blake gave it to his younger artist friend and patron John Linnell, among whose family papers the unbound leaves remained until examined and sorted by its first editors, E. J. Ellis, and W. B. Yeats in 1891 (who published a hasty transcription in 1893).[1]

The manuscript of the first Nights shows that Blake's basic plan was to inscribe his text in black ink in a flourishing "copperplate" hand (guided by ruled pencil lines, to be erased) on sheets of fine cream-colored Whatman paper about 16 × 12 inches, leaving ample margins for designs which were first sketched in pencil to be completed in ink with color washes, perhaps to be finished in fully pigmented colors as were Blake's Young and Gray projects.[2] Pages 3, 4, 5, and 7 are tinted in two to five colors each (blue, gray, brown, pink, black); page 15 in brown; 31 in gray and brown; 128 in black, brown, and pinkish purple); page 6 is painted clearly and carefully; page 22 has a touch of pink, page 131 a dark red streak. Pages 25, 31, and 37 are sketched in black chalk only. Most of the drawings are in pencil or pencil and chalk, several with chalk shading.

Blake evidently would have finished the whole work (and replaced the proofs with drawings) if he had found a customer. Failing that, he kept the leaves at hand, working over the text year after year, with increasing doubt that a perfected volume would ever be called for. The first revisions he made were done with care. He would erase words or lines and inscribe the revisions in as neat an engraver's hand as could be managed on the rough surface of erased paper. As he continued to revise, he subsided to a plain, workaday handwriting (sometimes in ink, sometimes in pencil). And finally, as the margins filled up—some of the original pages have their margins filled with many stages of revision and addition—he resorted to making fair copies on fresh sheets, but no longer attempting a fine copperplate hand, and often continuing to revise, both text and drawings. Sometimes Blake rearranged pages or marked parts of the text for transfer to other pages. Sometimes these rearrangements separated pictures from the text they had inspired or been inspired by. As time passed with no customer in sight, Blake made revisions with less and less attention to any finished appearance: a final draft of the manuscript would have had to be a fresh labor; this manuscript subsided into the category of preparatory sketches. At this stage of the game the drawings of bodies, for example, could be tried out in various positions, given more arms or legs than a Hindoo deity. And at this stage the easiest way to borrow designs from the published *Night Thoughts* (and to save paper) was to coopt the proofs that survived from that labor. Jesus, for example, was a prominent figure in Young's poem; when he became prominent in Blake's (in the Eighth Night, by necessity of the plot) there were several portrayals of Jesus among the proofs, including variant states of Blake's original plates. And there was space for the "Vala" text within the engraved box and on the entire verso. (If Blake had incorporated these proofs merely, as some have supposed, for the saving of paper, wouldn't his impulse have been to use the completely clear versos first before spilling over the design area?)

During all this physical cluttering of the manuscript, however, Blake's creative purpose and the power of his poetry were boldly sustained, and he brought the whole work to a triumphant conclusion on what is now page 139, writing, as his finish line: "End of the Dream".

Because many of the drawings are phallic or vaginal—the Dream constituting a deep probing of the buried primitive life of the psyche—there are erasures and scribblings in some areas that should be attributed not to the artist but to the exigencies of the manuscript's survival in a Victorian household. The work has also had to survive the predisposition of critics and scholars, until recent years, to dismiss the whole poem as a fragment, an unfinished work, or a failure. It should be recognized, rather, that at several stages the work was evidently finished, while at no stage was the parental artist ever done with it. At one stage Blake began a few changes of names to fit his later epic, *Jerusalem* (completed and etched and published by

1820); perhaps his giving up that impulse marks his putting down his tools. His giving the manuscript to Linnell perhaps saved it from further harm; even so, when it left Blake's workshop it contained several unresolved complications: revisions begun and canceled; revisions meant to be canceled but left as alternate readings; additions not clearly marked for insertion. Even the order of the early Nights was unsettled, Blake having erased "Second" from the chapter title "Vala, Night the Second" without deciding among alternate orderings which would make it First or Third. And he made two chapter titles for "Night the Seventh," with some, but insufficient, instructions in the margins to indicate which pages should stay in a final draft and which pages (if any: we agree that he needed them all) should be dropped.

In the Linnell family library over seventy years, the leaves got loose from whatever threads, visible or invisible, Blake had bound them with. (Some have stabholes indicating their having been tied together at some time; many have no holes.)[3] In 1889, Ellis and Yeats, wishing to include the text and some illustrations in their edition of Blake's *Works* (1893), were allowed to spend several evenings putting the leaves in order. There were enough clues in the manuscript to enable them to get most of the sequences right, though the two Nights the Seventh troubled them (and all editors since) and some leaves were put at the back as puzzles: the leaf now paginated 15–16 and the leaf paginated 111–12. By 1904 Ellis had found the answer to the first of these, but they remained listed in the Keynes *Bibliography* of 1921 as "additional leaves and fragments," though Sloss and Wallis got them located properly in their edition of 1926 (while leaving others out of place). Meanwhile the manuscript had reached the British Museum (now Library) in 1918, bearing the foliation that numbers those two leaves "69" and "79." When one of these was located as folio 8 a firm hand wrote in ink on the title page: "69 leaves." Soon after, the other (70) was located at 56, and a firm but more accurate hand wrote a new foliation running to "70 leaves."[4]

Our point is that the proper sequence is not a given but has been arrived at by editorial consideration. We concur with the judgments of Keynes and Bentley as to the sequence needed for textual continuity—except for the business of what have been called by editorial convention Night VIIA and Night VIIB. These we have conflated into one Night VII (going back to Ellis in this—to his argument rather than to his actual sequencing) after an extensive mail and telephone symposium with other scholars working with the *VALA* manuscript. (The results were published in the Fall 1978 issue of *Blake/An Illustrated Quarterly:* see articles by Andrew Lincoln, John Kilgore, Mark Lefebvre, and David Erdman listed in the Bibliography below.) The same sequence was arrived at independently by Landon Dowdey for his modernized transcript published in 1983. And guided by this textual sequence we have arranged the leaves of Night the Seventh to make the pictorial sequence correspond. The pictorial suitability of this sequence seems clearly to justify this choice.

(See the table of numeral equivalents, below.)

THE ILLUMINATIONS

From the provisional nature of the manuscript, once Blake had given up making each page a perfected graphic unit, we can understand why the designs are often the least finished part of the work and why some drawings even on the perfectly inscribed pages of the first Night were tampered with. Blake's giving the Vala figure on page 3 an alternative left leg, lifted toward a marginal gloss, was probably, like the gloss, an afterthought, though we cannot be certain about either point. On most pages, however, both text and design tend to exfoliate with variant or supplementary details, frequently alternative body positions. On other pages Blake has given himself only the sketchiest memoranda to remind himself of his intended ultimate designs.

It is this unfinished and multiple alternative quality of many of the drawings that necessitates our attending closely to nuances of sketching and to contextual and textual hints to deduce the author/artist's intent. We have proceeded on the principle that the strongest evidence to resolve such uncertainties may be available in the text. While the drawings are seldom merely illustrations, direct depictions of actions and details given in the text, they often contain detectable allusions to it while telling a separate story of their own.

Blake's Use of Night Thoughts *Proofs*

Blake's incorporation of proof sheets of his engraved designs for Young's *Night Thoughts,* writing his text in the empty box where Young's was to have been, and on the blank verso where he made margin room for fresh designs for his own night thoughts, presents a difficulty of a different kind—and further evidence of intent. It is a fairly common opinion—it was ours before we trained our eyes—that (as Bentley says: *BB* 457) "In general, the *Night Thoughts* engravings seem to have had little effect upon the text and designs of *Vala.*" Actually the effect is usually noticeable, sometimes striking. Beginning with page 43, *Night Thought* proofs are used steadily to the end (with one exception that proves the rule)[5] and (except for page 140) the engraved side is always a recto page—facing a verso upon which Blake again and again makes a drawing that echoes or opposes the facing (engraved) design, speaking a pictorial counterpoint. If necessity perchance dictated the use of proof sheets, it was more than mere ingenuity that made a virtue of their adaptability to Blake's poem—one of the manifest purposes of which was to rehearse and reinterpret the themes and visions of Edward Young, a process Blake had begun when he created, not without solemn ironies, his own designs to embrace *Night Thoughts.* Often the design drawn on the page facing an engraved scene mirrors or balances it. A body lying with slightly raised head is matched by a different body in the same position. A spear or dart in the engraving is matched by some weapon in the adjacent drawing. And the text too has its reverberations both ways.

Martin Butlin (*Text,* 275) suggests that some of the full-page drawings may have been made when Blake was drafting designs for the *Night Thoughts,* but notes that "Blake seems in many cases to have chosen the *Night Thoughts* proofs for their particular appropriateness to the text to be written on them." Obviously Blake's final illuminated manuscript would have required fresh drawings to replace these proofs in the process of becoming (as the early surviving pages indicate) a self-sufficient illuminated book, its designs highly finished (in Blake's sense) and more or less free of these preliminary sketches and engraved clues. These hypothetical assumptions are necessitated by the actual condition of the manuscript. But the particulars of our commentary will take us beyond the shelter of such generalized observations. And the reader will understand that, from the nature of the document we have examined and photographed and debated over (between ourselves and with other scholars), the firmness of our descriptions and interpretations of the "ornaments" of this manuscript, which range from simple illustration to hyperbolic illumination, must fluctuate over a wide field of probability as we move forward through the book, sometimes finding narrative sequences, picture stories, and at other times single emblematic designs.

The text itself has been our constant study; yet for the present enterprise we must stress that we cannot begin to do justice to the poem's integrity, its own completeness—so much of which is *not* represented in the designs; so much of which is entangled in its own problems of interpretation and uncompleted revisions (and undeciphered cancelations).

Of modern "readings" of the text of this epic, of widely varying emphases but increasing mutual reinforcement, there is no end, and can be none: witness the growing bibliography listed below. Our commentary frequently discusses the poetry but primarily those passages or motifs that have a definable relation to particular drawings.

Arrangement and Numbering of Manuscript Pages

In the present facsimile we arrange the leaves in the sequence now recognized as least departing from the textual sequences called for by Blake's own marks of instruction (where transpositions are indicated). Blake himself did not number the pages or leaves (except for a few in the first Night). In the twentieth century the leaves were first given folio numbers, in the top right corners—first from 1 to 68, leaving out two, finally from 1 to 70. Modern usage has been to cite these as 140 *pages* (with supplementary fragments now paginated 141—45).

We supply new page numbers, representing the more defensible sequence, but give the old numbers, when they differ, within brackets—since it is the old numbers that modern texts use, even when modernizing the arrangement.[6]

Twenty-four pages (twelve leaves) are thus rearranged:

19 [21]	87 [95]	95 [87]	105 [113]	109 [105]	113 [109]
20 [22]	88 [96]	96 [88]	106 [114]	110 [106]	114 [110]
21 [19]	89 [97]	97 [89]	107 [115]	111 [107]	115 [111]
22 [20]	90 [98]	98 [90]	108 [116]	112 [108]	116 [112]

The textual sequence for Night the Seventh in the new arrangement but old numbering (as in the Erdman *Complete Poetry & Prose* of 1982) is this: pages 77 to 85:22; 95:15–33; 96 to 98; 91 to 94; 95:1–14; 85:23–47; 86 to 90.

Numerals and Inscriptions Not by Blake

Folio numbers in the top right corners, running from 1 to 68, then corrected to 1 to 70, represent in their first series the ordering of the loose manuscript leaves achieved by Edwin J. Ellis and W. B. Yeats when they were preparing their 1893 edition of *The Works of William Blake*. Page 105, marked "Extra. 1." by Ellis, soon found its place, but the leaves containing pages 15–16 and 111–12 (as bound; now 115–16) were kept at the end as "69" and "70" and remained in the Keynes *Bibliography* (1921) as "additional leaves and fragments."

Ellis wrote two dated notes at the top of leaf "69" (page 25), the first stating the problem— "(a separate sheet: It cannot be placed as its sequel is missing.)—E. J. E.—1891"—the second, thirteen years later, giving the answer: "Perhaps it is all an insertion designed to preceed 'Enion blind & age bent wept upon the desolate wind,—[line] 373,—in the 1st printed numbering [now line 17:1].—Suggestion of Mr. F. G. Fleay 1904". Ellis's new edition was already in the press, though dated 1906, and failed to absorb this change.

Thus leaf "69" became leaf 8, and leaf "70" was silently inserted as leaf 56 (pp 111–12 as bound). The folio numbers were then advanced by one after leaf 8 and by two after leaf 56. The inscription "69 leaves" on the title page must have been made after the first discovery, the "70 leaves" on page 139 after the second. (Three scraps of draft material were numbered 71–73.) The editorial realization that leaves 10 and 11 were in the wrong order was not reached before the binding.

Other phenomena suggesting the disarray of manuscript leaves that confronted Ellis and his helpers include efforts to number the leaves, or "sheets," of Nights V and VI. The five leaves that constitute Night V are identified thus: "Kat. Ellis) Sht 3." (on p. 61); "(Kat. Ellis Sht. 4" (on p. 63); "Kat Ellis 5th Sheet" (p. 65). (Our conjecture is that someone in the Ellis family, a Kathleen or Katherine, was helping out.) For Night VI, "Kat" drops out, but someone signing with the initials "W. V." comes forward, correctly numbering sheets 2 to 7 of Night VI.

It seems to have been Ellis himself, however, who marked up the pages of Night V in ruthless ink. We can see from his signed notes on p. 15 that he wrote a "g" like an undotted "j" (twice in three g's on that page, the third somewhat more normal). In the chapter title of "Night The Fifth" on p. 57, Blake's erased "book" (under "Night") prompted Ellis to write, in bold ink on Blake's sky, "book 5 / Paje 1." Worse, on p. 59 he inked "Book 5 paje 3" right across Christ's halo (the page has no margin). On p. 61 someone has erased his "Paje 5" and written "Night V. page 5." and, on p 63, "Night 5" above Ellis's "Paje. 7." Ellis triumphs on p. 65, the "End of the Fifth Night" (where, again, he could see that Blake had written "Book" then "Night"), by inscribing: "Book 5 Paje 9" (over "8").

The particular difficulties presented by the discontinuities of some of the leaves now identified as Night VII are manifest in Ellis's notes on the pages we number 85–86, 95–98 which he fitted into a sequence numbered (and bound) as 86–90. He first considerd "5th N" for p. 98 and "?5th N. p. 3" for p. 95; at some point, in despair, he penciled "?what night?" atop p. 89. Then he considerd the group as perhaps a "fragment" (they did not seem to fit anywhere) of Night VII, and he marked pages 98, 85, and 86, respectively, "?fragment of 7th (1)", "?7th (2)", and "?7th (3), treating two versos as rectos. Ultimately, reversing his 1,2,3 order, the leaves were foliated 43–49 and bound as pages 86–90 (there is no text on 88–89); a position that was not changed until the new Doubleday edition.

After the Ellis edition was in print, or at least in page proof, someone made many pencil notes (usually within boxes or brackets and usually in the margins) collating the text with pages in the early edition, e.g.: "Ellis / p. 8" or "p. 21 / Ellis". (These are visible on pages 5–7, 9, 10, 24–35—the first two Nights—then: 63, 69, 70, 78–85, 87, 90, 92, 94, 98, 117, 118, 120, 122–24, 126, 128–30, 132, 134–39.) The boxed note on p 63, "Ellis p / 54", is apparently doubled-checked for the second edition, by "W. V." who puts those initials before the box and "Same / X" after it.[7] The note on p. 70 is heavy and full: "(Page 60 of Ellis / Vol III Night VI)."

On p. 123, above Blake's "howlings began", Ellis penciled the same words, displaying both his kinds of "g". On p. 23 he guessed correctly "Second?" at the beginning of Night II; the query "?for night 2" on p. 16 is also his. Ellis's hand appears once again on the p. 143 fragment: "(for 1st nijht—varied)".

The Nature of This Photographic Facsimile

The leaves of Blake's manuscript vary in size and shape, but most of them fall into a pattern of about 12¾ × 16½ inches (or 32.88 x 41.91 centimeters). Photographs we have seen in full size show less detail in faint places than do the 8 x 10 inch prints, many in infrared photography, obtained for this work, and we were advised to print from them without enlargement, to retain their sharpness of detail. The staff of the British Library and Museum have helpfully replaced weak photographs with stronger ones and have supplied detail pho-

tographs of some of the puzzling areas.

Where significant lines remain unclear, we have made tracings and sometimes partly conjectural redrawings of lines, to bring out particulars almost lost to the camera. We are grateful to the curators and scholars who from time to time have assisted us in checking these details against the original drawings.

The availability of G. E. Bentley, Jr.'s Oxford Press edition of 1963 is sometimes helpful, since it faithfully reproduces the full size of the pages of the original, but often almost nothing appears of the details which the naked eye, or good photography, can recover.

NOTES

[1] See Erdman on "The Editorial Problem," item 9 in the 1978 *BIQ*, listed below in "Bibliography."

[2] For examples of this coloring, see the color plates at the back of this book.

[3] See Bentley (1963 and 1977) but also Erdman (1968)—listed below in Bibliography.

[4] On the end leaf of the bound manuscript is written: "Examined after binding. C. M. H. 26 August 1960." Pasted onto this leaf from the earlier binding is a slip reading "ii + 73 folios December 1918 by E. J. E. [Ellis]" endorsed "Examined by E. S." The 73 would include the three additional fragments containing pages 141–43 given in our Appendix.

[5] Pages 87–90 (old system: 95–98) consist of two halves of a print of Blake's early engraving, "Edward and Elenor," firmly kept *out* of the poem: the picture cut in such a way as to remove its center, the *Vala* text inscribed on the backs only and in a sequence that makes the engraved halves face only each other.

[6] See *Blake Quarterly* items for 1978, listed in Bibliography, below.

[7] On p. 69 the note after "[Sheet 2" seems to read: "W. V. Same in Ellis".

BIBLIOGRAPHY

Few scholars have discussed these designs with any thoroughness. In the list that follows we believe we have included all the published modern criticism that has assisted our labors—and brightened our dreams.

1893

Ellis, Edwin J. & William Butler Yeats. *The Works of William Blake . . . With Lithographs of the Illustrated 'Prophetic Books', and a Memoir and Interpretation.*

The first transcript of the text, very inaccurate—as are most of the lithographs, some being just freehand sketches.

1921

Keynes, Geoffrey. *A Bibliography of William Blake.* Grolier Club, N.Y.

1924

Damon, S. Foster. *William Blake: His Philosophy and Symbols*. Boston.

1925

Keynes, Geoffrey, ed. *Writings of William Blake* In Three Volumes.
   The first reliable transcript.

1926

Sloss, D. J. and J. P. R. Wallis. *The Prophetic Writings.* Independent transcript.

1946

Schorer, Mark. *William Blake: The Politics of Vision.* Henry Holt & Co.

1947

Frye, Northrop. *Fearful Symmetry: A Study of William Blake.* Princeton University Press. (Current reprint, 1969.)

1949

Blackstone, Bernard. *English Blake.* Cambridge University Press.

1954

Erdman, David V. *Blake: Prophet Against Empire.* Princeton University Press. (third edn. 1977).

1956

Bentley, Gerald E., Jr. "The Date of Blake's *Vala* or *The Four Zoas.*" *Modern Language Notes* 71:487–91.

Margoliouth, H. M. *"Vala: Blake's Numbered Text.* Clarendon Press.

1958

Bentley, Gerald E., Jr. "The Failure of Blake's *Four Zoas.*" *Texas Studies in English* 37:102–13.

Miner, Paul. "William Blake: Two Notes on Sources. (1) Blake's Use of Gray's 'Fatal Sisters' (2) A Source for Blake's Enion?" *Bulletin of The New York Public Library* 62:203–7.

1961

Bloom, Harold. *The Visionary Company.* Doubleday & Co.

1962

Raine, Kathleen. *Blake and Tradition.* Princeton University Press.

1963

Bentley, Gerald F., Jr. (ed.) *William Blake, 'Vala or The Four Zoas':* A Facsimile of the Manuscript, A Transcript of the Poem, and a Study of Its Growth and Significance. Clarendon Press, Oxford. (For review by Erdman, see 1968, below.)

Bloom, Harold. *Blake's Apocalypse: A Study in Poetic Argument.* Doubleday & Company.

1964

Butlin, Martin. "Blake's 'Vala, or the Four Zoas' and a new Water-colour in the Tate Gallery." *Burlington Magazine* 106:381–2

Bentley, G. E., Jr. and Martin K. Nurmi. *A Blake Bibliography: Annotated Lists of Works, Studies, and Blakeana.* University of Minnesota Press.

1965

Damon, S. Foster. *A Blake Dictionary: The Ideas and Symbols of William Blake.* Brown University Press.

Erdman, David V., ed., with commentary by Harold Bloom *The Poetry and Prose of William Blake.* Doubleday & Company. (Fourth printing, with revisions, 1970; complete revision 1982.) Commentary by Bloom on *The Four Zoas,* pp. 948–67.

Harper, George Mills. "Apocalyptic Vision and Pastoral Dream in Blake's *Four Zoas.*" *South Atlantic Quarterly* 64:110–24.

1967

Beer, John. *Blake's Humanism.* Manchester University Press.

Stevenson, W. H. "Two Problems in *The Four Zoas.*" *Blake Newsletter* 1 iii:13–16. Continued in iv:6–8

1968

Erdman, David V. "The Binding (et cetera) of *Vala.*" *Library* 19:112–29 (vol. dated 1964, published 1968). Review of the Bentley 1963 facsimile.

1969

Beer, John. *Blake's Visionary Universe.* Manchester and New York.

Nanavutty, Piloo. *"Materia Prima* in a Page of Blake's

Vala." Pp. 293–302, 477–78 in Rosenfeld, Alvin H., ed. *William Blake:* Essays for S. Foster Damon. Brown University Press.

1970

McNeil, Helen T. "The Formal Art of *The Four Zoas.*" Pp. 373–90 in Erdman and Grant, eds. *Blake's Visionary Forms Dramatic.* Princeton University Press.

Paley, Morton D. *Energy and Imagination: A Study of the Development of Blake's Thought.* Clarendon Press.

Rose, Edward J. "'Forms Eternal Exist For–ever': The Covenant of the Harvest in Blake's Prophetic Poems." Pp. 443–62 in Erdman and Grant, eds. *Blake's Visionary Forms Dramatic.* Princeton University Press.

1971

Stevenson, W. H., ed., text by David V. Erdman. *The Poems of William Blake.* Longman. Annotated; punctuation modernized for the Longman series.

1972

Evans, James C. "The Apocalypse as Contrary Vision: Prolegomena to an Analogical Reading of *The Four Zoas.*" *Texas Studies in Literature and Language* 14:313–28.

Fletcher, Ian. "The Ellis-Yeats-Blake Manuscript Cluster." *Book Collector* 21:72-94.

Stevenson, Warren. *Divine Analogy: A Study of the Creation Motif in Blake and Coleridge.* Institut für Englische Sprache und Literatur.

1973

Curran, Stuart, and Joseph Anthony Wittreich, Jr. (eds.) *Blake's Sublime Allegory:* Essays on *The Four Zoas, Milton, Jerusalem.* University of Wisconsin Press.
  (1) Jerome J. McGann "The Aim of Blake's Prophecies and the Uses of Blake Criticism" 3–22.
  (2) Joseph Anthony Wittreich, Jr. "Opening the Seals: Blake's Epics and the Milton Tradition" 23–58.
  (3) Ronald L. Grimes "Time and Space in Blake's Major Prophecies" 59–82.
  (4) Edward J. Rose "Los, Pilgrim of Eternity" 83–100.
  (5) Jean H. Hagstrum "Babylon Revisited, or the Story of Luvah and Vala" 101–18.
  (6) Morton D. Paley "The Figure of the Garment in *The Four Zoas, Milton,* and *Jerusalem*" 119–40.
  (7) John E. Grant "visions in *Vala:* A Consideration of Some Pictures in the Manuscript" 141–202.
  (8) Mary Lynn Johnson and Brian Wilkie "On Reading *The Four Zoas:* Inscape and Analogy" 203–32.
Essays 5–8 deal particularly with *The Four Zoas;* Grant's (7) is the first intensive consideration of the designs.

Tayler, Irene. "The Woman Scaly." *Bulletin of the Midwest Modern Language Association* 6:74–87. (Reprinted in the Norton Critical Edition: see Johnson and Grant in 1978 list below.)

Wagenknecht, David. *Blake's Night: William Blake and the Idea of Pastoral.* Belknap Press of Harvard University Press.

1974

Mellor, Anne Kostelanetz. *Blake's Human Form Divine.* University of California Press.

1975

Di Salvo, Jackie. "Blake Encountering Milton: Politics and the Family in *Paradise Lost* and *The Four Zoas.*" Pp. 143–84 in *Milton and the Line of Vision,* ed. Joseph A. Wittreich, Jr. 1975.

Kaplan, Nancy A. "William Blake's *The Four Zoas:* The Rhetoric of Vision" *DAI* 36:2846–7A. Ph.D. diss., Cornell University. Relation of text and design.

1976

Lindsay, David. "The Resurrection of Man: A Short Commentary on Night Nine of Blake's *Vala or The Four Zoas.*" *University of Cape Town Studies in English* 6:14–23.

1977

Ault, Donald. "Incommensurability and Interconnection in Blake's Anti-Newtonian Text." *Studies in Romanticism* 16:277–303.

Bentley, G. E., Jr. *Blake Books: Annotated Catalogues of William Blake's Writings . . . and Scholarly and Critical Works about Him.* Clarendon Press.

Bidney, Martin. "Urizen and the Comedy of Automatism in Blake's *The Four Zoas.*" *Philological Quarterly* 56:204–20.

Myers, Victoria. "The Dialogue as Interpretive Focus in Blake's *The Four Zoas.*" *Philological Quarterly* 56:221–39.

Schotz, Myra Glazer. "On the Frontispiece of *The Four Zoas.*" *Blake Newsletter* 10:126–7.

1978

Bentley, G. E., Jr., ed. *William Blake's Writings,* vol. II. Clarendon Press.

Blake/An Illustrated Quarterly 46 vol. 12, no. 2 (Fall 1978).
  (1) Nelson Hilton "The Sweet Science of Atmospheres in *The Four* Zoas" 80–86.
  (2) Terence Allan Hoagwood "*The Four Zoas* and 'The Philosophick Cabbala'" 87–90.
  (3) Andrew Lincoln "*The Four Zoas:* The Text of Pages 5, 6, & 7, Night the First" 91–95.
  (4) David V. Erdman ". . . New Text for Pages 5, 6, &

7, Night the First" 96–99.

(5) Mary Lynn Johnson & Brian Wilkie "The Spectrous Embrace in *The Four Zoas,* VIIa" 100–106.

(6) John Kilgore "The Order of Nights VIIa and VIIb in Blake's *The Four Zoas*" 107–14.

(7) Andrew Lincoln "The Revision of the Seventh and Eighth Nights . . . 115–33.

(8) Mark Lefebvre "A Note on the Structural Necessity of Night VIIb" 134.

(9) David V. Erdman "Night the Seventh: The Editorial Problem" 135–39.

(10) Cettina Magno *"The Four Zoas* for Italy" 140–41.

Lindsay, David W. "Prelude to Apocalypse: A Short Commentary on Night VIII of Blake's *Vala or The Four Zoas." Durham University Journal* 39 (1978): 179–85.

Wilkie, Brian, and Mary Lynn Johnson. *Blake's "Four Zoas": the Design of a Dream.* Harvard University Press.

1979

Johnson, Mary Lynn, and John E. Grant, eds. *Blake's Poetry and Designs.* Norton Critical Edition. Pp. 214–34, annotated excerpts of *The Four Zoas.*

1980

DeLuca, Vincent A. "The Lost Traveller's Dream: Blake and the Seductions of Continuity." *Ariel* 11:49–69. (Urizen's journeying, in Night VII, as a lost traveller.)

Fairchild, B. H. *Such Holy Song: Music as Idea, Form, and Image in the Poetry of William Blake.* Kent State University Press. Chapter 4 examines *The Four Zoas* as an experiment in "The Musicality of Prophecy."

Grant, John E., Edward J. Rose, Michael J. Tolley, and David V. Erdman. *William Blake's Designs for Edward Young's* Night Thoughts. 2 vols. Clarendon Press.
The "Table of Engraved Designs" (17–35) compares states of engraved plates (incl. those in *Vala*) and the watercolors.

1981

Butlin, Martin. *The Paintings and Drawings of William Blake.* (For the Paul Mellon Centre for Studies in British Art) Yale University Press. 2 vols: *Text* (i.e. catalogue) & *Plates.* A catalogue raisonné; contains brief descriptions of all the designs, in the *Text* volume, pp. 274–94.

Lincoln, Andrew. "Blake's Lower Paradise: The Pastoral Passage in *The Four Zoas,* Night the Ninth." *Bulletin of Research in the Humanities* 84:470–78.

Mann, Paul. "Editing *The Four Zoas." Pacific Coast Philology* 16 (June 1981): 49–56. Not located until on the way to press; out-dated by the present project.

Miner, Paul. "Blake and the Night Sky: Visionary Astronomy" *Bulletin of Research in the Humanities* 84:305–36.

Worrall, David. "Blake and the Night Sky: The 'Immortal Tent'." Ibid. 84:273–95.

1982

Erdman, David V., ed., with commentary by Harold Bloom. *The Complete Poetry & Prose of William Blake.* Newly revised edition. Anchor Books and University of California Press, 1982.

Essick, Robert N. A detailed review of Butlin (1981) in *Blake: An Illustrated Quarterly* 16:22–65.

1983

Ackland, Michael. "The Embattled Sexes: Blake's Debt to Wollstonecraft in *The Four Zoas." Blake: An Illustrated Quarterly* 16:172–83.

*Deen, Leonard W. *Conversing in Paradise: Poetic Genius and Identity-as-Community in Blake's Los.* University of Missouri Press.

*DiSalvo, Jackie. *War of Titans: Blake's Critique of Milton and the Politics of Religion.* University of Pittsburgh Press. Concentrates on *The Four Zoas.*

Dowdey, Landon, and Patricia Hopkins Rice, eds. *The Four Zoas: The Torments of Love and Jealousy in the Death and Judgment of Albion the Ancient Man,* by William Blake, derived from his original drawings, engravings and the manuscript dated 1797. Chicago: Swallow Press. (Text rendered in carefully punctuated prose; design details selected and highlighted from about 55 ms pages, from a few of the *Night Thoughts* plates, and from other Blake works.)

Hilton, Nelson. *Literal Imagination: Blake's Vision of Words.* University of California Press.

Lee, Judith. "Ways of Their Own.: The Emanations of Blake's *Vala, Or The Four Zoas." English Literary History* 50:131–53. Argues that Blake used Wollstonecraft's *Vindication* as a "paradigm for his portrayal of women."

*Paley, Morton D. *The Continuing City: William Blake's Jerusalem.* Clarendon Press. Frequent references to *The Four Zoas.*

*Webster, Brenda S. *Blake's Prophetic Psychology.* University of George Press. In chapter 6, *"Vala* and *The Four Zoas,"* the readings of erased drawings are quite different from ours.

1984

*Brown, James Boyd. *The History of an Illusion: The Meanings of the Four Zoas in "The Four Zoas."* Ph.D. diss., York University, Toronto, Ontario.

*DiSalvo, Jackie. *War of Titans: Blake's Critique of Milton and the Politics of Religion.* University of Pittsburgh Press. A 72-page chapter treats thoroughly and insightfully "The Politics of *Paradise Lost* and *The Four Zoas."*

*Howard, John. *Infernal Poetics: Poetic Structures in Blake's Lambeth Prophecies.* Fairleigh Dickinson University

---

*Received too late for notice in our Commentary.

Press. The concluding chapter, *"The Four Zoas:* Epic Prophecy,"* gives a succinct account of the themes and structure of the poem and its place in Blake's oeuvre.

1985

*Ault, Donald. *Narrative Unbound: Re-Visioning Blake's The Four Zoas.* Barrytown, N.Y.: Station Hill Press. Detailed, comprehensive reading of *The Four Zoas;* clearly difficult but of great value.

*Bracher, Mark. *Being Form'd: Thinking Through Blake's Milton.* Barrytown, N.Y.: Station Hill Press. Minute particulars of the metaphysical and ontological structure of a Blake "prophecy."

*Essick, Robert N. *"The Four Zoas:* Intention and Production." *BIQ* 18: 216–20. A reply to Mann (see below). Finds some of Mann's conjectures possible, none proven; yet concludes that their exploration "may contribute to a better understanding of the manuscript and the intentions it never reveals." Neither essay touches on the fact that the pages of "the text" as we have it are now bound and kept in an order that was not Blake's.

*Mann, Paul. "The Final State of *The Four Zoas.*" *BIQ* 18: 204–15, illus. Considers possible evidence that Blake went through a series of plans for the publication and hence format of the work.

*Nanavutty, Piloo. "Blake & Medieval Christian Iconography." *Aligarh Journal of English Studies* 10:49–65. Discusses several of the "monster" designs in *The Four Zoas* and their possible medieval sources; hardly reliable in its conclusions but full of suggestions of sources to be examined.

---

*Received too late for notice in our Commentary.

ABBREVIATIONS

Blake's Works

America	*America a Prophecy*
Europe	*Europe a Prophecy*
F.Z.	*Vala or The Four Zoas*
Jerusalem	*Jerusalem the Emanation of the Giant Albion*
Job	*Illustrations for the Book of Job*
Marriage	*The Marriage of Heaven and Hell*
Milton	*Milton a Poem*
NT	Blake's designs for Edward Young's *Night Thoughts;* water-color number and engraving number are cited thus: *NT* 58:18E.
Urizen	*The Book of Urizen*
VLJ	Blake's Notebook description of a Vision of the Last Judgment

Studies listed (by date) in the Bibliography; or communications

Bentley	Either *Blake Books (BB)* (1977) or *Writings* (1978)
Butlin	*Paintings and Drawings* (1981)
De Luca	Vincent A. De Luca, personal communication
Grant	John E. Grant, "Visions in Vala" (item 7 in *Blake's Sublime Allegory,* 1973); also personal communication
Hagstrum	Jean H. Hagstrum, personal communication

Commentary on the Illuminations

Commentary on the Illuminations

TITLE PAGE

Page 1

TORMENTS AND JUDGEMENT

Flanking the inscribed title there were, before erasure, two naked, springing figures—human angels: human in that they do not have the wings that angels need in order to fly, angels in that they are trumpeters and thus messengers of the good news that will awaken humanity. Each has a left leg extended and a right leg drawn up tight against the buttocks, prepared for the next spring. But their positions are reversed, and at the top the arm of one overlaps the leg of the other.

The erasure may represent Blake's deciding to eliminate all but the large angel on the right, heavily drawn, who descends blowing a trumpet, which is held in both hands and extends to the date line (as if to mark "1797" as an urgent moment of Judgment, of descent and ascent, of going forth and returning). The figure of the angel on the left is erased, or was faintly drawn, with some extra loops that indicate trial variations, at the head and above the buttocks. The circle across them was perhaps the head of a barely sketched second trumpeter, whose arms, with left elbow crooked, hold to mouth a trumpet extending to a bell in the curve of the "A."

The long left leg of the rising angel still touches the words "of Nine Nights," but a triangular-headed serpent, recoiling from the angel's presence (as it were) indicates the "Ancient Man' with bulging eyes, open jaw (and presumably darting tongue). Staying outside the angelic circle, the ser-pent has coils based on the grave, which we see opening at the bottom of the page and crowded with about a dozen figures, variously responding to the trumpet—and to the title of the poem and, we hope, to the body language of the trumpeter: the naked perfect "human form divine" to which all fallen but potential humans, in the grave and among Blake's readers, must aspire.

Individual and seasonal resurrections are mentioned soon, but not until Night the Seventh will we read that "many of the dead burst forth from the bottoms of their tombs. In male forms without female counterparts or Emanations" (85:19–19). Not until Night the Ninth will "every species. . . Flock to the trumpet muttring over the sides of the grave" (122:34–35). Thus Blake declares the necessity for his "long resounding strong heroic Verse" (3:2) and the reward it offers to those who join the nocturnal and diurnal march of this "DREAM" (which is not a dream: he scores out the word) to the very last line, announcing "The dark Religions are departed & sweet Science reigns" (139:10).

All of these waking figures in the grave, components of the psyche of Albion, the Ancient Man, but also potentially *human* individuals, look like birds in a nest but range from bird-like to nearly human, some clutching themselves, only about half of them actually looking up. The four faces directly under the trumpet are all shouting back, or crying out, but only three of these are humanoid, the fourth and loudest mouthed being a vulture or eagle. At the center and bottom of the picture a bald, apparently human figure clutches the edge of the grave with desperate fingers—and beside him a gentle horse, with ears alert to the trumpet, has one hoof over the edge. On the other side of the bald one is a lion grasping the grave's edge with both paws. (For similar lion, and eagles, see Blake's painting of *The Fall of Man*.) Above horse and lion the drawing is tentative, including what may be flames—or another pair of horse's ears—and a circle that might have become another human head.

To the left of the lion is a human head, with chin turned far up, to see the whole heavenly scene (and direct us to the whole title of the poem). At far left, beneath the serpent, is a sinister faced, heavy bodied humanoid with no neck, clenching his fists under his chin; his mouth is open for surly speech; he does not look up but (like the serpent) over upon the others.

It was not Blake but a modern editor who wrote "69 leaves" here, before discovering there were 70.[1]

[1] For a variant sketch of this design, see Butlin, plate 853A.

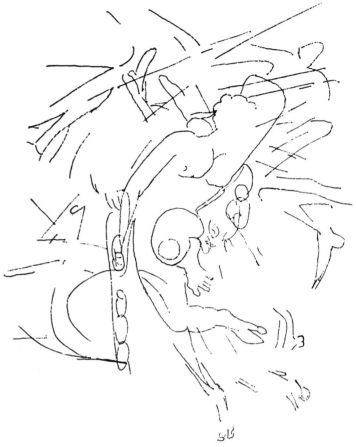

Page 2. "Rest before labour."

FRONTISPIECE

Page 2

"REST BEFORE LABOUR"

After the dynamic soaring and dramatic trumpeting of the title-page, this variation upon the motif of the naked human-angelic figure springing up or about to spring is startling in its contrasts. Neither leg is in a position to propel a springing up. We might think of the right leg as retracting after a kick, but the face and left arm seem to contradict that impression. The eyes are bandaged, though the right eye if opened might be able to see below the blindfold; the right leg was first drawn with unbent knee, then partly bent, finally half bent, and it has curiously knotted muscles (or shagged fur?) and a cloven right foot in all three versions (too carefully repeated to be a sketching error). The left foot is more goat-like and less ox-like than the cleft left foot of Jehovah in Blake's much later design, *Job* 11.

This figure is not the poet as trumpeter but the poet as workman; he must respond with labor that will create the poem, moving it from Death to Judgment. Is he something of a Satyr (identifying with "wood notes wild")? Are we to compare him to

Jove's crippled blacksmith Hephaestus? Blake implies this comparison when he defines his creative genius as Los, fallen form of the poet-blacksmith "Urthona, limping from his fall" (137:8). In the final plate of his epic *Jerusalem*, Blake pictures the laboring Urthona in a similar position, seen from behind, carrying the sun (with many radiant beams) on his shoulder like a hod of mortar.

If this is now Urthona resting, perhaps some of the lines behind him are rays of sunlight; yet most of the lines scattered across the background of this drawing suggest rather a random heap of building materials. The poet's grip on the chain (of six links, held by or holding his right hand) is ambiguous.[1] (The irregular loops beside his left chest look a bit like the chain links but more like locks of hair.)[2] When the trumpet sound reaches his ears, Los can be counted on to spring into action; yet that action must include (we are soon told: 3:9–4:4) *his* "fall into Division & his Resurrection to Unity"—his as well as the other Zoas'.

Myra Glazer Schotz (1977) sees in the contradictions between upper and lower torso the tensions of "a dreamer rising as he dreams or perhaps even dreaming that he rises." (She sees the eyes as closed—and may be right about that.) He seems on the threshold of the "demios oneiron," the numinous state in which the Greeks imagined that dreams and myths were created.

On the final page of the poem (139), under the caption "End of the Dream," Blake will show us this figure or its "counterpart" in fully naked human form, springing into wakeful life. He might have captioned this frontspiece "Beginning of the Dream"—for the poet's work is done in one moment's sleep of creative inspiration. Both his sleep and his dreaming are creative, since within his "rest" the sound and sense, the form and function, the nascent analogies of the "materia viva" moving the poem, will combine, ready for the laborsome creative purpose. We come to realize that this figure is simultaneously Los and Blake and Albion, mediating between time (and space) and eternity.

[1] By contrast, the chain-dangling naked man in Plate 3 of *America a Prophecy* is wide awake, soaring upward, holding his chains for all to see. (He too has a cloven right foot, in the preliminary sketch, Butlin 226[r], which is reversed to left in the etched plate.)

The cleft foot is human, without the goat's hoof, though it has a sort of platform like a cloven sandal. Compare Blake's drawing of the right foot of the Belvedere Apollo (Butlin 115[v]). Two cloven human feet may be seen on the two rising or swimming figures on page 66, below.

[2] Compare the four loops of hair on the top of his head.

earth, is the archetypal image of femininity which art and literature have conjured to appear to any man at the dawn of his puberty. Her improbably pliant limbs convey an idea of the various forms she will assume in the mind of man, while her palm and foot tell that her shifting will occur within the reality of earthly forms. Her open-mouthed gaze fixes in wonder—and perhaps alarm—upon the space where living substances are solidifying and taking shape between the tawny earth and the blue air and water.[2]

Vala, then, defines herself as the image of external reality (Nature) conceived by the first mental act of Primeval Man. Her conception or creation (stated in the biblical language of Genesis) will be determined by the poet's giving her identity through a name, as we see he is doing at the top of the page.

[1] The King James Version of the Greek passage at the *top* of the page reads: "For we wrestle not against flesh and blood, but against principalities, against powers, against the rulers of the darkness of this world, against spiritual wickedness in high places. Ephesians 6, verse 12.

[2] For an illustrated article on this Titian-esque position, see Paul F. Watson, "Titian and Michelangelo: The *Danae* of 1545–1546," in *Collaboration in Italian Renaissance Art*, ed. W. S. Sheard and J. T. Paoletti (Yale 1978).

Page 4

CUPID AND SERPENT

The poet's description of the mental division between the sexes—"Why art thou Terrible and yet I love thee" (21)—is represented by a drawing that associates a scaly phallic serpent with the classical symbol of Cupid with bow and arrow, a powerful stroke of candor by Blake that transforms the classical tradition.

The Greeks had represented Venus and Cupid by crystallizing the meaning of the myth in the external beauty of marble. The early Christian painters had changed the pagan myth into a frank but unreal emblem of blithe serenity; in the catacomb of Saint Domittila, in Rome, Cupid is depicted without wings, shooting flowers into a basket, while a winged Venus-Psyche gathers them in a bunch. Blake, with a different kind of innocence roused by a more energetic impulse, transforms the myth by relating the hidden and manifest actions it represents. The determined stare of Blake's Cupid reverses boldly the tradition (rather more recent than sometimes thought)[1] of the *blind* Cupid. His Cupid is shown as supported by a phallic serpent—also not blind—on which scales

NIGHT THE FIRST

Page 3

BEGINNING OF NIGHT THE FIRST

The small female figure beside the title-word "VALA" enacts the springing up which was implied in the Frontispiece and directs us into the poem.

The voluptuous figure reclining below the text in a V shape is evidently Vala herself, a Female Counterpart of the Ancient Man. Her right foot and left palm press upon the earth; one of the positions tentatively sketched for her left leg puts the heel on the ground just beyond her left hand, but another (also tentative) extends her left foot up beside the Greek text from St. John indicating the indwelling of the Savior ("And [the Word] . . . dwelt among us").[1] This naked female, with long flowing hair and firm, pointed breasts, body voluptuously curved, and hand and foot firmly in touch with the are forming and whose coils are immersed in the sea, thus identifying the source of energy that shoots his arrow into the space of earthly time.

Variant versions of the serpent's head are sketched; both give pictorial meaning to the theme, "We hid in Secret," of lines 8–10. In the version sketched beside these lines, the head has the shape of an eyed triangle, or cone, similar to an upward-pointing yantra triangle whose central dot stands for the original point of energy of the male seed. The second extends the serpent's body, with a more Satanic head (like that on page 1) with open mouth and leering eye alongside lines of text added at the top of the page. In these Tharmas, the Zoa of the sea and touch, defines his counterpart Enion as an expanding and contracting (and flower-like) vagina: "Sometimes I think thou art a flower expanding; Sometimes I think thou art fruit breaking from its bud" (41–42). The pointed, searching head recalls the phallic heads which the Gnostics used to display to initiates during the rites of the worship of Priapus. Both sketched versions are crude, but their crudeness causes the secret meaning of the pagan sexual myth to become manifest and therefore innocent and human

[1] "Twas the Greeks love of war / Turnd Love into a Boy / And Woman into a Statue of Stone / And away fled every Joy." Blake's Notebook, p. 56.

Page 5

THARMAS SINKING DOWN

In these pages the arrangement and condensing of visual and verbal images of the primeval sexual act and of the sensory perceptions that flow through the memory of Albion, the Ancient Man, make them appear before us like pictures on a scroll. After the Blakean Cupid, this winged figure appears as the optic enlargement of Tharmas, the Zoa of touch, who "groand among his Clouds, Weeping, then . . . stoopd his innocent head" and finally "sunk down into the sea" and "flowd among [the] filmy Woof" of Enion (lines 8–14). Gathering all his strength, he sinks his organs of sense in the billows of time and space. He accepts generation, the "circle of Destiny," and so becomes the agent of a new myth of creation imagined from "within" the human emotions of fear of chaos and oceanic wonder.

The pensive pose of Tharmas—his face buried in his hands and body outstretched (out of drawing, but partly visible through his transparent left wing)[1]—foreshadows the emotional potentials which are going to burst chaotically from all sexual acts of mankind—and to bring about a consequent division of sensation into the separate modalities of sight, sound, odor, touch, experienced by the solitary male or female longing for communication. The closing of "the Gate of the Tongue" by the Daughters of Beulah "in trembling fear" (43) seals this division—from which the Babel of languages will arise.

[1] Compare the seated angel in the *America* frontispiece, chained but strong with potentiality.

Page 6

THE PROUD SPECTRE OF THARMAS (TOUCH)

With many deletions and additions in the text, pages 6 and 7 record the toilsome sexual struggle of Tharmas and Enion. The male figure stretched in sleep on page 6 is identified as Tharmas by his wings (compare page 5) but now is present only in his spectral form, "drawn forth" on Enion's loom, a proud Narcissist repining in solitude before he awakes to command Enion as his slave. When awake he has been flaming up in "self-admiring raptures"; here he rests after coitus, in which he has been conscious only of his own "glory" and "wondrous beauty." With his legs tucked under and his eyes shut, he lies huddled as though determined to refuse any intellectual communication with the female. Yet our prophetic eyes must recognize in the wings of his sleeping humanity his potentiality for soaring.

Faintly sketched above Tharmas' left wing is the triangular head of a large serpent whose body curves down the left margin, originating perhaps in the top right margin—or from the suggestion of a tree there. We see the top of the head, with eyes bulging at the sides. Compare the smaller but similar shape of the serpent's head in page 1; the larger upper head in page 4. (Suggestion of Vincent De Luca.)

Page 7

"A BRIGHT WONDER . . . HALF WOMAN & HALF SPECTRE (9–10)

This contrasting picture of Enion awake illustrates the daytime life when male and female join, "mingling their bodies . . . in burning anguish" (deleted reading). (We quote the deleted wording, since the drawing seems to have been made before revisions of text; the revisions, in turn, interpret the drawing.)

From her perspective, his body takes serpent form while hers remains human. While the relationship is seen from the male point of view on page 6, it is shown on page 7 from the female: "Mingling his . . . brightness with her tender limbs . . . she soar'd . . . a bright wonder . . . Half Woman & half Serpent" (revised to "Half Spectre," with an intermediate wording of "half beast") (8–10); the male has become a half of one body, which she perceives as her own.

The image of primeval sexual mingling is an astounding example of Blake's "consummate Art" (to use a term he applied to Jesus' in "The Everlasting Gospel" 17). Each metaphor of his volcanic language is matched in pictorial terms with almost syllogistic wit. Enion is immersed in the dark waters of her sexual baptism and appears electrified by the Spectre's bestial energy. Her sinuous body turns under the pressure of energy being converted to motion. Her lifted face and anguished eyes direct us to the words "wandering on the earth" (13), "incessant thirst," and "fell despair" (deleted lines) as though interpretations of her sorrow. The serpentine energy makes her hair stand on end—or is her head in flames?—and she opens her mouth and covers her ears with her hands, overwhelmed by the bursts of the male call.

No ancient seafarer, projecting his desire into the water of a solitary sea and watching it take shape in the dazzling figure of a mermaid, can have had a finer stroke of imagination than Blake's. Insofar as we see this "monster" as a female body, half serpent rather than half fish, we attribute the traditional guile and treachery of the serpent to Eve herself, as a stage of exorcism. Visibly opposed to the sleeping but human spectre on the opposite page, Enion appears to embody the loathed part of himself which Tharmas scorns.

Paintings of "Leda and the Swan" (e.g. by Rosso Fiorentino after Michaelangelo) depict a comparable union of beast and woman as Leda leans backward and is coupled by the serpent-like swan with large opening wings like those of Tharmas.

Page 8

ENION'S CHILDREN: BRIGHT OR FIERCE?

The "fierce pain" of sexual mingling ends suddenly with the birth of "two little Infants," who will be named Los and Enitharmon. Regarding them with "pity and love," the mother supplies "strength" to them "like richest summer shining" (1–5). But then the "glories" that beam from their heads elicit in her a contrary mood of "drooping mother's pity, drooping mother's sorrow" (7). This requires at once a "Council of God" (canceled line 8).

The picture was evidently drawn before the deletion of the center of the text—a revision that jumps directly from the Joy of the "bright boy & girl" (7) (first changing "bright" to "fierce," then restoring "bright") to the Sorrow of the infants, who sulk upon their "woful" mother's breast. (The titles "Infant Joy" and "Infant Sorrow," of contrasting poems in Blake's *Songs of Innocence and of Experience*, seem appropriate here.)

Before the central deletions, the text celebrated not only the birth of children, with fields of corn to shelter them, but the birth of trees (fruiting), birds, and goat and sheep. Motherhood at the dawn of nature remains the theme. The mother's flowing, robe of flesh emerges and runs along the surface of the earth, growing like the grain beside her and the tree on which she sits and leans, as though the tree and its roots were an extension of her body, opened to bring forth the infants "upon her breast" (8)—as well as the flying creatures imagined as peeping forth when "the rough bark opens," a dawning of animal existence. The named and pictured trees merge into one Tree of Life, supported by and supporting the arched back of the mother.

Three rather diagrammatic flying things are sketched to the left of the line beginning "The rough bark opens; twittering peep forth" (del.9); two more are just visible six lines above, and others may be guessed at. The upper branches of the tree bend over the text, and the division of the upper trunk may be meant to remind us of the double tree behind Tharmas on page 6. The pictures are shaped to blend in our vision, enabling us to put all biforked, double, created things into one matrix, one conglobation beneath the Tree.

After the textual deletions, when perhaps the flying creatures and other trees were erased, the text and picture concentrate on the human scene, the male and female children sucking as if still incubating in the pitying and loving mother's all-comprehensive body. Yet they are already using their eyes; they have already "fallen" into this world and begun to sulk. And the mother's energy, flowing into them, leaves her "Weaker &

weaker . . . her bright Eyes decayd" (9–10). The picture richly expresses both the glory and the fierceness, the joy and the sorrow, of giving life.

(Compare the standing woman, in *NT* 4, with her rejoicing twins.)

Page 9

"EMBRYON PASSIONS" (25)

Hostilities intensify. Nine years have passed, and while Enion is said to be shaking off the spectral inhumanity which she drew forth from Tharmas and to be "rehumanizing from the Spectre in pangs of maternal love" (9:3; see 6:1) the process is incomplete. The children have developed "a dread repulsive power" (5); the mother has gone quite blind and feeble. She may be oppressed by her own passive acceptance of the sorrow attached to maternity by the Bible curse: but what is she doing with her outstretched hands, as she follows her ten-year olds in "stumbling" woe over "rocks & mountains" (2)? One of her elongated index fingers touches the line of the boy's garment (or of his leg, perhaps drawn in a variant position). The sadistic aspect of her sorrow is what the "ingrate" boy and girl draw from her, even as they try to drive her off "Into Non Entity . . . in dark despair" (4–6)—a phrase applicable to all parties.

The picture shows the children "drawing" the "Spectrous life" out of their mother "in pride and haughty joy" (7). "Thus Enion [gives] them all her spectrous life," which manifests itself as "embryon passions" towards each other, of "Love & Hate . . . Scorn & Jealousy" (8,25,24). The youth Los is gliding away from his mother to dance the dance of love; yet his gaze is still upon her and he seems to be measuring the spectrous fibers drawn from her. Indeed he and his sister are acting the roles of two of the Fates. Like Clotho, their mother has spun the thread of life; like Lacesis, Los is measuring it; Enitharmon, like Atropos, is about to cut it with the scissors in her left hand. In cosmic terms, Los can now "controll the times & seasons" and Enitharmon "the spaces" (27–28). But by divine dispensation the universal mother, Eno, and her "Sisters of Beulah" (spirits of "Silent Hope & Feminine repose") have opened windows for imaginative freedom in each moment of time and atom of space (14,18,11–12). The girl has "no power to weave a Veil of covering for her Sins" (2)—after all, veils and fig leaves are only the Accuser's stigmata—and while she may appear to have the

Page 9. Saviour in globe.

power to sever the thread of Life, she must realize that in the cord she is cutting is only the brutish "spectrous Life": the umbilical attachment is not forever.[1]

As for the atom of space, to show us what lives within the symbolic circumference of infinitude, Blake has drawn a globe at the top of the page (see tracing). In its center, contradicting Old Testament fatalism, Jesus is shown sitting on a curve of this earth, with his legs drawn up and his arms outstretched in a gesture that corrects the jealous tilt of Los's arms (below) and offers the radiant immortality of the creative imagination to all earthly creatures, lest Enitharmon's space and Los's time should decay. The text closes with the children "Conversing with the visions of Beulah in dark slumberous bliss" (33). The "bright" or rather "fierce prophetic boy" can, in such converse, appreciate his sister's "mild voice," which "fills all these Caverns with sweet harmony"—while "our Parents" (he has to add) "sit & mourn in their silent secret bowers" (35–37).

[1] Line 29, added in revision, may express an idea that Blake felt was implicit when he made the drawing, or it may represent the drawing's influence on the text; on the other hand, the drawing may have been made only after the revision.

Page 10

"I HEARD HIS VOICE AMONG THE BRANCHES" (16)

Enitharmon, sounding like Vala, sings a "Song of Death"; yet within it she laughs in her sleep, because "in the visions of Vala" she walks with Albion—although *he,* "the mighty Fallen One," and all his Zoas are asleep (9,15). She has "heard his voice among the branches, & among sweet flowers," scolding her for being a "terror" and darkening the "pillars" of his "halls" with death-threats to Los, "who devotes himself" to Albion (14–24).

Sketchily pictured are the pillars of Albion's halls, pillars which might be human bodies turned into forest trees. Floating dreamily in the margin at the left is (we assume) Enitharmon/Vala, with scroll-like gown, the scroll curve of which is repeated in the body of a coiled serpent directly below her. At the other side of the forest, with left elbow against the crotch of a tree, stands Los/Albion, his legs crossed indolently, his large left hand holding his head as if in pensive boredom. Why is she being a terror to him who devotes himself to her (in the Albion/Los account)? His devotion, we see, is expressed in a sadistic birch-rod held in his right hand.[1] His whole stance defies her to come closer.

[1] Or perhaps we are to see only his right hand, resting in a cleft of the tree.

Page 11

"I SEE THE SWORDS & SPEARS . . . IN THE BRAIN OF MAN" (14–15)

"I awoke in my sweet bliss," says Enitharmon ending the tale of her dream vision. "Then Los smote her upon the Earth; 'twas long eer she revivd" (2–3). In the drawing, both Los and Enitharmon appear wide awake. Her dream-garment of scroll-cloud is gone; gone, too, is the forest. He begins arming his head (we know from the next picture); their positions are reversed, seeming almost to mirror those on page 10 (as Bentley notes, 1091).

On one level (in the vision which Los shares) these two are Albion "the Fallen Man" seeking to comfort Vala, weeping for her lost Luvah (6–9). On another the man is Los, whose face can be seen through a sort of face-guard or mask (which his hands seem engaged in sewing—compare the man sewing a net in page 29—or tying over his head), predicting invisible knives and bloodshed. Making certain that the veil of rationalization and experiment *does* descend upon human nature and human action, Enitharmon's response is to match threats with threats and summon the Zoa of reason, Urizen, to "descend with horse & chariots" (21).

Page 12

THE SEXUAL DUELING

The benighted combat between Los and Enitharmon grows more violent, and it is necessary to introduce some fencing rules—"the one must have murdered the other if [Urizen] had not descended" (6)—yet the entrance of a referee at first only complicates the falseness of the positions of both combatants. And we see Urizen descend, with grinning human face but serpent body, swinging down from a tree to hover between them. Indeed, his kind of brainwork only leads male and female to adopt incompatible modes of defense.[1] Los now sheathed in protective clothing from head to foot—the shapeless mask of page 11 replaced by, or tightened into, a round helmet resembling a fencing mask—adopts a righteous fencing posture, and his left leg and Enitharmon's right are getting entangled; indeed the sword he aims at her is a winged phallic object. Her mouth and eyes indicate a vituperative response, but she bends back in defense with an appeal to the referee for pity, while her reclining body half invites another kind of attack from Los. (Behind her head, to make the sexual point, is a shadowy serpent with two coils—or two heads?) See detail figures on next page.

Four lines inserted (partly in erased pencil before what had been the last line of the page) momentarily (and prophetically?) report a quick swing by both persons away from dueling to embracing:

Los saw the wound of his blow; he saw, he
  pitied, he wept
. . . . he felt love arise in all his
Veins; he threw his arms around her loins
To heal the wound of his smiting

(40–43)

The implication is that the appeal to reason (Urizen) can work *if* it coincides with forgiveness and a healing surge of love.

[1] Vincent De Luca, who has helped us recognize the wedge-headed serpent of pages 1, 3, and 6, sees in the soaring Urizen here, "once again, the face of a serpent. It looks directly at us, triangular snout pointing down, orbed eyes near sides of head, neck sweeping to the left and up the left margin." The drawing is very difficult to make out; one photograph seems to show two small round eyes near each other like a pair of glasses (as in our tracing); but another seems instead to reveal two rather smaller eye-circles further apart. There is something appropriate, however, in Urizen's descending *as* the serpent!

Page 12. Urizen descending.

Page 13

"ELEMENTAL GODS THEIR THUNDEROUS ORGANS BLEW" (22)

A great Victory Feast of Los and Enitharmon climaxes in a Nuptial Song from "thousand thousand spirits Over the joyful Earth & Sea," with "elemental" music that creates Delicious Viands (20–23). Pictured is a Demon of the Waves (or of the Air) with firm cheeks, who has been blowing a "serpent" (a three-looped deep bass horn favored by military bands). The Demon has a broad, not-quite-human face with horn-like brows and shut eyes; the mouthpiece of the instrument rests below his right eye. His left hand holds the middle loop of the horn. (Blake gives a similarly crumpled bell to the serpent held by a sleeping horn blower in his 8th illustration for Gray's "Bard.")

Fairies and Demons in Blake are amoral creatures. (Consider the merriment of the two trumpeters in *Europe* 9 who are blowing mildews to blast the wheat.) The viands at the Feast will taste delicious if the Victory (indicated by Los's momentary repentance in 12:41) is one of Pity and Love over Hate and Jealousy.

Ominously, at this banquet Urizen sits "beside the Seat of Los" (12:30); Luvah and Vala stand aloof and alone in the "bloody sky . . . forsaken in fierce jealousy" (13:4–5) and unable to "avert their eyes" from each other to take note of Eternity, which appears "above them, as One Man infolded in Luvah's robes of blood & bearing all his afflictions" (7–9). So we are not surprised to learn that Los and Enitharmon sit "in discontent & scorn" in spite of the sunshine and heavenly music. But the Elemental blower of the serpent, and his companions with "doubling Voices & loud Horns wound round sounding," will continue "the mighty Song," whatever its hearers make of it.

(The curved lines in the left margin are something like those in page 6; too indistinct to "read.")

Page 14

"LET US PLAT A SCOURGE O SISTER CITY" (20)

In this context of male-female jealousy under Urizenic rule, the song at the Feast is heard as a universal rejection of peace, for war. The men (Brother Mountain calling to Brother Mountain) choose the refusal of Plow and Spade, the burning of Corn fields, the drinking of "the lives of Men" (8–14). The women, Sister Cities, protest the feeding of children with blood instead of milk, the nourishment of children "for the Slaughter" (21–22). Do they propose reversing the cruelty? No; they plan rather an escalation, to fight fire with fire. "Let us light fires," Blake began to write, then, "Let us plat a Scourge" (braid a whip; plan a desolation) (20).

In the drawing we are shown three sister heads growing out of one body, a united committee of outrage with eloquent mouths and eyes. All seem agreed on the combat demanded by the outstretched right arm with upraised palm. Above that palm, two spirits spring into action, the furthest one shaking rain from the moon (a circle which its arms encompass), the second following with arms ready for the whirlwind (see tracing). Is it too fanciful to imagine these spirits as notes arising from the bell of a trumpet, drawn behind the forearm of the commanding Sister? This does seem to be the bell of a serpent horn similar to the one on page 13, only sketched in a more crumpled form (as if Blake

Page 14. Spirits of rain and wind.

needn't explain again just how it works). Butlin supposes that the serpent shape and the three-headed woman constitute a "serpent with three female heads" and sees the rain and whirlwind spirits as simply "two small figures" that "flee" the serpent.

Page 15

"O SPIDER . . . EXALT THYSELF" (3–4)

With "the Sons of men muster[ing] together to desolate their cities" (5–6), even the light of dawn enlists for battle and is "clad in steel" (11). His "Mighty Father" (Urizen as Apollo) puts out his own light, with rage seizing "his bright Sheephook" and swinging it like a shillelagh to cut down the sun (12–13). We are shown the white-bearded, robed, and winged Father of Jealousy "reddning with rage" (12) (brownish tints are given to shadows of face and arm) and intent upon his effort: to plat a scourge, that is, to twist into a heavy rope fibres that are symbolic of the various acts of desolation that fill the War Song.

The face and the rope should remind us of the final plate (28) of *The Book of Urizen*, where this same father figure is proudly tangled in a web woven of ropes like this—a symbol, in that poem, of the "thirty cities divided . . . but bound down" (*U* 27:43–46).

In the ironic mode, however, this self-binding is what happens when, at the taunting of the Tyger and the Lion, the Spider king does "spread [his] web! Enlarge [his] bones & . . . attain a voice" (1–4).

Page 16

"THERE IS NO CITY NOR CORN-FIELD NOR ORCHARD!" (5)

The Nuptial War Song seemed to culminate at the end of page 15, with nothing but "a barren waste sunk down Conglobing in the dark confusion" (18–19). But then a momentous statement of no apparent moment was made: "Mean time Los was born, And Thou O Enitharmon! Hark, I hear the hammers of Los" (19–20). But this birth, or rebirth, of the human Imagination *at work* could make all the difference between barren wastes and thriving cities.

Page 16 is in effect a coda, in which the concluding verses of the Song repeat the depiction of chaos—within the context of the hammering,

Page 16. Saviour with feet in flames.

which in smithy imagery melts the bones of Vala and of Luvah "into wedges" (1) (no longer alone in the sky but closed in the furnace) until Luvah's impatience "no longer can endure" (8). The hammering, as an act of sex, has planted Luvah (whose infant form is Orc, whose adult form is Jesus) in the womb of Enitharmon. Finally, "Distracted Luvah" bursts forth "from the loins of Enitharmon" and the song urges Los to "Smite his fetters" with more hammering, to "mock the fiend who drew us down From heavens of joy" (8–12). But as the song ends, Urizen's influence wanes (16–18). And the drawing, mostly veiled by the text, introduces Jesus walking in the furnace, his feet in flames yet unconsumed, mocking the mockers.

There is some similarity to *Jerusalem* 62, in which an apocalyptic giant stands in a similar textual furnace. But here the Jesus of Resurrection is indicated by a kneeling and bowing winged angel in each lower corner (somewhat like the angel in the Resurrection picture of *Night Thoughts* 1). Above the text Jesus' hands extend in benediction, his head bent sadly back and his eyes looking back, the silhouette of his body visible down through the text to his flaming feet in firm motion forward, his weight on the forward foot and lifted from the other.

The small, gowned figure watching from the lower corner must be Vala; recognizing her Luvah, she moves rapidly and holds her arms over her breast. (In *Jerusalem* 62 there is also a small figure down near the flaming feet, but there it is Los, between the feet and viewing them with alarm as blocking his path either way.) The pertinent text, as Bentley notes, is from page 31, lines 9–10: "I see not Luvah as of old. I only see his feet Like pillars of fire, travelling thro' darkness & non entity."[1]

[1]Bentley (1979), cautious and lacking a strong photograph, sees the feet as unrelated to the sketch of Christ; simply "two feet walking toward the right." Butlin considers the Christ figure as erased before the inscribing of text; he does not note the flames on the feet.

Page 17

WHY FALL THE SPARROW & THE ROBIN? . . .
WHY HOWL THE LION & THE WOLF?

(3,8)

We saw Enion "blind & age-bent" on page 9, and in the same condition she begins now her great Lamentation. But the emanation pictured here is probably not Enion, for it is neither blind nor age-bent but soaring—and has three faces, though only two heads—unless we are to imagine the too-wide central head, which has two upward facing profiles sharing one eye (faces 2 and 3 in our tracing), as about to separate—or converge. The triple motif reminds us of the three-headed Sister Cities of page 14, and perhaps face 2 is meant for the large central Sister. We can imagine her open mouth chiming in with Enion's lament. Face 1, on the smaller, level head with grimly closed mouth, is not in disagreement.

The upheld arms, drawn somewhat double, terminate in a sort of basketless cluster of flowers or fruit, or flames. (Butlin sees but a single female, who "floats above the text, her hands touching her apparently very dishevelled hair.") A third pair of arms from the same shoulders, extending much too far into the margin to be human, was erased before the hands were more than sketched loops.

The furnaces of Los are hot enough to make the feet of Luvah and the hands of his Emanation Vala (perhaps) burst into flames. When will the creative hammering begin?

Page 17. Sister cities' three faces.

Page 18

"WATCHING . . . WITH LOVE & CARE" (15)

The text originally intended to conclude this Night ended with the quiet line, "This was the Lamentation of Enion round the golden Feast" (8). The drawing was evidently begun at that stage; the descending body would have just curved below the first rubric "End of The First Night," now covered by additional lines and a new rubric. At that stage Blake apparently felt that the reader would be sufficiently comforted, despite the lamentation, if he depicted the Eternal Saviour descending to repeat Urizen's rescue operation with a difference. Later Blake decided to spell it out:

> Now Man was come to the Palm tree & to
>   the Oak of Weeping,
> Which stand upon the Edge of Beulah, &
>   he sunk down
> From the supporting arms of the Eternal
>   Saviour; who disposd
> The pale limbs of his Eternal Individuality
> Upon the Rock of Ages. Watching over him
>   with Love & Care.
>
> (11–15)

Presumably the bundle of lumps and fibres in the lower right corner constitutes the pale and battered limbs of Albion, not of much use until Judgement Day.

As Bentley points out, the head of Christ has two bodies, one descending, the other kneeling upon the Rock of Ages. It is evident that the kneeling figure was drawn later, to fit the smaller space left after the addition of lines of text; but Blake's leaving the earlier image unerased enables us to see both Christ's rapidity of response and his patient watching. (Butlin sees two figures, one swooping to seize the other.)

Page 19 [21]

"SHILOH IS IN RUINS . . . ALBION . . . IS SICK" (9)

No identifiable shape can be made out of the few pencil lines and curves on this page; indeed Blake did not attempt to illuminate the long extension he added to Night the First when he inscribed this and the next three pages on two leaves made by cutting up an old pencil drawing of a large face— although he did finally make some tangentially relevant sketches on two of them.

In the early twentieth century when the loose leaves of the manuscript were being put in conjectural order by E. J. Ellis and, later, Geoffrey Keynes, these two leaves were arranged in a mistaken order for text. We have put them in the proper order in this facsimile, renumbering them [with the traditional numbers in brackets]. (The small folio numbers on the first and third of these pages, first "9, 10" and then "10, 11", were not put there by Blake.)

Page 20 [22]

"URIZEN WITH DARKNESS OVERSPREADING ALL THE ARMIES" (32)

No drawings were added when or after the text on this page was transcribed, but the slicing up of a portrait of a bearded old man may have been felt by Blake to be suitable for the acts of paternal oppression recorded in the poetry. The face and hair look something like those of Death on page 101; a much closer resemblance has been noted to "the fine pa-

Pages 20–21. Reconstruction of drawing on uncut sheet.

triarchal portrait called by Keynes *Head of Job*" (Grant, "Visions," 151) a pencil drawing dated by Keynes c. 1823 (*Drawings*, 1970, no. 74).

Before the sheet was cut, the top edge of page 21[19] was in line with the top edge of 20[22]; the face was severed just across the upper lip.[1] Why the six inches including the portrait's right cheek were cut away may be explained by Blake's fresh use of the remainder. See comment on page 21[19].

[1]See the composite tracing of the drawing that was on the sheet before it was cut into the leaves constituting pages 20–21.

Page 21 [19]

"HIS CHILDREN WANDERING OUTSIDE" (15)

The underlying drawing which Blake cut and placed sideways for manuscript paper has a statuesque quality suggesting a study of some motionless marble effigy on the tomb of a king or bishop, made when Blake was copying such effigies for the Antiquaries. The symmetry of the stonily parted hair (repeated in moustache and beard) and of cave-like nostrils and blind eye-sockets expresses such rigidity as might, when thus sliced apart and turned sideways, signify (to a Shelley) a fallen Ozymandias or to Blake the impotence of Urizen when he gave command for an orderly retreat, and "Sudden down fell they all together into an unknown Space" (20:38). Or Blake may have intended to convey the realization that all these Zoas are merely acting out ideas in The Man's head.

In his sleeping stony form, of course, the Eternal Man is only Urizen. On *his* face the marble expression illustrates the lines which, at this point, stand at the "End of The First Night":

> His inward eyes closing from the Divine
> vision & all
> His children wandering outside from his
> bosom fleeing away.
>
> (14–15)

What Blake's witty pencil does in the space offered by this fallen stone head is to cover its right eye-socket with a formless rock, treat the whole face as a forest background, and picture a dwarfish Cupid as sprung from the Man's right temple. This Cupid is mounted on a triangular or conic saddle, like the phallic head of the sea serpent which a different Cupid rides on page 4, or the head of the giant penis which is being worshipped on page

Page 21. Cupid astride.

88[96].[1] What he instantly performs is a William Tell parody with his bow and arrow. When we look, the arrow has entered the genital space of a woman (Vala?) whose hand is already in it. She has been urinating into a large, tilted taper-neck jug. (The area is heavily erased, but see Grant's account, p. 150.) And her inclined, silent face suggests willing cooperation. The sequel, on the next page, shows the nature of the arrowhead.

[1] Butlin: "an arrowhead phallus."

Page 22 [20]

"PERVERSE ROLLD THE WHEELS OF URIZEN & LUVAH"
(14)

This last addition gives a sense of continuity and hope to Night the First, as the Daughters of Beulah hide Jerusalem in the Porches of Enitharmon's bosom, brain, bowels, and loins. The very faint drawing seems to depict the result of Cupid's action: a supine female figure with uplifted breasts and a slit of a vulva, and in it the arrowhead (a pink-colored penis)[1] which can be a warning to readers of the strange Cupid's antics that are to illuminate the following Nights. (See tracing.)

Barely visible in our photograph is the woman's companion or guard (in the text Enitharmon, "the bright female terror," refuses to open her "Inner gates"—but perhaps that has not to do with the picture) (2–7). This large, grinning figure has a human head and face, turned toward the fallen woman, but his body has the shape of the three-looped serpent-horn blown by elemental demons for the Nuptial Feast. Or rather, the looping ser-

Page 22. Cupid's arrowhead planted.

pent (the first coil of which rolls against the woman's right knee) seems an extension of the fellow's arms, while we may be seeing the curves of his back that indicate a body submersed in the ocean. (Actually, above the three coils the looping line makes some further curls up under the top lines of the text.)

[1]Butlin suggests this pink image might be an infant's arm; "if an arm, this would parallel the design on plate 3 of *The Marriage of Heaven and Hell*"; a remote possibility: but there we see two arms, face, and chest, though the woman's position is similar.

NIGHT THE SECOND

Page 23

"THE BODY OF MAN" (11)

Man (Albion) weary upon "his Couch of Death" (1), invites Urizen to take possession, and what that god of "druidical mathematical proportion" can see of "the body of Man" (see Blake's *Milton* 4:27) is pale and cold and eloquent of the "horrors of death" (11). Albion's wrist is manacled, and only his head and right arm retain human shape. The very act of his "Rising upon his Couch of Death" (1)— with supplicating eyes, a nose lacking visible nostrils, and thick closed lips—is pictured as a collapsing. (The logic of abdicating to the deity of common sense is to melt humbly back into the clay.) Albion's hand thins out into vague parallel lines. His beard and body trail off into shapelessness, crumbling (or bending back?) at about where the knees would be. The sketched leg and foot, on a line with his head, seem not connected to any trunk and are perhaps close to losing form altogether.

Urizen's ideas for the shapes of bodies—"Trapeziums Rhombs Rhomboids Parallelograms" (page 33:34–45)—may be responsible for the angular redrawing of the elbow, the proto-triangles in the foot and what might be another foot at the edge of the page. The body we are shown reflects "the horrors of death," the dread of a birth inseparable from old age, decay, and loss of form; also the paradox of "Turning his Eyes outward to Self, losing the Divine Vision" (2).

Page 24

LUVAH AND VALA TREMBLING AND SHRINKING

Luvah and Vala shrink as the pyramid-builder, Urizen, commands the construction of "the Mundane Shell around the Rock of Albion" (8). Both of these human figures have lost their heads.

If we turn the page sideways, we can see a picture of Vala struggling in the twisted ropes and nets of Urizen's rationalizations. Her left leg is drawn up, her right extended, in parody perhaps or echo of the leg positions of the resting figure on page 2 ready to rise. Beside Vala's extended leg is a swirl of what may have been her gown but now functions as part of the corded net surrounding her whole body and tightening about what remains of her head.

In the left margin of the page, beside the line in which Urizen commands the building of the Mundane Shell, is depicted the torso of a female with legs apart but with neither head nor feet. At the place of her vulva there was something (much erased) resembling a keyhole—perhaps symbolizing the guilt that forbids sexual intercourse.[1]

Urizenic vision annuls the capability of the body to use its head for viewing the sublime, or for living.

[1]Butlin sees "a phallic form, perhaps a figure." The figure does have a phallic appearance; yet knees, even the right kneecap, can be made out; also the double bulge of breasts. Perhaps the "keyhole" was originally simply a vulva.

Page 25

GOLDEN COMPASSES: IRON POWER

Urizen's bands of workers, singing and shouting and constructing "anvils of gold" and "harness of silver & ivory" and "golden compasses" (24:9–13), are nevertheless all employed to "avert" the despair of the "great Work master" and, "with iron power," to "keep The evil day afar" of his loss of hegemony (25:42–44).

The impossible and perverted use of golden compasses is represented in the artist's struggle— note the muscular effort expressed in legs and body—with what must be either three pairs of compasses or one pair that won't hold still—won't stay "fixed" at one angle but must divide with three angles at once. (This might be simply three trial sketches, such as we sometimes find of heads or legs, but it would be unusual for Blake to draw all three trials with the same strong penciling and no erasure.)[1]

[1]On the compasses, see Grant, "Visions in *Vala*" (1973) pp. 152–53.

Page 26

FROM EARTHWORM TO DRAGON

Under Urizen's dominion, Vala forgets her lover—"her Luvah With whom she walkd in bliss, in times of innocence & youth"—and Luvah laments his nurturing of a love that has turned to hate. But the artist, in a progressive cartoon that can be read from the top of the page to the bottom, analyzes the sexual union which we first saw in the "half Woman, half Serpent" of page 7 into four stages of metamorphoses which combine love and hate, humanity and monstrosity, and are depicted with such sympathy and amusement that they constitute a prophecy of true progression. Compare the face of the worm-child at the top to the face of the dragon-woman at the bottom—whose coiling vigor should remind us of the children-and-serpent pictures in *The Book of Thel* and *America a Prophecy*.

Fortunately the vandaliser who erased many of the erotic drawings in this manuscript could not bring himself to obliterate anything here, except the male genitals of the figure second from the top. The first figure—appearing when Luvah "call'd forth the Earth-worm from the cold & dark obscure" (7)—depicts a "worm" in butterfly form, already in the air, an emblem of hope and humor: a droll creature with girlish, winking face, bushy hair (her arms stretched back to pat it), moon-enameled wings, pendulous breasts, and fat short thighs. Her belly looks swollen; and perhaps erasure has obscured a vulva.

The second figure, with wings changed from moth to bat, from feathered and rounded to webbed and pointed, has an erect penis (Butlin defines this as a monster "riding a small penis") which thrusts the small creature's head aside but is embraced by her/his arms where it rises (with pubic hair on both sides) above testicles that end just above her kneecaps.[1] Human calves are forming, but the feet are just narrow strips.

The third figure, with wings elongated but reduced from five "fingers" to three, shows male and female organs fused into a unity—and appears incapable of flying, walking, or swimming. Where

the female head and male genitalia were is a goose-necked vulture-beaked cipher of a head, with one blank eye and the beak inclined (futilely) toward the prominently drawn slot of its own vulva. Legs and feet have turned into scaled thighs growing together into a mermaid's body that trails off into four absurd filaments.

The final figure is a great delight and horror, from extensive and splendidly coiled tail to adult woman head: "a Dragon winged bright & poisonous" (13), richly prophetic of apocalyptic transformations to come. The great bird-bat wings match the lithe tail. Arms and hands are forming: the worm-girl had none, just sprouting arms. The bat-girl had arms without visible hands; the bird-mermaid had only wings, narrowing perhaps toward becoming arms. The complexity of sexual development since page 7 is impressive; the fanlike spread of the hands and the style of hair and profile suggest a woman ready for the drawing room.

Students of alchemy and mandala symbolism see the four figures as representing in turn the earthy, airy, watery, and fiery species: the worm as butterfly, then the bat, then the mer-figure; then, combining all these when fused "in the furnaces" (lines 1, 4), the human. Fluidity is implied in the dragon-woman and the mandala of the four components. The traditional multiple breasts of "mother" Nature are also suggested. If we read the four figures as interacting, the phallic bat is impregnating the cocoon-butterfly; the nameless mer-bird-bat explodes into the exaggeratedly female and exaggeratedly male Dragon, which, however, has no male face.

From the furnaces of affliction (or desire ungratified) Luvah can be thought to "see" what is happening to Vala's genital and nurturing organs even as she becomes a monster to his loving eyes. It would be misleading, however, to compare this vision to Freud's concept of the unconscious production of the fearful sight of a toothed and castrating vagina, for Blake's vision is not castrating. In his representation, the movement of the hair and wings, the hands fanned like all-reaching pinnae, the swollen breasts and the belly and legs assimilated to the phallic serpent tail: all express the passion of the female—to capture the male organ?—to transform it into a baby to feed.

For Vala, plunging herself into generation is a sexual act but not a fearful one. We must recognize that Blake, as we discover him in all his work and life, knew very well what he was doing—and what he was implying—as he adapted traditional emblematic and symbolic connotations to the realities of his own mental-emotional experience and vision.

[1] Nelson Hilton (1983, p. 165) sees only one figure here, "the spectre as a bat-winged genital that dominates the body."

Page 27

"BONDAGE OF THE HUMAN FORM" (18)

Under the sway of Urizen, "who was Faith & Certainty" but "is changd to Doubt" (15), Luvah and Vala feel as far apart as prisoner and jailer, he in the furnaces, she stoking them, he in bondage, she wandering—both together only in the sense that both are trapped in a vision of the human form as "bondage" (18), of generation as a "fortuitous concourse of incoherent discordant principles of Love & Hate" (12–13)—Blake's parody of the ancient belief in form as a fortuitous concourse of atoms.

In this drawing the body of man is shown as dependant on the womb of woman and destined to be generated and brought into life but with the seal of death and old age. The body of the woman appears young, sensuous, alluring, her destiny to assure the eternal continuity of the cycle described by Luvah in the text. As if balancing between love and hate, the two figures are linked by the same tissues of blood and flesh, and by speaking countenances. Their eyes diverge and meet, haunted by the question the sexes will eternally put to one another: "Is it life or death you give me?"

When we examine the translucent integument that encloses Luvah, we see, at first, that it encloses both figures. It is much less evident around Vala, whose head seems almost free. When we notice that she has no arms, or only a suggestion of a left arm, we may suspect that the integument serves her in place of arms as a means for embracing the male. Below their heads, is his body all bones, hers only flesh? Why has his skeletal right arm no finger?[1] Is its fist a cloven hoof? His left arm goes out of sight around her waist.

[1] Though lines of the veil dropping below the wrist may seem to suggest fingers.

Page 28

"SILENT . . . IN THEIR FAMILIES" (16)

The fourteen lines of text inserted in the lower margin before or after the erased drawings beside them seem to offer comment on the unhappy people in the picture. Some "Children of Man" could see visions of Luvah melted with woe and Vala faded and the Bulls of Luvah dragging the Plow (3–11),

> But many stood silent & busied in their
>   families
> And many said, "We see no Visions in the
>   darksom air."
>
>   (16–17)

The picture suggests that both the unseeing and the unseen share a common fate, "Reasoning from the loins in the unreal forms of Ulro's night" where the ambition of Urizen has placed them (2; cr. 27:17–19). The two figures most visible in the partly erased drawing can be enacting the separation of Vala and Luvah; they certainly look silent and uninspired. The one at the left, a woman with a pained look, clutches her head with her left hand and her belly with her right. She has been kneeling beside a person with long curly hair (who is identified when he reappears on page 31 as a version of Luvah whom Vala cannot see). He lies with legs apart (the left leg is drawn in two positions) and with a large pillow behind his head, and he holds something like a fan or wing—or a bird?—in his left hand. So close to lying together, these two are exhausted with woeful separation. Apart from them, in the right corner, stands a small child (almost completely erased except for its bare feet; but the feet and height identify this figure with the unerased child in the same corner in page 35). Far apart in the upper left margin is a rather clearly outlined drawing that suggests the curved back and head of a woman cradling a baby in her lap.

Ironically, all four figures appear to be simultaneously "busied in their familes" and yet individually isolated.

Page 29

GOLDEN NETS TO ENLIGHTEN THE DEEP

Darkness and light alternate in the text (pages 28–29) with the spinning and weaving of contrary atmospheres of reason and emotion (the alternative influences of Urizen and Luvah), a process which separates "the furious particles" of air and blends them "into mild currents as the water mingles with the wine"—the nerves and blood of creative life. The Lions of Urizen prepare the space, dividing the deep "with compasses" (compare page 25). When "many a net is netted" (16) the great "universal curtains" are borne by "strong wing'd Eagles" and hung abroad "on golden hooks"—that is, they are "spread out from Sun to Sun, The vehicles of light" (8–12).

Since the Eagles are said to appear "in Human forms distinct," we may recognized one of them in the naked, garlanded young man shown working on a section of the net curtain which extends vaguely up the left side of the page. One of the hooks (suns) can be seen beside the word "Begin" in the last line, and its circle is repeated in the human circle of the net-maker's knee. The twine extends from a needle held in his left hand and loops down across his left knee; he holds the net in the toes of his right foot and the fingers of his right hand. His attentive eyes and expression, the tension of his arms, his balancing from one foot to the other convey the full involvement of the human body in this mingling of the ratio (the sun) and the infinite.

Page 30

"MANY A SPIRIT CAUGHT" (1)

The making of seeds, despite accompanying music from "many a flute," involves "condensing the strong energies into little compass" (1–5). Opposite this line Blake has drawn a vague sketch of a female torso, bent towards these words. The impression conveyed is of a broken statue abandoned as a dead thing in the cellar of an archeological museum—one of the "bulbous roots, thrown up together into barns & garners" (7). But we know what kind of death is compacted into seeds and bulbs. Farmer Urizen may preside over their garnering; Luvah will know what to do in the spring.

Butlin suggests this figure may be Urizen's "Shadowy Feminine semblance" (24).

Page 31

"I SEE NOT LUVAH AS OF OLD" (8)

The huddled Vala figure clearly illustrates the reduction of human form to the shape of an egg

(compare Blake's *Milton*, plate 4). Abasing herself as "the weak remaining shadow of Vala" (16), the bride of Luvah can "only see his feet"—like pillars of fire, she says. But that was so when she was still upright and running (in the design on page 16); these words are added in the margin here, as if to "bring in" that earlier picture. She has now returned to the egg, a lump of sorrowful flesh and blood, withdrawing from all human contact. She holds her arms (or arm) in a way that will offer Cupid a gripping place for his leading strings (see pages 38, 39, 40 in Night III), but all that is internalized, now, in consequence of the worshiping of Urizen's hermaphroditic restraint and repression.

Luvah's body is quite firmly drawn in pencil, with a shadowy outline behind it to indicate his illusory shifts of form:

> Luvah in vain her lamentations heard; in
>   vain his love
> Brought him in Various forms before her;
>   still she knew him not.
>
>   (18–19)

His breasts, face, and long curly hair may be intended to suggest a hermaphroditic image. He seems to stand naked before Vala, arms behind his back (in trickery?) and pelvis forward, to let her see his/her? sexual organs (heavily erased) or to urinate (like the female in page 21), but Vala is in another world. Her pitiful acceptance or internalization of Urizenic restraint gives birth to social structures—the world of Urizenic creation—which consist of masses of oppressed and sacrificed humans—"We are made to turn the wheel . . . to mix the clay with tears & repentance" (6–8), led by self-worshiping oppressors.

Page 32

"STILL LABOURING IN THE SMOKE" (2)

Vala and Luvah, in the first words of this page, are still hating and "still professing love, still labouring in the smoke." Another couple, Los and Enitharmon, are introduced, then canceled, then brought in again (3–5), rejoicing in "the sorrow of Luvah & the labour of Urizen." Enitharmon joyously plots "to rend the secret cloud, To plant divisions in the Soul of Urizen & Ahania." Yet planting is what it is all about; an "infinitely beautiful . . . Golden World" (7–8) is arising, though the Planters and Sowers go forth in sorrow and in bondage to Urizen.

Page 32. Planters and sowers.

We may not recognize any of these couples in the naked figures in the design (see tracing) but all suggest variants on the theme of planting and the theme of love, "in various forms," unrecognized (31:19). At the left, almost obliterated by erasure, is a couple that occupy an oval space below the word "They" in the last line (see Commentary on *FZ*, p. 40). On tiptoe and arching her back, with her breasts near that word, is a naked woman. Behind and below her a man kneels, with his face in her long hair. He may be attempting to approach her anally somehow; yet their bodies are far apart: can there be a small figure between?

Further right, unerased, is a naked, almost faceless woman sensuously outstretched across the prone figure of a sad-faced man whose right arm cradles his head. (Compare the woman on page 28 and the turbaned woman on page 128.)

Below these two couples is a woman lying prone on a mound of ripe, lodged wheat, as if to take the ripe grain as seeds into her body. Her extended arms and legs taper without apparent hands or feet. (Blake may not be responsible for the dark scribbles on head and feet.) The woman's rump is swollen as if it were a pregnant belly.

The most curious couple, standing to the right of busier planters seem at first glance a fairly normal, unsmiling pair. Then we notice that the woman, facing us, is holding a small penis in her right hand (planted in her vulva like the one on page 22[20]), presumably the subject of their discussion. On second glance we may suspect that both figures are women, being struck (as Bentley is) by similarities to the sisters Gwendolen and Cambel in *Jerusalem* 81: the stances of those sisters are quite similar to those of this curious pair, though "reversed and slightly altered," and Gwendolyn holds a "falshood" in her left hand and crosses her legs while Cambel holds her left hand (not her right) to hide her pudendum (not display a penis). But on third glance the similarities fade, for we see that the Cambel figure here (on the left) is not covering her breasts, that both are talking—and that the Gwendolyn figure far from hiding anything is also displaying a tiny penis. Can these be a pre-Freudian variety of "the phallic woman"?[1] We suddenly realize that the lower part of this body fronts toward us, as revealed by the bending of the knees and the position of the one visible heel (pointed away from us).[2] And perhaps something odd is happening to his right arm. ("Still she despised him . . . knowing him not" would be appropriate here.)

What of the drawing at the far right? If we expect to see another couple, we are startled to discover a large and somewhat shapeless penis, standing up from the ground like a toadstool. (In later pages we shall see similar phallic giants.) The primary image is certainly a penis, though it also suggests a standing couple embracing, perhaps an intended visual pun.

[1] See the discussion by Jean Hagstrum in Curran & Wittreich (1973), 108ff.

[2] Some lines suggest that Blake had begun to change the lower part of the body to make it consistently a back view. He drew a spinal line right across the arms and down to the penis and some curved lines suggesting buttocks. He left the knee and heel unchanged, however, still signifying a frontal view.

Page 33

"TO BIND THE BODY OF MAN . . . FROM FALLING" (17)

The design sketched on this page seems to be drawn on top of a previous one. Possibly it is the silhouette of a figure in childbirth, or perhaps simply a formless body taking shape. In the text Urizen, comforted at his sons' workmanship, sees the "wondrous work flow forth like visible out of the invisible" (10).

Page 34

All the large margins are filled with text, and no drawings appear to have been there before the additions.

Page 35

"WHAT IS THE PRICE OF EXPERIENCE?" (11)

The phallic growth in the wheatfield of page 32 has prepared us for the gathering of such sexual vegetation as that upon which the three central female figures drawn here concentrate their attention. (The prude—see the irony about "laws of prudence" in the last line of text—who erased Blake's drawings of erogenous zones in this manuscript has added scribbles over erasure here, darkening the central female—but apparently uncomprehending of the plucked stems.) The basket of symbolic fruit held on her head by the woman in

the margin links the picture firmly to the poetry. Her mouth half open to pitch her voice, she is calling her wares—evidently phallic totems which the scribbler has obscured with loops—alongside Enion's cry that "Wisdom is sold in the desolate market . . . And in the witherd field" (14–15). (Of the six buttons down the front of her jacket, someone has circled the fifth, to suggest a vulva beneath."

If we look again at that field, we see a lover's head behind the central woman, who receives his kiss on her neck, and a shadowy figure (another lover?) behind the woman picking the mandrakes—to take a hint from the action of the mother depicted in Blake's first emblem in *The Gates of Paradise*, who finds vegetable-shaped infants "beneath a Tree."

Observing the scene from the far right is a squatting figure, doing such business as attracted the prude's eraser. A small naked girl beside the observer watches with arms and hands raised and a look of wonder—and her legs crossed at the ankles. Does the line of emphasis drawn on her vulva signal the falsehood of her alarm? (Compare the girl watching a boy urinate in Hogarth's *The Enraged Musician*.)

Page 36

"NEVER FROM THAT MOMENT COULD SHE REST" (19)

Enion's "Wisdom" reaches even to the great Workmaster on his couch, as "the youthful harlot's curse" reaches the poet and reader of *Songs of Experience*. Hearing the lamentation, Ahania, while Urizen sleeps, is "drawn thro unbounded space Onto the margin of Non Entity" (16–17) and we see her falling through the space of the page, her hands ineffectually shielding her eyes from the vision of "Enion in the Void" (18).

NIGHT THE THIRD

Page 37

MOURNFUL "BEFORE HIS SPLENDID FEET" (2)

Ahania, shaken by her pre-dawn vision of Enion's fall into Non Entity while Urizen was asleep (36:15–19), now bows herself down before Urizen "high upon his starry throne" (37:1). Her words (echoing those of Blake's Dalilah in the *Poetical Sketches*) define her as "like a mournful stream" embracing her Lord's "splendid feet" (2–3).

Lines apparently indicating water in the foreground show that Ahania is still on the "margin" of the abyss, a margin of self-humiliation; she is ready to extinguish Urizen's fault by her flattery and to charge it upon Luvah. As she kneels, holding Urizen's left heel, her face is within kissing distance of his big toe, her eye is a dark mask or cave, and we see that his right foot, pressing on her head, grasps her with talons in place of toes. (Blake originally drew the left foot as cloven, then changed it to human shape.) Ahania's worship of his human foot while in the grip of his feral one emphasizes her collaboration in sustaining the illusion of "present joy" (10). While she is in this tyrant's clutch, her account of Albion's dramatic splitting apart at the vision of Vala is faulty yet seductive and illumined by flashes of truth.

Urizen huddles in "dark fear" of the message that a "Prophetic boy Must grow up to command his Prince" (38:6). (Blake first gave Urizen an open mouth, then a closed one, fist against chin, left hand pressed against the side of his head.)

Page 38

"THOSE WHO EAT OF MY WIDE TABLE" (5)

In the left margin our friend Cupid, with wings outstretched above outstretched arms, appears to be mounted (as in page 21) on a vague phallic erasure (see Grant and Butlin)—which, on analysis, however, proves to be some incredible extension of a human leg thrust upward from the cluster of naked copulating bodies at the bottom of the page. (See tracing.)

There are at least four bodies in the heavily erased cluster, and two small heads of onlookers peering from behind the group. Bending away from it, while keeping his left leg (presumably both legs) underneath the active bodies, a stout Silenus figure (with vine leaves in his hair?) twists around to embrace a plump woman who seems to regard the whole "feast" with horror. His right hand is buried between her arms and breasts; the fingers of his left hand *may* be what we see on the top of her head (repeating the talon motif of page 37); yet the effect is that of stiff curls of hair, unusual for Blake. The woman's arms are held in a curious position, perhaps keeping something from the grasp of her seducer, but also anticipating the relationship to

Page 38. Society unclothed?

Cupid which becomes clear in page 40.

Does this multiple erotic embracing illuminate Urizen's fears expressed in the text? He sees himself "set here a King of trouble commanded . . . to . . . do my ministry to those who eat of my wide table" (4–5)—a sort of Ulyssean lament at the feasting of the suitors. Is the Cupid atop the phallic shadow "that Prophetic boy" whom Urizen "must serve" (6)? Does this anticipate Orc's Oedipal desire for his mother in Night the Fifth? Perhaps so, but we have discovered a contemporary analogue to this sensual feast which gives it a peculiar frame of reference—which suggests, indeed, that Blake in this social cluster of naked bodies is offering an undressed version of the cluster of elegantly clothed bodies in illustrations of Pope's *The Rape of the Lock*!

In 1797, the starting date of *Vala*, Thomas Stothard, Blake's old acquaintance whom he claimed to have "found . . . blind" and taught "how to see," painted a series of watercolours which were engraved for the 1798 Du Roveray edition of *The Rape*. One of these (see engraving) depicts a deck party of belles and beaux on a boat on the Thames. At the top of the painting is "the merest suggestion of the ship's mast and rigging to set the scene on the 'painted Vessel' " in Canto II (to quote Robert Halsband's recent study).[1] Atop the mast, with arms and wings outstretched, rides

Thomas Stothard and Anker Smith, engraving for Canto II of Pope's The Rape of the Lock *(1789) (Halsband, Fig. 19).*

[1] Robert Halsband, *The Rape of the Lock and its illustrations 1714–1896* (Oxford: Clarendon Press, 1980) pp. 39–43, plate I. For the watercolor see Halsband, Plate I.

[2] This sylph, Halsband observes, is a folk-lorist fairy, Stothard being "one of the first" to convert sylphs to winged fairy–like creatures—a conversion said to have been suggested by "a friend" whom John Adlard conjectures to have been Blake himself. (Adlard, *The Sports of Cruelty, Fairies, Folk-Songs, Charms and Other Country Matters in the Work of William Blake,* 1972, pp. 77–78, cited by Halsband, p.39n.) No other cupids in Blake's manuscript are so much like Stothard's, though the one on p. 21 shows his wings to better advantage. The children on p. 39, however, are like Stothard's in other of his *Rape* designs, and the wings of the cupid on p. 42 suggest Stothard.

[3] The small face below and beside "O Prince" may have been suggested by the small faces backstage in the painting.

Page 39

"LUVAH HID THEM IN SHADOW" (18)

As Ahania narrates her "vision" of what occurred when Urizen slept and Albion "was smitten" (15–16), she tells that Albion, ascending the steps of fire (whence passion will spring), sees the light of intellect (Urizen's power) fading. In the next lines (page 40) Ahania reports this change as the dominance of Luvah, dismissively called (by the spirit of reason) a mere shadow from Albion's "wearied intellect." (In *Jerusalem* 4:22–24, a "perturbed" Albion turns away from the Divine Vision because he mistakes it for a "delusive Phantom of the over heated brain! shadow of immortality!") In Ahania's vision, Luvah appears pure and perfect in white linen, and she sees this as a belittling of Urizen and a deluding of Albion, because she—being under Urizen and obsequiously partaking of his fear—must put all blame on Luvah. (Compare Enitharmon's vision in Night VII, page 85.)

In the drawing, nobody is wearing linen, but the threatened rape of the preceding scene, symbolic of Luvah's dominance, is proceeding apace. It is now the woman (Vala) whose whole lower body is stretched flat along the ground, while the body of the man (Luvah) rises on top of her (slightly reminiscent of the gnome perched on the maiden's breast in Fuseli's *The Nightmare*). In the left margin Cupid's post has taken the fleshly shape of a great penis, with hanging scrotum. One testicle is so close to the head of the taller of the voyeurist children that he would bump against it if he straightened up. Cupid is nowhere to be seen; yet the arms of Belinda/Vala are oddly fixed in the same, now reversed, position as before, as if symbolic of Cupid's continuing control. In the poem's terms this Mars and Venus are Luvah and Vala, and the boy and girl who witness and perhaps authenticate

the sylph Ariel, "with purple pinions and azure wand . . . at his commanding post."[2] Blake's Cupid is mounted on a similar post of command, and we can see that the faint broken lines that slant down from there represent the faintly indicated rigging in Stothard's depiction. We can recognize the two small "onlooker" faces behind the huddled bodies as two of Belinda's attendant ladies.[3] But most striking of all, we can recognize the tight curls and the face of Silenus' victim as those of Stothard's Belinda. The scene is Blake's version of the Baron's pursuit.

That absurdly long leg which emerges from Blake's cluster of bodies (and rises to turn into, or support, Cupid's command post) is a parodic version of the largest bodily part in Stothard's painting: the gleaming, tightly stockinged right leg of the standing Baron, the only visible leg in the scene, an only slightly absurd long barrel with hardly an indication of knee (rectified in the engraving). Blake has stripped away the clothing of the whole party to get down to basics—what *The Four Zoas* is about—from a point of view that sees the proud masculine phallic leg as a stanchion.

the sexual embrace are not sylphs but Los and Enitharmon as small children. Ahania says that Albion "saw not Los nor Enitharmon for Luvah hid them in shadow"—his attention dwelling on the central scene. (See canceled lines 39:18, 40:1, and the rest of page 40.) But *we* see them, the taller child clearly the boy, though erasure has removed their genitalia; and they can see Luvah and Vala,[1] for the blindfolds (bandages?) have slipped onto the children's foreheads, and they are making gestures respectively of curiosity and revulsion. They are, in effect, standing in for Cupid, who will return in the next picture.[2]

[1]Grant notes that the figure of Luvah was drawn and redrawn, in two, perhaps three, positions, with the curly head closer and closer to Vala's; also that Vala in at least one version was bent away from him with both her breasts on the pillow which is now under her back and head.

[2]Hagstrum agrees, but wonders whether there is not a suggestion of a bow in the shorter child's right hand.

Page 40

CUPID ASTRIDE, WITH SPUR AND BRIDLE

On this page the erotic scene is continued. The body of Vala is now prone, and we see that both her hands are so oddly bent over her head because they are being pulled back by bridle-straps that must connect to the reins held in the extended arms of the winged Cupid—who now has the face of a gaunt old man and is wearing spurs, with sharply spiked rowel. He is astride not the female but the male, the Luvah figure who in turn is astride Vala, in the posture of coitus from the rear. Luvah's head appears to have been drawn twice, once plunged into the woman's back. His arms are difficult to make out; probably they are tangled in some way with the leading straps. Recognizing here the climax of the scenes on page 38 and 39, we may also compare the earlier Cupids of pages 4, and 21 [19].

We will next, as the text reminds us, shift the focus to Albion himself (still within Ahania's vision). What we have been seeing demonstrates that Albion has become "idolatrous to his own shadow" (12), giving himself up to the phallus worship of the religious and sexual rites that will haunt the human sexual experience with many fatal types of totem and taboo. Vala, who now trembles "and cover[s] her face," spreading "her locks on the pavement" (9)—so much for the outcry at their rape—will in the next scene have a strong reaction to Albion's

Page 40. Cupid as jockey.

withdrawal into the "Unformed Memory" of "a Worm seventy inches long That creeps forth in a night & is dried in the morning sun In fortuitous concourse of memorys accumulated & lost" (to quote *Jerusalem* 29:6–8).

Page 41

CAN LOVE SEEK FOR DOMINION?

As the perspective changes, Vala is shown in smaller but more finished outline, her hands reaching out to male genitals with no spurring Cupid between. This is now (according to the text) "Albion, the Awful Man," and not one of his Zoas. He lies upon his back with his head flung back almost out of sight. His left thigh seems to end at the knee, with no visible calf. (It was erased, or never drawn.) Vala holds the palm of her left hand under his scrotum and with her right directs his extended penis to a position from which the "balmy drops" (1) of his sperm fall onto her forehead and hair.[1] (See tracing.)

It is as though Vala's reaction to Albion's withdrawal into a self-worshiping shadow were expressed by her turning from her prone position (of page 40) and twisting her body over a couch to distend her breasts and free her hands (of all straps or bridle) to seize his tumid organ. (It is difficult to say whether there are curls of hair, or her fingers, at its base.) Her breasts distend with the milk or sap that nourishes all the forms of nature. Luvah has now obtained obsessive dominion over Albion's sexual energy. The voice of Tharmas, calling for Enion, startles Albion to confront the question, "Can Love seek for dominion?" (11–13)

Ahania, with a flash of liberated vision, understands that the fall from unity, of the Zoas within Albion, occurred with the change of universal affection into maddening passion, when the Zoas were "rent from Eternal Brotherhood" (9). She does not know that Urizen's cruel reasoning derives from the struggle between the Light of Intellect and the Fire of the universal Passion, dividing the sexes in Albion's brain and causing his female emanation, the Jerusalem within him, to hide under Vala's veil. (See also *Jerusalem* 21–23).

[1] Butlin's reference to "an enormous penis of a headless male" must mean that he mistakes the man's left thigh for a penis and does not see the fairly small penis, nor that the head is presumably bent back.

Page 41. Man's "balmy drops."

Page 42

CUPID AS PLAYTHING

Ahania continues reciting her vision of Albion's reaction to Luvah's maddening his heart with passion. Albion sent Luvah to "die . . . for Vala" (1) and to sacrifice himself to the libidinal energies of Nature. He bade the Zoas to entwine their functions within the natural organs, causing the four senses to live *for* the Ears, Nostrils, Eyes, and Tongue, not *through* them; causing "the Human Blood" to foam "high" (10), rending the Human Heart with jealousy, fury, and rage; causing all the senses to perceive "the vast form of Nature" rolling like a Serpent (13 and 17) between Heavens and Hells created by mankind's chaotic displacement of mental faculties and bodily parts—which were spread and divided all over the earth by their dichotomy into sexualized Bodies and spiritualized Souls. Urizen's power, the function of his fear, then covers his Light with dark thoughts ("heavy clouds

around him, black, opake") (21), preparatory to casting the blame on Ahania and flinging her from his "obdurate" bosom (43:24), a deed performed on the next page.

In the illustration the phallus appears to be shrinking to the condition of a captive bird and vegetated child.[1] At the left of the drawing a woman who may be Enitharmon (from her head band) with a gloved hand suggestive of falconry (the line above it is not part of the design) threatens to strike a bat-winged penis—which is not free to fly away but is controlled, loosely, by a long string which is held in her left hand and runs over her left thigh.[2] This leading string is evidently a variant of the reins connecting Cupid and Vala on page 40 and, perhaps, 38—Blake's way of redefining the relationship indicated in those pages.

In the center of the partly erased drawing is a figure which seems to sprout up from the ground like a tree stump (or a mutant of the large phallus), but its upper body is like a child's—rather like the Cupid's we have seen before. He has a child's face and cupid wings and casts an anxious glance at a large woman, sitting or kneeling beside him, who faces him severely, eyeball to eyeball, while her right hand apparently measures his penis.[3] Perhaps she is Vala. Luvah is hardly anywhere to be found; sex is reduced now to an object for young girls to leash and play with, for women to fondle or pluck like something growing in a garden. At the right a young girl with left leg crossed in front of the right at the ankles, and left arm over her head, smiles and reaches out her right hand to stroke Cupid's left wing. The girl's left hand *may* be holding the ribbon of a broad-brimmed hat beside her face.[4]

The erased head of another figure can be seen below the word "black"; it had a left arm first raised toward the word "storm" and then lowered to the right of "opake."[5] A wall or curtain is suggested by some crude shading (perhaps not by Blake) at the right.

Page 42. Penis on a string.

[1] See our comment on page 35.

[2] Nelson Hilton, not seeing the string, describes this "bat-winged genital" as having "separated from [the body] and taken flight on its own, becoming a fairy-spectre that another misguided soul wants to make her own." (Hilton, 1983, p. 165).

[3] Butlin seems to mistake the space between Cupid's wing and the woman's arm as the arm of a child seen "through" Vala.

[4] The hat line turns up in a photograph, but it is not apparent to the naked eye.

[5] Butlin may be right in identifying this as a large "robed figure stooping to the right, echoing the figure of Death in the facing engraving."

Page 42. Cupid center stage.

Page 43 (NT 108:30E)

"SO LOUD IN THUNDERS SPOKE THE KING" (23)

Blake's "King of Terrors" design, among his *Night Thoughts* engravings, was a natural foil for the text of this page in which Urizen, identified as "King" and "Prince," asserts himself as "the active masculine virtue" (8) and hence the natural law-giver. This assertion ironically is accompanied by the mustering of heavy clouds, rolling of thunders, and darting of lightnings while "his visage changd to darkness & his strong right hand came forth To cast Ahania to the Earth" (2–3), whereupon the very "bounds of Destiny" (27) crash and both Urizen and his Emanation fall into the Abyss.

The Jehovah in Young's text—"This KING OF TERRORS is the PRINCE OF PEACE"—served Young's purposes ambiguously: "death is the crown of life," "we fall, we rise, we reign!" In Blake's illustration his strong right hand unrolls the scroll of destiny in which Blake's difficult and reversed Hebrew lettering apparently indicts Jehovah himself as Death, a judge separating fire and dust.

Accompanying Blake's own text here, the scroll suggests Urizen's condemnation of Ahania, whom he accuses of having become like Vala as "the steps of ice" freeze "around his throne" (4–5, 22). With his saddened but domineering visage, Jehovah/

Urizen simultaneously (according to the text) petrifies "the immense" and bursts "its bonds" (27, 29). With his white and flowing hair, falling like snow, he forbids the fire of Luvah and freezes all desire—as though serving notice on the sexual play on the opposite page. We know from the many depictions of Urizen with his book of laws, elsewhere in Blake, that they are the Commands of prohibition. "Thou Shalt Not!" is the message of the sharp spears of lightning that project from beneath his scroll: "So loud in thunders spoke the King folded in dark despair" (23).

Page 44

"STRUGGLING TO TAKE THE FEATURES OF MAN" (18)

As the "bounds of Destiny" break, the sea bursts "from its bonds in whirlpools," and Urizen and Ahania crash down into "the Caverns of the Grave & places of Human Seed" (43:28–44:3). Among "the wracking elements" a sort of resurrection of the dead begins. "One like a shadow of smoke" appears, "human bones" rattle together and struggle "to utter the voice of Man" (12–18), and our old friend Tharmas emerges from the smoke, his eyes watery as if irritated by the marine salt. Blake's drawing captures the moment when "Tharmas reard up his hands" and before he "stood on the affighted Ocean" (21).

Tharmas laments the disintegration of his body into "sea jellies" and "little monsters / Who sit mocking upon the little pebbles of the tide / . . . & on dried shells that the fish / Have quite foresaken" (44:24–45:1). His features are now firmly human, and his right arm has taken shape, but there are lumps where his chest should be, and perhaps little monsters and snail shells are scribbled on his shore-like body; the dark wave where his right leg should be seems bubbling with life. Despair is emphasized in the text; yet his hand and face appeal for help.

The other body, taking female shape in the smoke, has no hands or feet yet visible, no nipples, a small head stuck into a large neck, crown-like horns rather than hair, and a triptich or Gothic chapel outlined in her genital zone. She may be expected to emerge as Enion (compare Enion's face on page 46) yet bears symbols fitting Urizen's recent characterization of Vala: regality, chastity.[1] No human relatedness between male and female figures is indicated—except to the viewer who can see that raised arm as matched in the facing engraving by the raised arm of Lazarus, brought to life by Jesus after four days of death in the tomb. After the Urizenic law-giving of the preceding page, the spiky female can be seen as what becomes of Ahania when her femininity is reshaped by the moral code. Like Enitharmon fallen (in *Jerusalem* 88:17, 19) whose response is to "Create secret places" and weave a "triple Female Tabernacle for Moral Law" (or, from another point of view, to make the "places of joy & love excrementitious" 39), Ahania's genital zone bears the triple seal of a sanctuary, an altar, and an imperial cathedral; a saintly Byzantine figure stands at the place of her vulva and uterus; her ovaries are replaced by two bowing angels.[2] She is a scourge and blight like the Wife of Bath, who has a similar spike or cone on her headgear in Blake's illustration of the *Canterbury Tales*. If we count the fourth spire of her crown hat as double (and so it is drawn) she bears on her head seven points for the seven capital sins.

If the head and the genitals represent, respectively, the "Caverns of the Grave & places of Human Seed" into which Ahania has fallen, we can see that while the picture seems to indicate both places as in a hopeless condition, the text differs, saying that in these places "the impressions of [both] Despair & Hope enroot forever" (3–4). The head needs replacing but the human statuary in the Gothic shrine can resume the drama of regeneration.

[1] The "interrelationship of sexual and religious idolatry," observes Ackland (1983, p. 176), is demonstrated with brutal frankness" by this sketch "in which the female genitalia are pictured literally as an altar for secret worship."

[2] Butlin finds indications of another, smaller tabernacle between her breasts.

Page 45 (NT 148:40E, first state)

"WHAT HAVE I DONE?" (29)

When Blake drew the picture of Tharmas raising his head and arm for help, on page 44, he must have planned to use this *Night Thoughts* design depicting the Saviour's response to Lazarus' similar gesture for the facing page, to assure us all that Tharmas' plea for sympathy will not fall on deaf ears. For Blake uses the same device (repeating the same engraving) when honest but desperate Tharmas gets even closer to the end of his tether on page 97.

In his design illustrating Young's argument for the unique efficacy of the touch of "the cross"— "That touch, with charm celestial heals the soul / Diseased, drives pain from guilt, lights life in death"—Blake changed the symbolic touching to a direct human eye-and-body communication between the despairing Zoa of touch, Tharmas, and an instantly ready Saviour. Young had dodged the question, "when?" Blake's text on page 45 needs only his picture for answer—as will happen again on page 97.

Tharmas is said to confuse "both rage & mercy" (45:29) as he bellows for his lost Enion. She is "too far off And yet too near" (2–3); he loses her, then finds her, not surprisingly an "Image of grief," conditioned by his own hatred—and love (28–31). The text gives no hint of the Saviour's presence, but both lovers take steps that could bring him near. Enion repents, regretting her "sin" and rebellion; Tharmas recoils from his "fierce rage" and instead of seeing the female as mere shadow of the male, he recoils "into [her] semblance" (32). He sees her face as "piteous" and feels that Love and Hope would end if Enion, already "only a voice," should fall into Non Entity (46:5–12).

When this Lazarus engraving is used again, on plate 97 in Night the Seventh, the text—in which Tharmas, behaving as "the Demon of the Waters in the Clouds of Los," recalls his original separation from his "crystal form"—seems to afford no glimmer of mercy or hope; yet again, in a more utterly desperate situation, Blake rescues his worthy Demon by holding forth the silent promise of Christ's hand. (Compare the similar role of Christ's presence in page 9.)

Page 46

"NOTHING BUT TEARS! ENION!" (1)

Enion's "piteous face" has begun to "Evanish like a rainy cloud" (45:32), as the drawing seems intended to indicate. But whatever Tharmas may say, despairingly, he does not give up. He has now not only "reard up his hands" and "reard up his Voice" but also can stand, unfrightened, "on the affrighted Ocean." The contrast of the two figures seems to indicate that as Enion "melts," his subsiding into her semblance ceases. Although he fears that "Rage shall never from my bosom," we may deduce that since "both rage & mercy are alike to me," his rage is for merciful life, not ruination.

As Enion vanishes into an echo, "Only a voice eternal wailing in the Elements" (7), her place as the eternal wanderer is taken by Ahania, but there is no visual depiction of that fact. In the drawing it is clearly Enion, vanishing, who is being sought by Tharmas, calling her name. The picture is a sort of cross-section of the watery element: we can see Enion hidden by a great wave and Tharmas striding down the trough between two waves, walking on water, his element, but unable to see her through it. Yet he seems able to suspend the next wave, with his left hand, a wave which Blake sketches as the curved lower torso of a female. And we soon learn, from the text (pages 47 and 48) that Tharmas has been able to check the waters and so prevent another deluge.

The drawing of Tharmas' body does not seem to have been erased (except in variant sketches for the head) but seems to lack genitalia: the problem of sexual efforts by touch (Tharmas) without energy (Orc/Luvah). The hands are more lobster-like than human.

NIGHT THE FOURTH

Page 47 (NT 87:26E)

"THEY ROSE . . . RED AS THE SUN" (4–5)

This is the Night of Blake's poem in which the Protean Zoa Tharmas asserts and declines godlike power, and his billowing alternation of pity and wrath shakes through the structure of the poetry and is matched by an alternation of designs from page to page: *Night Thoughts* proofs on recto pages faced by matching or contrasting pencil drawings on versos.

This sunflower picture, designed for Young's Night the Third, was made to illustrate Young's complaint of the death of his step-daughter Narcissa and his search for the reason why, despite her untarnished virginity and youth, birds of omen and birds of prey had called her "before her hour." Blake seems most attracted to the passages praising "Song, beauty, Youth, love, virtue, joy" as a "group of bright ideas, or flowers of paradise," while failing to share Young's passivity, his feeling of guilt, his blaming the sun of southern climes for failing to heal his beloved, and above all, his brooding and reasoning upon death. Far from blaming the sun, Blake pictures it as a passionate Apollo whose orb fills the sky, a young man driving three galloping steeds against the encroaching dark of sky and sea, against clouds of dim and opaque fear of mortal death. The dark vapors (painted with blood-red streamers in Blake's original watercolor) cross the hooves and manes of the horses and the sun-god's hair but not his face.

Instead of the "lilies" chided by Young for not sharing human sorrow, Blake paints a tall, large-leaved sunflower, whose stem surpasses the limit of the earthly mound and from whose flaring, Catherine-wheel petals a young girl with face uplifted to the human sun seems to appeal, with arms outstretched, for the liberty to enjoy that "group of bright ideas" praised by Young. The gesture and mouth of the kneeling man in gray (royal blue in the watercolor) identify him as the complaining poet, with the dying Narcissa outstretched at his side. Blake, we are sure, sees them as the separated youth and maiden of his Song of Experience, "Ah! Sun-flower," the youth pined away with desire and the pale virgin shrouded in snow who arise from their graves to go where Blake wishes they should aspire. Yet the similarity of features of the pictured Young and of Apollo, indicating they are both poets, suggests that Blake put himself into the picture as the solar Apollo, the human form of the sun, displacing the poet Young, who could think only of a sun that sustains mortals inadequately.

The surface details are apt, almost parodistically, for the purpose of a ready-made illumination of the *Four Zoas* text. Apollo can be Tharmas, in the first line, riding "on the dark Abyss," and later "Red as the Sun in the hot morning of the bloody day" (1,5).

We can imagine him[1] inspiring the pining couple to rise "in strength above the heaving deluge" (4); in the text he impresses Los and Enitharmon with his determination to escape the "endless corruption" (48:8) of mortality. Though wailing for his Enion (his Narcissa) and tossed between pity and compassion, he knows that he is "Deathless for ever" (12). The perpetual motion of his ride over the sea causes him to divide and unite, fall and rise, immortal though in despair.

The power of Tharmas' waters, like the galloping of the horses, cannot stop despite his knowledge (and fear) that he is approaching the dark clouds of the solidification into mortality of Los and Enitharmon's senses. Though filled with pity and doubt, Tharmas places them under the power of the fallen Imagination, the Spectre of Urthona, the spectral form of this earthly experience, so that they begin the chain of earthly families—in the roles of a "pale virgin" (mother, daughter, and wife) destined to "weave soft delusive forms of Man" (48:6) and of a father, son, and husband who is condemned to sacrifice himself in the name of Natural proliferation, rather than Human regeneration. The sunflower's counting countless sunsets illustrates the hammering of the chains and fetters of time and space upon the Universal Mind.

[1] Apollo = Tharmas = Blake.

Page 48

"O HOW LOS HOWLD AT THE RENDING ASUNDER"

From the picture of Young's poet passively complaining to the Sun, while holding his lost Narcissa's body at his side (the engraving used for page 47) Blake offers a giant leap of imagination to this bloody picture of Los protesting the rape of Enitharmon from his side, by Tharmas momentarily playing God. The text is on the facing page:

[Tharmas] in a wave . . . rap'd bright
    Enitharmon far Apart from Los. but
    coverd her . . . balming her bleeding
    wound.

O how Los howled at the rending asunder
    all the fibres rent
Where Enitharmon joind to his left side in
    griding pain
He falling on the rocks bellowd his Dolor.
    till the blood
Stanch'd, then in ululation waild his woes
    upon the wind

                                        (49:4–10)

Remembering the Bible account, we can see that Los has literally lost a rib and has a serious wound. His upward look suggests he is cursing his god, Tharmas.

(Faint traces of an erased drawing in the right margin, near lines 13–17, suggest a standing human figure, with its legs in the area now filled by Los's upper body. The erased sketch was obviously made before the present drawing and seems not related to the poem.)

Page 49 (NT 27:7E)

"MAKE FIRST A RESTING PLACE FOR LOS & ENITHARMON" (20)

Fourteen lines after having carried Enitharmon away from Los, Tharmas relents and instructs the Spectre (called forth from its dislocation) to "bear Enitharmon back to the Eternal Prophet" (i.e. to Los), though the best he can offer them is "a bower in the midst of all my dashing waves" (18–19).

The Night Thoughts proof chosen to suit this text, and to face the picture of Los trying to stanch his bleeding, echoes the Genesis story in another way. The bleeding arises in the shape of a serpent symbolically whispering into the ear of a collapsed Adam. Eve (Enitharmon) is trying to control their infant (Orc) who has the impulses of a Cain toward an endangered lapwing (or is this Cupid, seeking wings?).[1] Blake's original purpose with this design was to illustrate and rebut Young's complaint that all earthly "joys" are treacherous, like "bosom friendships" that sour, yet that the souring and other "misfortunes" are heaven's tests, especially those that seize "our vitals" with stings that double our distress. The bosom of Los, bereft and bleeding on the facing page, serpent-encircled here, suffers agony for which Blake will use this engraving again on page 77 (Night for Seventh). There Urizen, still acting like Young's God, is oppressing Los with such guilt that Los feels "the Envy in his limbs like to a blighted tree" (77:27): Los the tree, Envy the Serpent. (In 77 we can see the serpent-entwined man as Orc, also.)

In short, Young, as Blake read him, was trapped by the same Urizenic caveat against "all joys" that holds the Zoas under the tyranny of despair, represented here by Los's separation and his "falling on the rocks" (9). This we can recognize in the fallen man's not simply resting upon a great rock (which is sometimes Blake's image of Britain as island) but his pressing his arms and body against it like a Prometheus. The picture is echoed later in Jerusalem 69, where the giant Albion is in a similar position, arms outstretched and head collapsing, the victim of Druid priestesses ready for his blood, near a phallic altar stone; also in *Jerusalem* 25, where three Fates are examining a serpent shape that must be his own vitals.

The family trinity and the business of the present scene inaugurate a chain of jealousy that will go and return from father to mother to son and back; it is woven by threads of natural pity and unnatural love. In the next Night, Orc will desire his mother and be chained by his parents under the tree of good and evil.

[1] The mother helping the bird escape from the child, or not letting the child grasp the bird, was first depicted in plate 5 of *No Natural Religion* (a). Butlin notes the contrast of "the man dying from the attack of a snake with the carefree mother with her child".

Page 50

"HERE BEFORE THINE EYES" (34)

Tharmas recognizes Los as his "old companion" Urthona, the unfallen Imagination in the days of happiness before "Urizen gave the horses of Light into the hands of Luvah" (28–30). (Blake uses the Phaëthon myth to define the disorganization of the Zoas of reason and passion, Urizen and Luvah.) Tharmas understands Los's need for his "loved Enitharmon" and also somehow realizes that Los has the power to return her, by what seems to Tharmas a simple correction of perception: "But now come bear back Thy loved Enitharmon. For thou hast her here before thine Eyes" (33–34).

The picture, matching the picture on page 48, shows blood spurting from Enitharmon's side as from Los's. The magic carpet she is borne upon seems a trough in one of the waves of Tharmas' sea, with a foaming crest at each end. That her breasts lack nipples implies a solipsistic condition long before the fall.[1] If we compare the cursing anger in Los's face with the bitter reproach (perhaps) in Enitharmon's, we may understand why the blood is not yet dried—and why we are still far from Night the Ninth, where we shall find (p. 138) the contrary picture, of Enitharmon after having "walkd tho fires" unconsumed. Los and Enitharmon now face the hardening of their organs of sense so that they perceive the world as divided into Nature and Matter, but their facing it together, thanks to Tharmas, will carry them to the preception of the contrary of their fallen condition.

Why has the drama of lost male and lost female shifted from Tharmas and Enion to Los and Enitharmon? The change implies a generational progression from the acts of feeling to the acts of imagination. Los has the ability to see Enitharmon despite the waves—and to see her bleeding as his own.

And Enitharmon appears to be pulling something along with her right hand. Perhaps she pulls an inchoate Orc, suggests Hagstrum. See page 56.

[1] Nipples are often lacking in these sketches, possibly from mere haste of drawing, possibly from the intent to give special emphasis to the drawings in which they do appear. The contrast to the drawing on page 52 concerns us here.

Page 51 (NT 60:19E)

"IS THIS TO BE A GOD?" (29)

Tharmas feels he is exercising god-like power in reuniting Los and Enitharmon; yet he finds himself feeling only "weak hope, hope sister to Despair" (6). What hope there is lies in his recognition that being able to "rage God over all" is not to "be a Man," and in his seeing in himself a tendency to repeat the mistake of Urizen and Luvah, who were properly "Prince of Light" and "prince of Love" but yielded to the temptation to rage over all: "O why did foul ambition sieze thee, Urizen . . . And thee, O Luvah?" (20–29).

The perfect illustration of Tharmas' moment of insight is Blake's engraved design for Young's admonition ("mene, mene, tekel, upharsin") to the unprophetic Proud. Tharmas, like Belshazzar at the feast, is dashing the cup and swearing off ambition. But the damage has been done. "The eternal Man," says Tharmas, "is sealed never to be delivered . . . . the sea encompasses him & monsters of the Deep are his companions" (15–17). (So much for intuition without imagination.)

Young's application of the Bible story (Daniel 5) was a warning to his dear Lorenzo to beware the dial of mortal death; Blake, illustrating these lines, probably fancied the doom-sayer as the poet Young and the drinker whose hair stands on end as Lorenzo:

> Should not each dial strike us as we pass,
> Portentous, as the written wall which
>   struck,
> O'er midnight bowls, the proud Assyrian
>   pale,
> Erewhile high-flushed with insolence and
>   wine?
> Like that, the dial speaks; and points to
>   thee.

The King's sin had been ambition in the sense of

tyrannous rule and lifting himself up against the Lord of heaven; and the message was that the kingdom was to be divided. "In that night was Belshazzar the king of the Chaldeans slain."

The seven coils of the worm around the corpse in its winding-sheet, pictured at the top of the text box, can be taken as the seven accusations of deadly sin. In the vision of Tharmas the dead body is the corpse of the Eternal Man, sealed by winding-sheet and worm. Los-Blake would understand that as a vision of the doom of any king, or Zoa, who chooses to rage over all.

Page 52

"TERRIFIED AT THE SHAPES" (53:23)

In this text page and the next occurs a further fall of Los and Enitharmon into the world of matter, where their senses will be crystallized into organs. The Prophet of Eternity, after having bound "round the limbs of Urizen" the chains of chronological time and having "linked hour to hour & day to night & night to day & year to year" (53:1–3) and lashed this chain of sorrow "on the limbs of Enitharmon," is "terrified at the Shapes Enslaved humanity put[s] on" and becomes what he beholds (53:22–24). Thus the "Limit of Contraction" is reached, the point when all the Zoas have fallen and divided, and Albion's Eternal Mind is bound by the threads woven in his brain by their division. The divided perceptions enter man's universal spiritual body as organs of sense formed by male and female beings (p. 54).

In the drawing, Los and Enitharmon are holding each other at arm's length, unhappy at the lineaments they behold and apparently comparing their healed wounds (of pages 48 and 50). Blake as artist was perhaps too unhappy to decide on the proper positions of Los's arms and legs.[1] Enitharmon is holding two circular objects in her left hand, perhaps to stanch the blood or perhaps to add nipples to her body to distinguish it from what she beholds of Los's. Or is she making comparison of their hearts? No genital organs are to be seen;[2] her gesture may hint that she holds her partner's emotions so possessively that he is unable to allow human love and sexuality to emerge from his hardening body. (Their situation is comparable in *Jerusalem* 85). We are to be reminded that the human body is just being formed at this stage of the epic; they are trying it on with misgivings. A breast/apple association is suggested. (At the other end of the process, note the detachable breast of Vala in Night the Eighth, page 114.)

[1] De Luca observes that "Los on his knees was drawn in two positions; first, frontally, with his knees spread apart and the crotch area front and center, then with knees together, and torso and legs twisted part way to our left. Signs of erasure in the former crotch area suggest that genitals may once have been present; in the second position they would be hidden from view."
Butlin, evidently conflating these positions, describes Enitharmon as warding off "a kneeling man, apparently with an erection." (Los, he notes, has "the curly hair usually characteristic of their son Orc"—but, of course, also to be found on Los himself, as on page 2, "Rest before Labour.")

[2] Hagstrum observes that Enitharmon's gesture does suggest lactation and recalls many representations of the Madonna and Child, some indeed in which milk spirts out between the Virgin's divided fingers as pressure is applied. This may be a frustrated maternal gesture here, he concludes.

Page 53 (NT 18:4E, second state)

"TERRIFIED LOS BEHELD THE RUINS OF URIZEN" (52:11)

We are told that Urizen "slept in a stoned stupor" while Los labored to bind him day and night (52:20). But this picture from Blake's file of *Night Thoughts* proofs nicely illustrates how "frightened with infectious madness" (52:28) Los felt, all the same.

In Young's poem the poet himself was imagining, at his labors, "gorgeous tapestries of pictured joys, / Joy behind joy, in endless perspective!"— until he woke at the toll of Death's bell, "whose restless iron tongue / Calls daily for his millions at a meal." With Young and Los so similarly frightened as they forge joys to dispel mortality, it is hardly surprising that the number of cross-references between texts is considerable. The extension of chronological time seems to have been wrought by the Spectre to stop the contraction implicit in Los's binding of the Urizenic "grey oblivious form Stretched over the immense" (52:23–24). Los, like Young, waking in the middle of the night beholds "the ruins of Urizen beneath, A horrible Chaos to his eyes, a formless immeasurable Death" (52:11–12)—the exact image here, if formless it may be called. In the next moment will Death, as Urizen in 52:22, freeze "to solid all beneath" him? Los manages to stay on top, yet at the cost of becoming Urizen in his stead: "He became what he was doing; he was himself transformd" (55:23, spelling out 53:24).

In page 71, for which Blake uses another print of the same picture, we learn that Urizen has collaborated in the binding, i.e. the transforming of the concept of time from imaginative to rational—and the changing of creation and recreation to procreation—all under the compulsion of the tolling bell, the fear of death and decay.

Blake shows the Fall as reflecting the war of the Zoas in the Universal Mind at the dawn of human experience. In this Night all the divisions have been accomplished, and Los and Enitharmon assume the spectral forms the others have already assumed.

Page 54

AGES "PASSED OVER" (19)

"The Eternal Mind bounded began to roll," the text begins, and the picture gives us a glimpse of the first results of the labors of Los's hammer: a brain "lockd up In fetters of ice," until "a roof shaggy wild inclosd In an orb his [Urizen's] fountain of thought" (1–10). The next ages described, after completion of the "first age" which includes extrusion of the spine and skeleton, bring in the "red round globe" (17) of the heart, and then eyes, ears, nostrils, and so on.

The drawing apparently depicts the formation of the skull or roof. Ideas of circularity, developed from whirlwind eddies "of wrath ceaseless Round & round," have concretized into a globe, moving like a vortex between a snowy mountain on the left and a higher mountain faintly sketched on the right—though these can equally well be seen as crests in Tharmas's ocean, "the sulphureous foam surgeing thick" which settles into "a Lake bright & shining clear. White as the snow" (2–3). One can even fancy the human head of Tharmas forming on the higher crest. Butlin notes that Margoliouth saw the globe as supported "by a reclining figure, head to the right."

Another means of support, faintly indicated by Blake and perhaps erased by him, is a large hook, dangling a chain link attached to the top of the orb, and suspended by a long line or cord that begins beside the word "began" in the top line of the text (noted by De Luca).

Page 55 (NT 143:38E)

"THE COUNCIL OF GOD . . . WATCHING" (10)

The ages of creation of man's body are finished—and his fall has reached bottom. Council must be taken: Christ is the answer. Having chosen this engraving of Christ among the families of man for the concluding lines of Night the Fourth, Blake came to realize (after inscribing "End of The Fourth Night" beside Christ's elbow) that the picture afforded a nice counterpoint for a passage (perhaps inspired by the picture, perhaps waiting in draft for insertion somewhere) introducing "The Council of God on high watching over the Body Of Man"—a Council only taking on flesh in the body of Christ below on earth. In the revised ending, the Council is at once described as putting on Luvah's robes of blood (the robes of the crucified passions) and "Descending" as "the Divine Vision" to the world's comfort—a contrast to the warlike descent of Urizen (10–13). In continuation, on the next page, Jesus finds the Limits—of Opacity, naming it Satan, and of Contraction, naming it Adam "While yet those beings were not born nor knew of good or Evil" (56:19–22).

Jesus, on high though on level ground, is haloed by a star of light shaped like the Sunflower's petals (page 47). His right hand is upon his thigh, his left is offered in friendship. And the families behind and beside him form a balance of human identities weaving between the contrary states of innocence and experience. Those furthest behind feature an aged blind man, the flesh of his hands shrunken in decay, a mother possessively cherishing a baby, and between them a contemplative teen-aged girl. Peace is among them. Beneath the text area a small boy holding a mother's hand is watched calmly or sadly by a slightly older sister. An independent lad with a charmed look marches behind Jesus. Another boy, his brother or the same lad grown older, stands courteously preparing his countenance and body for his presentation to Jesus by a strong, black-bearded man—Joseph of Arimathea?—with concern in his eyes; his wife, it may be, at his left shoulder. It is a solemn procession; humanity still and sad, but calm: accepting contemplatively the sad-faced Saviour. His mouth is open in speech. The silence is for his words of comfort.

The passage in Young's poem, for which Blake designed this scene, is a paean of self-abasing praise of Christ as the "great PHILANTHROPIST!" Young stresses His "omnipotence" and the pleasure He takes in relieving distress. His benevolence makes "us groan beneath our gratitude, Too big for birth!" In that context we can read Blake's silent folk as confounded by the immensity of the debt they owe: with Young they must feel that the "stupendous heights" of Christ's favor "leave praise panting in the distant vale! Thy right too great defrauds

THEE of thy due." Blake can hardly mean to en-
dorse Young's view of "life, death and immortality"
and debt-paying. But whereas this plate comes
near the end of the fourth section of Young's poem,
called "The Christian Triumph," which Blake fol-
lows the author in treating as completing a four-
night work, in the fourth Night of *The Four Zoas* the
Divine Vision in human form has only begun his
active role.

Page 56

"LIMIT . . . PUT TO ETERNAL DEATH" (23–24)

The curly haired boy of page 55, who implores
Young's Christ, reappears here with a cheerful look
and a ready commitment to the work of benev-
olence. His charitable action is more strenuous
than that of the smaller boys in "London" (*Songs of
Experience)* and *Jerusalem* 84 who lead aged cripples
through dark streets. Kneeling, he sustains the
grip on his extended wrists of a human form which
would, we may suppose, without this support col-
lapse into the utterly fallen position of the wrapped
corpse we saw atop page 51.

This youth (Orc he must be) impressively en-
dorses the "bright group of ideas" about how life,
death, love, hate, desires gratified and ungratified,
all achieve their balance of vision, of hope and
despair in the heart of man. Setting a Limit, he
balances his energy against the gripe of one who
chooses not to die, transforming mummy into
man. The scene closes Night the Fourth and opens
progress toward the poem's end, for the balance
between life and death—in Blake's myth the mercy
of visionary time given by Jesus in Beulah—will
allow Los and all creative visionary men, as Spec-
tres of Urthona, to resurrect in continuous mental
creations—exemplified in Nights the Seventh and
Eighth.

A small watching figure behind Orc, mostly
erased, has a face and a large folded wing that
seem to identify him as Cupid, an indication of
Orc's power, as love, to animate the mummy. (This
figure is not to be confused with the lines of the
tall, standing Christ which show through, in the
photograph, from the engraving on page 55.)
Written in pencil and erased before the drawing
is Blake's comment: "Christ's Crucifix shall be made
an excuse for executing Criminals." If the boy Orc
is engaging in criminal action in raising the dead,
he is in the company of Jesus, Thomas (Tharmas)

Paine, Luvah (whom "Albion brought . . . To Jus-
tice in his own City of Paris, denying the Resurrec-
tion"— *Jerusalem* 63:5–6) and William Blake the
"terrible."

NIGHT THE FIFTH

Page 57 (NT 117:32E)

"MAJESTY & BEAUTY . . . BUT UNEXPANSIVE" (13)

The engraving chosen to open this Night depicts
a climactic confrontation between brutal power and
naked humanity. To illustrate Young's view of life
as a lawless mutual hunt "of noisy men . . . Pursu-
ing and pursued, each other's prey" until "death,
that mighty hunter, earths them all," Blake
focussed on Young's concept of himself as an inno-
cent bystander, "like a shepherd gazing from his
hut," who thinks he is, psychologically, merely
fighting "the fear of death." Blake does not show
men fighting men like wolves but a naked strong
man pushed to his limit of contraction by a Nimrod
who has wolves on leash, a king (this is to take
Young's word "ambition" in the political sense)
whose crown's points have grown into horns and
who leans on a spear but wields power by men-
ace—his mesmerizing stare, magnified by the glare
of his close-mouthed policing hound.

(The engraving Blake chose for the concluding
page of this Night—p. 65—will dramatically re-
verse the pressure and subtly transpose the theme,
while offering a parallel of confrontation.)

Only imperfectly can the engraved victim *in ex-
tremis* signify the condition of Los at the limit of
contraction: "Now fixd into one stedfast bulk his
features stonify From his mouth curses & from his
eyes sparks of blighting" (2–3). We can see his body
turning to marble, and his mouth cursing. But only
from the text can we know that he has the wit to
fight back, not only with curses but with the self-
confidence that can say to a Satanic, grinning Nim-
rod: "Truly . . . thou art but a Dunce!" (See *Gates of
Paradise*, 19.) We can see that the hound is also
turned to stone, but not that Los, when "Infected
Mad," can dance "on his mountains high & dark as
heaven" (1).

In Night the Fourth, Los and Urizen had been
mutual pursuers. Now Los, maddened by the deed
of chaining the light of Urizen, who had in turn
bounded Los's imagination, cannot go on in that
way. Enitharmon too, we are told, feels "her im-

mortal limbs freeze stiffning pale inflexible" (6). Both have shrunk "into fixed space" (12). Yet their stasis is only superficially that of Young's hunted man. For their contraction is compared to the withering of plants, "leaves & stems & roots decaying," and the hardening and survival of seed: "while the seed driven by the furious wind Rests on the distant Mountains top" (9–11). Los, though the anvil is "cold," can yet dance "with the hammer of Urthona" (imaginative power: 4; see 17), and Enitharmon can shriek "on the dismal wind" (20). Their "senses unexpansive in one stedfast bulk remain" (19), but the dance and the outcry mark the beginning of labor, both transforming and procreative.

(We may think there is something wrong with the victim's toes until we see that they are simply hidden by grass.)

Page 58

ENITHARMON, AND THE EARTH, IN LABOR

Below the text lies Enitharmon in labor on her "weary couch." Is the curve of her body repeated in the carved back of her couch, with pillows? Or are those faintly sketched lines the soaring body and head of some sympathetic demon responsible for "the faint harps & silver voices" that "calm the weary couch" (10)? Butlin suggests that this is Los "crouching over her." Enitharmon's legs and feet are intertwined and taut, her right hand clutches her head, and her left (we are to understand) her husband's feet. "Her pale hands cling around her husband & over her weak head; Shadows of Eternal Death sit in the leaden air" (1–2). The poet conveys a sense of "solemn revolutions" of contraction and exhaustion by reporting the "labring Earth" as participating volcanically in the birth, accompanying the mother's groans with a convulsed rocking "to & fro" (16, 9).

We should not be surprised that when the "terrible Child" is born he "springs forth" like lava, not from her womb but "from her heart" (17–18). He is born "In thunder smoke & sullen flames & howlings & fury & blood." And as soon "as his burning Eyes" are "opend on the Abyss," the Demons in it utter from their "horrid trumpets" a Nativity song to "the new born king" as "Luvah, King of Love" and "King of rage & death" (18–22). The setting is, by proper contrast, wintry. The "Shadows . . . in the leaden air" are personifications of Winter, Frost, and terrible Snow:

But from the caves of deepest night
  ascending in clouds of mist
The winter spread his wide black wings
  across from pole to pole.
Grim frost beneath & terrible snow linkd in
  a marriage chain
Began a dismal dance.

(11–14)

In the left margin are puffs of mist or snow, and as we try to make out the faintly penciled but unerased figure that stands with his feet exactly *in* Enitharmon's belly and his head beneath lines 3 to 7 of the text, we are tempted to see a personification of Winter spreading "his wide black wings across . . ." (12). But in fact what looks like a bat's wing in the right margin is the edge of billows of cloud—as will be recognized if we turn to the full-page design on page 108 [116] where a tall, naked Jesus is pushing back similar cloud-curtains. (Holding a photocopy of page 58 against a photograph of page 108 [116] we find an almost exact matching of the positions of arms, head, and body down to the knees.)[1]

The Saviour on page 16 was a variant of different proportions; His flaming feet—the only part of Luvah that Vala could see—now stand chill and still. But their presence indicates the presence of the Divine Human form—the presence, we might say, of Luvah at the birth of Orc.

For the whole of the Demons' song and of the situation, all of pages 58 and 59 should be read closely, the several possible relations of text to drawing pondered, and both time (narrative) and space (picture) recognized as not necessarily sequential. At this point in the poem, "expansion" is potential rather than actual. Enitharmon may think she is grasping at "her husband"—but the figure shown beside her looks like Orc at or approaching puberty. We may think, from the looks of her body, that her pregnancy is an illusion. In the Demon's Song, addressed to the "new born" Luvah, he is told that "Enitharmon's womb Now holds thee soon to issue forth" (59:17–18). The poet then explains that the Demons have been (are) singing "round red Orc & round faint Enitharmon," that Los, perspiring "Sweat & blood" in a sort of trance, "rouzd" and "siezd the wonder in his hands & went Shuddering & weeping . . . down into the deeps," and that "Enitharmon nursd her fiery child in the dark deeps" (59:21–25).

But there are indications that Blake is dealing with an immaculate conception myth (see his lines

"On the Virginity of the Virgin Mary & Johanna Southcott") and that Enitharmon simply "cannot know" (nor can we) who is father, who is son, when she grasps at "her husband" (1). Blake uses the term only this once in the whole poem. He will use it also on only one occasion in *Milton:* "God your Lord & Husband" (*M*33:23 & 18); in five places in *Jerusalem,* twice with similar connotations: Mary says to Joseph, "I hear the voice of God In the voice of my Husband" (61:9–10); Jerusalem says, "And wilt thou become my Husband O my Lord & Saviour?" (62:6). In the present scene, if Enitharmon thinks she is clinging round her husband Los, we may take it that she hears the voice of God in his voice. When we next see Los, however, we will recognize his agony as that of a Joseph, and Enitharmon's passionate interest in her son as complicated beyond the vision of Freud.

(Enitharmon was first drawn lying on her back, with the feet of Jesus—as Luvah, as Orc—standing on her belly. In the final position, this is more clearly illusory and her crossed legs indicate her resistance to penetration—or to giving birth.)

[1]Butlin suggests that the drawing was made before the text was written.

Page 59 (NT 131:34E, second state)

"THE DIRE STEEL"

Blake makes Jesus immediately visible by introducing a proof from his Young designs showing a Christ almost as bewildered as Los, crucified with black steel that is hammered not into a tree but into flames of wrath—the crucifixion that will be made an excuse for deadly vengeance (see Blake's marginal note on page 56).

The design in this proof works with one slant of prophetic irony for Young's poem, another for Blake's. The reader will find it rewarding to ponder as context the entire respective pages of Young's poem (121) and of Blake's (59). Young views the nails of crucifixion with a phrensied fascination, which the expression on Christ's face[1] warns us to consider carefully:

Draw the dire steel?—ah no!—the dreadful
    blessing . . .
There hangs all human hope!!! that nail
    supports
The falling universe!!!

(In something of this spirit, Los will shortly decide

to chain down Orc, his "fiery" son, to keep his own universe from falling.)

The "Enormous Demons" who hail Luvah as king of "rage & death" call upon Vala to "draw" her steel in an opposite sense—not that of withdrawing a nail but of drawing a bow, to shoot:

Draw thy bow, Vala; from the depths of hell
    thy black bow draw
And twang the bow string to our howlings:
    let thine arrows black
Sing in the Sky . . .

                                                        (5–7)

(Here and elsewhere Blake's "black bow" is a periphrasis for iron gun.) The flames, in contrary perspectives, can represent the "secret fires" which the Demons define as the true "soul" of Vala, or the "torrents of consuming fire" which rage within the breast of Urthona. Los is, in effect, repeating the Crucifixion when he siezes "the fiery boy" and nails him down on "the iron mountain's top" (60:24–28). Even as he begins the building of Golgonooza, the city of art, Los almost encages Enitharmon in "pillars of iron," architectural nails, though adding at once the brighter "brass & silver & gold fourfold" (59:28, 60:1–3). No wonder he labors "in howling woe."[2]

[1]Achieved by Blake only after having tried a different face in the watercolor drawing (and in the engraved proofs used for pages 111 and 115).
[2]Butlin suggests that Blake chose this engraving of the resurrected Christ among the flames of Hell to illustrate 59:1–2, the Demons' inquiring the whereabouts of Vala, "the lovely form That drew the Body of Man from heaven into this dark Abyss."

Page 60

"NOW LOS BEGAN TO SPEAK HIS WOES ALOUD" (22–23)

In this and the next pages fear and hope, pity and wrath alternate within the now contracting and now expanding senses of Los, Enitharmon, and Orc "the ruddy boy" (7). An expanding fabric is the structure of Golgonooza, built by the collaboration of Los and Tharmas on the border or Limit of Translucence—the place where any creative man can build "forms sublime" while living in his earthly mansion. A contracting structure is the gate of Golgonooza named Luban, the vagina, which opens into this world. "Tharmas laid the Foundation & Los finish'd it in howling woe" (5).

The drawing dramatizes the human form of the "chain of Jealousy" (23) which is forged by the oscillation of these contraries among father, mother, and son. Blake's impressive poetic voice assimilates the dramatic fables of the *Oedipus* and *Prometheus* of Aeschylus without waiting for Freud's analytic structuring. The roots from which each human child is destined to be born are discovered in the inmost roots of a universally generating Family Tree—in terms of cold steel, a "chain of Jealousy."

When the manchild reaches fourteen, puberty fills him with pining for a female body, the only one near being his mother's. The father thinks he discerns "plain" that the son plots his death and so develops "a tightening girdle" of jealousy "like a bloody cord," keeping its growth secret as long as he can: "Forming a girdle in the day & bursting it at night," a sort of male Penelope's web (9–16). The design on page 60 pictures the family relations in this secret period; that on page 62 shows the fatal result when Los finally "began to speak His woes aloud to Enitharmon, since he could not hide His uncouth plague" any longer (22–23).

The father, hands on the floor and sitting on his under-folded legs, adopts the pathetic stance of the infant, looking sadly and silently up at the adults. Yet the clenched fingers of his left hand resemble the possessive talons of Urizen (page 37) clutching his wife Ahania as she foretells the birth of Orc. The single girdle oddly surrounds his naked body. Son and mother are oblivious to the pitiful Los. Orc fixes his eye on Enitharmon's, indeed fixes all his organs of sense on his mother's organs. Son and mother seem tightly bound in *their* girdle, an umbilical linkage that binds them to a Urizenic destiny of moral, social, and religious taboos.

Intensities are of pain; all joys are forbidden: the mother's freedom to choose both husband and son; the son's freedom to choose a woman, not a virgin; the father's freedom from legal linking to the "marriage hearse," Blake's grim emblem of the intertwining roots that close the Family away from free brotherhood and sisterhood. It is suggestive that the girdle around Los is at the same angle as Orc's leg around his mother's.

(In the similar portrayal of this Oedipal triangle in *Urizen* 21, the son is much younger and the father is still able to stand.)

Page 61 (NT 141:37E, first state)

"HIS LIMBS BOUND DOWN MOCK AT HIS CHAINS" (11)

Blake's Promethean, Orc/Luvah, has eyes which,

as "the lights of his large soul," contracted "behold the secrets of the infinite mountains" with "veins of gold & silver & the hidden things of Vala" or, expanded, "behold the terrors of the Sun & Moon, The Elemental Planets & the orbs of eccentric fire" (18–23). The design in the proof used here was Blake's interpretation of the position of Young's "good man" whose soul "acts a God":

His hand the good man fastens on the
   skies,
And bids earth roll, nor feels her idle whirl.

Climbing from a world of pollution, "His heart exults" and his soul "mounts to reason's region, her own element."

In Blake's depiction the good man's whole body, not his hand only, is supported by a heaven-spanning cloud, and the planet he calls attention to is the earth, with Africa and the Mediterranean at the lower left and the British Isles just under his pointing finger. Indifference to the earth's "idle whirl" is hardly the spirit the artist conveys. These things, the pointing finger implies, are happening right now in London!

The expanding and contracting of Orc's powers of sense is said to occur despite, indeed immediately after, the binding down of "the fierce boy" by Los, "obdurate," while Enitharmon "howld & cried" (60:28–30). Orc is chained to the Urizenic family tree; yet the potential of "his ceaseless rage," expanding his vision and enlisting "ten thousand thousand spirits of life" to bring him "wine & food" (13–16) is as astounding and as repressed as the revolutionary potential of a silent and oppressed but universal people.

In this context the good man is pointing out a new way, imaginatively transforming, rather than Urizenic, to understand and speak for the oppressed millions. "In Equivocal worlds up & down are Equivocal," remarked Blake while illustrating Dante's Inferno (Design 101, a diagram of the 9 circles of Hell). Knowing that Orc is the product of an equivocal or ambiguous world, Blake represents a third possible position from which to view the earth and the human potentials within her womb, "the hidden things of Vala" (20). Fertilizing rain (a frequent Blakean image) streams from the good man's cloud, while his head and upper body gleam like an Apollonian fire awaking the earth to "the harvest & the vintage" (28) where "the spontaneous flowers Drink laugh & sing."[1]

Young's text for which this design was first made

represents religion, providence, reason, and the deadly "groans of Calvary" as the only "firm footing" or "solid rock" on which to rest his pen. Blake takes that to signify that Young was poetically inspired but looked at the fallen world as unequivocal (all upward or all downward). Blake replaces the groans with wrath and rejoicing, and his vision contracts and expands at will, chained by the world's double- or triple-faced masters.

On page 60 the signal of hope for this new kind of vision was Los's building of Golgonooza, the city of Art. In Night the Ninth, on page 119, this dynamic view of the earth is repeated as a reminder of the contractive/expansive range of vision: even chained to the family Tree of a life fabricated by Urizen, Orc can arise as Luvah, the "Tree of Mystery" go up "in folding flames," and the tyrants be "cut off" (119:4–13).

[1]David Worrall observes (see his 1981 *BRH* article) that in Blake's astronomical symbolism, Orc as the Demon star Algol, a pulsating variable known as the Blinking or Winking Demon (its 2½ day cycle discovered in the 1780s), has taken over the energy of Los, a Demon who stops blinking ("his fiery Eyelids Faded" 59:22–23). As the "new born king" (58:21) Orc has become a solar system fed by journeying comets, "Enormous Demons . . . going forth & returning . . . with wine & food"— an adaptation of Newton's hypothesis that comets reactivate planetary vegetation with their vapour tails—bringing good vintage, according to popular legend.

Page 62

"IN VAIN THEY STROVE NOW TO UNCHAIN" (26)

As directed by the pointing finger of page 61, we now return to the family center. Los and Enitharmon, having chained Orc, had returned to Golgonooza and there developed the creative and loving impulses that made them able to feel "all the sorrow" human parents feel, and to weep "towards one another" (9–13). Undertaking an immeasurable journey of "nine days" (running through the earthly time and space which they control), Los takes Enitharmon "by the hand," hoping to give her back "her son in tenfold joy & to compensate for her tears" (19). They reach "the iron mountain's top" where Orc howls "in the furious wind," but they see in horror and grief that the Chain of Jealousy, which they considered a reversible act of negation, has incorporated Orc into the world of vegetation. The chain has "strucken root into the rock," and fibres from the chain have "inwove themselves in a swift vegetation" which covers rock and cave and even "the immortal limbs of the terrible fiery boy" (17–25). The picture omits the vegeta-

tion, but Orc's hair may be growing fiery like Los's.

Each day's girdle had formed a link; each of Orc's limbs is pinioned by a link of steel (with another link visible beneath the one around his right wrist). The parents cannot or dare not "draw the dire steel"; releasing an infuriated Orc would be comparable to daring to create a tiger. Los and Enitharmon are depicted as thunderstruck by the result of a deed they do not identify as their own.

Blake had drawn a similar picture for the "Preludium" of *America,* but with the hair of Los simply standing on end; here his hair approaches the flame-like hair of the thunder-god on page 65; There is also—a very different effect—a resemblance to the thorns of a crucified Christ. But the greatest difference in this picture is in the figure of Enitharmon, who in *America* seems wholly involved in self-pity, clutching her head but also covering her eyes. Here she covers her ears against her son's outcry, but her whole face addresses the child and she bends down, kneeling to his level. Los, standing, is about as slender as in *America*, but Enitharmon's legs are heavier and ungainly—for symbolic reasons, we suppose: perhaps to emphasize her matronly concern.

The eyes of Orc do not appear to be looking back at his parents but to direct us to the text and "the power of Luvah's Bulls," appealed to in the penultimate line. The youth is concentrating on his "Father's business," like Jesus in *The Everlasting Gospel*.

Page 63 (NT 44:13E)

"ORC RENDING THE CAVERNS" (16–17)

The shift of models and symbolism from the grieving family of page 62 to the confident family of this facing page, a design borrowed from the *Night Thoughts,* is startling—and masterful. Blake's treatment of Young's text had been contrapuntal in this case. The line marked for illustration read "We censure nature for a span too short," and Blake depicted an infant supported by a mother's giant hand and almost "spanned" by a father's. Both these parents seem happy at their attempt to enclose the child within the span of mortal life; we can see, however, that the whole scene takes place inside a stone tomb guarded by angels. A trial proof shows that Blake at first let his infant submit to the span; in revision he had the baby flinging its arms above its head to escape the mortal span. And we are freed to suppose that the parents' joy lies in that very escape. Only the literal follower of Young must read them as censuring nature (the faces Blake gives them do not look censorious) for not chaining the child to the rock of vegetation. The visual allusion to the holy family reminds us that joy is reborn even in the tomb when Christ is reborn within it.

The *Vala* text inscribed on the proof of this birth-and-resurrection scene, however, seems at first only to prolong and deepen the anguished story of page 62. We need all the symbolic comfort we can obtain from the engraved picture to hold back our own anguish as Orc's "Parents" in the text appear quite trapped in the mortal span and incapable of breaking out of the jail of the grave. They are so inwrapped by "Despair & Terror & Woe & Rage . . . as they bend howling over The terrible boy" that they fall "fainting by his side"—and we are told that "all their after life was lamentation" (4–9)!

Yet the tomb does break open (as the picture on Page 1 had promised) and since all are within the Limit of Translucence, Enitharmon feels "the inmost gate Of her bright heart" burst open and again close (11–12). During that moment "when the Gate was open," Vala, trapped within the mother's heart, is able to see the "dreary Deep" where Ahania is weeping—and to see also the "infernal roots" of the chain of Jealousy that binds Orc (14–15).

Within that moment of vision, Vala is able to feel "the rendings of fierce howling Orc" (16). And somehow even Urizen, although as far away "as furthest north is from the furthest south," poles apart from Orc and not to be identified with the pictured father, is enabled by the same momentary break-through (a moment in which the poet's work is done?) to hear and tremble "where he lay" (18–19). The real breaking, which is "Rending the Caverns" and now reaches the perceptions of Parents and King and Vala (Nature), is the force of the fierce boy "like a mighty wind"—visually represented by the infant's flung hands, and by his eyes and mouth which look and speak directly to the perceiver.

(This page is a striking instance of Blake's using a *Night Thoughts* design for a tangential, not directly illustrative, relation to his own text. The Urizen of this fifth "Night"—which will end in two pages—is a weary old man, unable to compete with the vitality and originality of his son Orc; afraid of the future and unable to face the present, he can only repeat the untrue story of a happy past.)

Page 64

"THE WOES OF URIZEN" (63:23)

Urizen, "shut up in the deep dens of Urthona," sings the loss of his mountain throne and "gardens of wisdom" (63:23,30). He realizes that he erred in refusing to serve the Eternal Man. "O, I refusd the Lord of day the horses of his prince"—and, subsequently, in dragging down others in his fall:

We fell. I siezd thee, dark Urthona. In my
   left hand falling
I siezd thee, beauteous Luvah; thou art
   faded like a flower
And like a lilly is thy wife Vala witherd by
   winds.
When thou didst bear the golden cup at the
   immortal tables,
Thy children smote their fiery wings
   crownd with the gold of heaven.
                              (64:14, 28–32)

There may be some hope in this myth-making of Urizen's, though it rumbles with paternal ambiguities that remind us of the expression on the face of the father attempting to span the infant, on the preceding page.

The drawing brings us down from planetary Miltonic allegory to family concerns once more. The love-making at the right may illustrate the scene between Albion and Vala which alarmed Urizen when Ahania described it, in Night III. The fish-net at the left may remind us of the web of War in Night I, when Urizen cut down the Sun with his sheep-hook (15:3, 13–15), or the net-making during the building of the Mundane Shell in Night II (page 29). But in sequence we can recognize the family trio of Los, who seems to be putting his girdle of jealousy to good use as a fish-net, and Enitharmon and Orc (curly-headed) whose advanced love-making Los seems to be ignoring.

Closer inspection is less reassuring. Los may be turning his back on the two, but his fishing is like the father's attempt at spanning: just as the infant's hands fling out of the span, so one fish, sprier or luckier than the one in the net, has broken free and is eyeing Los with a lively expression like the infant's. As for the love scene, Orc and his mother (who grasps his penis in her left hand) have moved beyond the legwork of page 60, prodded perhaps by the grinning jester-cupid of Night I, who ap-

Page 64. Jester with cap and bells.

pears in miniature below the woman's crotch, in the shape of a crab standing on a sort of toy penis—one more of the sea creatures we saw on Tharmas in page 44—except that this looks like a tiny human wearing cap and bells.[1] Human existence is still at the water's edge; in fact, all three bodies are partly in the ocean indicated in the foreground (and see page 65).

(Traces of earlier drawing indicate that the trunk of the person now fishing was first bent back, perhaps with its head where Enitharmon's head is now: perhaps the first drawing depicted a preliminary kiss, with Los out of the picture.)

[1]John E. Grant (in Curran and Wittreich, eds., *Blake's Sublime Allegory* [1973], p. 171) suggests that "This scene may be regarded as a version of the cuckolding of Hephaestus by Aphrodite and Ares."

Page 65 (NT 133:36E)

"WHEN THOUGHT IS CLOSD IN CAVES" (12)

In Young's poem, for which this design was made, the question was, "Oh tell me, mighty mind! Where art thou?" The poet wonders whether to "question loud The Thunder," no doubt waiting for the still small voice. Blake pictures Young perched on a grassy mound precariously close to the ocean waves, his body half blanketed in what ought to be a scroll for prophetic writing. He seems only mildly interested in the Thunder, who is an earnest demon beautifully and powerfully declaring that the only way to go from here is *up*.

In Blake's text Urizen, concluding his lamentations, has all the right ideas without comprehending them. He remembers his draught of "the wine of the Almighty" at Luvah's table (5), he remembers Luvah's and Vala's children whose "fiery wings" were "crownd with the gold of heaven" (64:31), he remembers "the divine effulgence" (2)—but he blames his fall ("from *my* throne") on Luvah's getting him drunk "with the immortal draught" which he thinks of as "stolen wine" (7–8). Urizen has

reached the Limit of Translucence built by Los in this Night, and Blake indicates a visionary milestone, the Limit of Contraction given by Jesus at the end of Night IV. But Urizen is not the Prometheus of his own fable, and he is not the demon whose flaming hair and trail of lightning offer the apocalyptic way of the prophet whose just wrath is the inspired voice of honesty.

Urizen has a hunch (like Young, who did at least ask the question) that "perhaps this is the night of Prophecy & Luvah hath burst his way . . ." (11). But he is a man of logic and experiment. For the present, he "will arise" and "Explore these dens," to find what is giving his caverns (his skull) "that deep pulsation"—which we realise must be a beating heart (9–10). Not a user of quotation marks, Blake leaves it for us to conjecture whether the concluding line is only his own comment or perhaps Urizen's first grasp of the message: "When Thought is closd in Caves. Then love shall shew its root in deepest Hell." The reader-viewer of this page is prepared, in either event, to explore the full-page design that comes next without any faltering of imagination.

Page 66

"LOVE SHALL SHEW ITS ROOTS IN DEEPEST HELL" (65:12)

To see Los's "mighty bulk" from behind is to see him at work, beginning to give the blank paper the illumination—we can imagine rainbow colors—of the new vision which he and Enitharmon will draw in Night the Seventh. Now Urizen has just begun his Odyssey, and we are still in the deepest deep, but the adult human form of Los, standing tall as the Saviour, is putting up the heart, the "globe of life blood trembling" (*Urizen* 15:13). This emblem of prophecy placed between Nights the Fifth and Sixth marks a dramatic change of direction, a peripetaia or "falling round" in the poetic action.

Blake had described and depicted (in *Urizen* plates 14–17) the bloody globe's being born as Enitharmon's falling from the head of Los—a divisive separation called Pity. In several senses the direction is now reversed. In the early version Los pressed his hands against his head (in self-pity) and the globe was extruded. He now stands upright and is beginning to walk forward to light the dens (compare Christ's harrowing of Hell) that are to be explored.

He places the globe carefully above his head at the top of the vision, like a sun on a horizon. But all life is still under water, amniotic; the globe emits no rays yet, although the clustering curves that seem to form a basket to hold it—orbital, if this were a globe in space—may be recognized as a new use for the cords which Los was weaving into the Urizenic net. When the water draws away we may expect them to straighten into lines of radiance. The resurrection of creativity has begun. (We may contrast this to the trembling hesitation of the poet Young, on page 65.)

Where now is Orc? Who are the four figures around the living tree or cross-like body of Los/Urthona? The two swimming, one facing away, one toward us, but both looking up at Los, seem to have cloven left feet, like the man resting before labor in page 2. Their bodies seem like those of the two figures sitting on the ocean floor beneath them, female on the left side, male on the right. Perhaps each has first learned to sit up, then to rise up: Los's Emanation on the one side, his Spectre on the other. There is much redrawing of hands and heads and positions; the rising female was given wig-like hair but later given a variant outline with nose and lips that turn the head and show a face. Whatever the specific identifications Blake was working out, the whole group suggests a strong contrast to the family scenes earlier in the poem. As the individual pre-human forms wake and rise, they approach the light with open arms, without repulsion or hesitation. (Compare the outflung arms of the infant in page 63.) In the title-page we saw a nestful of bestial and human forms responding to the trumpet's blast. The more fully human figures here responding to the globe of Los and preparing to step forward out of the "caverns" of threefold existence are precursors of the Blakean Adam and Eve whom we see at the triple-arched doorway in the next page.

The swimming posture of the male figure on the right is similar to that of Urizen in *The Book of Urizen* 12 (as De Luca notes), but there his head is bent sadly back and we cannot tell whether he is trying to rise or sink. Here, if this is Urizen arising to explore his dens (65:9), his effort to rise is manifest.

NIGHT THE SIXTH

Page 67 (NT 119:33E)

THRESHOLD FIGURES

A direct rendering of Young's lines, "sense and reason shew the door, / Call for my bier, and point me to the dust," would show sense and reason leading the poet out of his house door, ordering his coffin, and directing his burial in the earth. (He had been saying that his life, as he grew old, had become so "shallow" and "vapid" it would make sense to order his funeral now.) The design which Blake engraved shows Sense and Reason confronting Young on a Gothic threshold and pointing (both of them) in contrary directions. With warning fingers they point to the dust under his feet (and to him as dust); with open palms they indicate an opposing choice, the doorway to heaven (an ascent visualized in the archivolt as angels offering a wreath of fame and a crown of fire). Blake's Sense and Reason are wearing, not Edenic fig-leaves, which would indicate that they are in the fallen world, where dust is dust, but vine-leaves, signifying their potential for regeneration. Reason's right hand indicates the geometric rigidity of the stone doorway; Sense's left hand demonstrates how illusory such structures can be. Adam as Reason straddles the threshold and accepts the rigidity of the stone.

The same design chosen now as entry gate for "Night the Sixth" offers no obvious correspondences with either Young and his Sense and Reason, or Blake's own text on this page. If we regard the two naked figures as Enitharmon and Los, however, and the gray bewildered figure with stretched legs unable to stride as Urizen, who will be seen striding decisively enough in page 74, we can find in this design an attractive introduction to Night the Sixth as a sequel to Night the Fifth.

The Adam and Eve figures stand, reversed, in the same front and back positions as the swimmers we recognize as spectres of Los and Enitharmon in page 66. Now on dry land they have achieved completely human forms. Their contrary pointing indicates two ways of stepping in and out of the door of life and death—one being that of the Urizenic ratio, which Urizen is to use in this Night, the other being the building of the city of Art, the artistic Calvary of Golgonooza announced by the living Gothic of the archway.

In the text of this page we are told that Urizen, exploring the "dark air" of his dens, comes to a river threshold and takes off "his silver helmet" to drink. He is at once confronted by "three terrific women," daughters of his (he soon discovers), memories hidden in his mind's caves, on the level of the unrising figures at sea bottom in page 66. The "Eldest Woman" is a sybil pouring forth "mighty waters" from her urn, and then filling and pouring again. The next is a "terrible woman clad in blue" whose "strong attractive power," creating vortices, makes her "mistress of . . . mighty waters" (2–15). The "youngest Woman," in green,[1] who divides and rules "the current," we shall meet in page 69. They answer Urizen's questions with silence: he had deprived them of the gift of the word. We may take them as symbolic of the unawakened condition of humanity bound in Urizen's nets and cords (see Night II), the druidic, pagan, and Old Testament religions of wars and sacrifice. The gesticulate, vineclad humans in the Gothic doorway offer a perspective from which we do not see a Urizen clad in shining armor, "leaning on his Spear" (1) but a shame-faced wretch stripped to his underclothes.

[1]Butlin finds a symbolic analogue: Sense and Reason pointing the poet, Young, "to the dust" match Urizen's daughters barring him from the river.

Page 68

"URIZEN KNEW HIS DAUGHTERS. THEY SHRUNK . . ." (2–3)

In a position repeated by Blake in his picture of Eve in the second plate of *The Ghost of Abel* and in his tempera painting of "The Body of Abel found by Adam & Eve," Urizen's youngest daughter (representing them all) is shown as a wilted lily of a human body, head drooping, a stiff-limbed arch of shoulders and arms, with no hands. In the text we are told that when the daughters confronted Urizen—"They reard up a wall of rocks and Urizen raisd his spear" (1)—daughters and father recognized each other. The daughters screamed and hid themselves "in rocky forms from the Eyes of Urizen" (4). He bewailed the "dreadful state" of their once "radiant colours" and proceeded to pour his fury on them, cursing "Tharmas their God & Los his adopted son" and ordering them all to "go forth"—forgetting that all of them were now in the desert (6–9, 24–27).

The abased fragment of human form in the drawing embodies the Urizenic curse of a religion of war and sacrifice: "I will reverse The precious benediction; for their colours of loveliness I will give blackness . . . For crowns [see the fiery crown at the top of the Gothic arch on page 67] wreathd Serpents . . . I will give Chains of dark ignorance & cords of twisted self conceit And whips of stern repentance & food of stubborn obstinacy"—in short, his own diet. The arms of the young daughter flow down like two parted streams whose course will be directed by the tyranny which Urizen's "labourd fatherly care" has become (14–23).[1]

[1]Hagstrum notes a parallel to the cascading hair on the last plate of *America*. Chayes notes a similarity to Fuseli's *Silence*.

Page 69 (NT 151:41E)

" 'TIS REASON'S INJURED RIGHTS HIS WRATH RESENTS."

We take our caption from one of the lines in Young's praise of reason, illustrated in the engraving used for this page, since the words can be applied—taking "his" to refer, not as in Young to a "father in the skies," but to Urizen himself—to the sense of injury and the spirit of vengeance in Urizen's obstinacy toward "The ruind spirits once his children & the children of Luvah" (70:6). The young girl receiving instruction in the use of balances can be recognized as the "youngest Woman" of page 68, obviously drawn to match this figure. Arbitrariness and secrecy are implied in the invisibility of one side of the scales, and the gowned and crowned woman instructing the youngest may be considered the "terrible woman clad in blue" who sits "mistress of these mighty waters" (67:15). The instruction is about dividing good from evil. "Reason," says Young in the text Blake illustrated, "rebaptized" him when adult, weighing "true and false in her impartial scale" and causing his heart to become "the convert" of his head.

In Blake's text, the presence of Urizen is freezing the vital juices into a "dreary waste of solid waters" (2), and Tharmas, overwhelmed by his responsibility for "The Body of Man," the "Eternal Man," although impressed by its capacity even under the ice to surge forth "in fish & monsters of the deeps," balances the woes of living forever "in these monstrous forms" against the quiet of death, and calls on Urizen to "give me death." He proposes to Urizen a mutual withholding of sustenance—light and food—to destroy themselves and Man. But Urizen doesn't bother to reply; he is intent on finding man's jugular, Urthona. Tharmas knows he would need the aid of Urizen for his desperate proposal, but if the Zoas were ready to collaborate, their objective would be peace in life not death.

Page 70

"URIZEN BEHELD THE TERRORS OF THE ABYSS . . . THE FORMS OF . . . DISHUMANIZED MEN." (5, 31)

Urizen, "wandering among the ruined Spirits, once his children & the children of Luvah," finds them "Scard at the sound of their own sigh" and unable to go beyond "the bounds of their own self." Some "wander Moping," others in vast troops, "women marching o'er burning wastes," "multitudes . . . shut Up in the solid mountains," some "dishumanizd" in "the forms of tygers & of Lions" and serpents and worms and "scaled monsters, or armd in iron shell or shell of brass" but uncomprehending. "So in regions of the grave none knows his dark compeer." (5–12, 31–35).

None answered his questions, for "His voice to them was but an inarticulate thunder, for their Ears Were heavy & dull." He persisted in "Questioning in words" the howling victims (39–41), and the drawing on the page suggests that he too is one of the "howling" compeers. Los cannot see "Urizen with a Globe of fire Lighting his dismal journey" (2), and neither can we (until the picture on page 74), for Urizen has become what he thinks he beholds. The hands and feet on this fiery crocodile (as on a Sendak monster) reveal his human form, however. Ultimately scales will cover them, we learn from the detailed description in 106:25–31 which also points out that he is tongueless and has a "triple row" of teeth (not all visible in profile).

The omphalos at the center of his belly is a graphic emblem of the center of the vortex described on this page as a whirl of clashing ruins of separated human forms. This monster is the aggregate image of the warring elements, the laws of the jungle and of past civilizations, a whirling fountain drawing all to the rock of death, an amphibian form incorporated within the bodily and mental identities of all dead and yet living beings within mankind's heart and brain.[1]

The polymorphous symbolism of this howling, shining figure (the lines of radiance from head and tail suggest that Urizen has become his own "Globe of fire," self-illuminating) reverberates with echoes of traditional emblematic figures expressing the mysterious links among sacerdotal and natural and imperial powers. Blake's mastery of the combination allows him to make the transformation that will be seen on page 100 (in Night VIII) where we shall see the energy emanating from the tail of this creature majestically employed in putting the tiller hard over, changing both face and direction, to stride leftward metamorphosed into the living Urizen—as an absurdity.

[1]Blake may have been commenting wryly on Urizen's plight when he wrote, in crayon beside the text:

Till thou dost injure the distrest
Thou shalt never have peace within thy breast.

Page 71 (NT 18:4E, first state)

"THE BOOKS REMAIND" (39)

This picture of Young's warning bellman, used earlier on page 53 where Los, after the binding of Urizen, becomes Urizenic himself, is brought in here for the bedside properties of quill, lamp, and open book—in which Death's arrow seems ready to inscribe a final word.

Urizen discovers, however, the fallacy of the final word. Through all the "revolutions" of "falling, falling, falling" he must carry his books. Though as a seed he falls "wearied, dead" into the "bosom of slime" created by the Saviour ("the ever pitying one"), and though he undergoes one "resurrection" after another "to sorrow & weary travel," he must carry his books with him—as must William Blake. "Nor can the man who goes The journey obstinate refuse to write time after time" (23–42, 72:1). With this as text, we must see the Bellman not as announcing the End for our weary traveler but as compelling him to rise and write. Urizen must collaborate in this poem with all the other Zoas. His mortal garments may be "rotted by the winds," but the books remain, "still unconsumd" and indeed "Still to be written & interleavd with brass & iron & gold Time after time" (39–41). As written on by the fallen reason, the leaves may have seemed to be leaden, but with the process of that prophetic interleaving that brings out the golden meaning, the leaves are revealed to be diamond ("adamantine") (42).

Thus quietly, to keep the poem alive, is introduced the Saviour whose mercy sets limits and can extend deadlines. This extension of earthly time was assured us in Night the First: "a mild & pleasant rest, Namd Beulah . . . Created by the Lamb of God" (5:29–32). In Night the Eighth, Jesus will descend as the seventh Eye of God to die "willingly" for mankind—and Blake will give us a whimsical depiction of the Spectre of Urthona, pitiful donor of time, in the first page of that Night.

The immediate result of the tolling bell wherewith Urizen condemns his daughter to a "vegetating" life in death (cf. 109:22) is depicted on the next page.

Page 72

"O THOU POOR RUIND WORLD" (35)

Blake hints that Urizen's travel will not be forever, thanks to the "Divine hand" (2), and indeed now he is not simply wandering and inquiring (itself an improvement on cursing) but "Creating many a Vortex, fixing many a Science in the deep" and "throwing his venturous limbs . . . Swift, Swift from Chaos to chaos . . . a road immense" (13–15). And here pictured we see his three daughters, weary but not dehumanized. Yet the way is still "downward all" (32). And this is not "the once glorious heaven . . . where joy sang in the trees and pleasure sported on the rivers" (38–39).

One daughter, perhaps the eldest, lies in the background behind the others, her head and arms sunk in the vegetation—perhaps becoming vegetation. Her legs seem sunk up to her thighs in a bog (as Urizen is "sinking thro these Elemental wonders swift to fall" [25]). A second daughter lies on her side in the foreground, her arm reaching toward something the third is hiding. Beneath her arm is the handle of a scythe, the long blade of which curves to the bottom edge of the page. After that tolling bell of Page 71, the grim reaper seems to have gone to work. But the third woman, head nodding but body almost upright, seems drowsy yet quite alive. Her features faintly resemble those of Michelangelo's "Pieta." Yet her closing eyes and mouth and her nearness to the dead trunk of Urizen's tree of mystery—a double trunk, however, almost able to move, to take shape as human legs—invite us to view this woman as representing Blake's view of a Virgin Madonna, whose utmost pity lets her accept the sacrifice of her son because she is unable to rebel against the blighting darkness of her father's Tree. (See "The Everlasting Gospel"; and see what these three daughters are doing in Night the Seventh when they knead the "bread" for Orc.) It is, in fact, within the remaining sap of this leafless and shattered tree that Urizen creates and recreates the Vortices of his rationalizing and lucubrating mental light in a process of which he cannot see the end: "No end I find of all" (33).

Page 73 (NT 78:24E)

"AND ALL FUTURITY BE BOUND . . ." (20)

The engraving used here, when fitted to Young's text, bore simply the title of Young's "Night the Third: Narcissa." In the design Blake employs a prophetic image from Revelation, chapter 12. A woman crowned with stars, escaping her mortal body, is to deliver Christ. Young's poem invites us all to "Spring from our fetters, fasten in the skies" (1797, P. 63). The woman of spirit strides past the closing gate of the serpent's body and mouth—like the infant Christ on page 63 escaping the parental spanning—yet though her knee and foot rest on an inverted crescent moon, the stride is extended too far for any springing up: she seems, rather, prepared to receive the vision which her hands implore and her face opens to. It may depend on what we expect, whether we see her as reaching for something we cannot see or as attracted by the gems and gold of the phallic serpent.

We can recognize the serpent as a traditional symbol of Eternity, an ouroboros, since it is about to swallow—or has just released—its own tail. (See the description of this engraving in the 1980 *Designs for Young's Night Thoughts*, I:36.) But the serpent, too, is looking ambiguously upward and need not, if he wills otherwise, become as inhuman as a chain. In the text of this and succeeding pages we encounter several images which wind round like serpents but could open "into Eternity at will" (74:1), choosing human rather than chain-like form. Urizen, who is determined to bring the world under his own will, "himself being King," wishes to bind "all futurity . . . in his vast chain"—which he attempts to form of "gold, silver & iron" (a perverse sequence: 16–20). This great python may, indeed, be seen as one symbol of Urizen himself (as Grant observes), another being the headless tree on page 72.

What actually happens, rather against Urizen's will, is that the familiar "Web of a Spider, dusky & cold," which shivers behind him as he travels "from Vortex to Vortex, drawn out from his mantle of years," itself aspires to human form (32–33). In birth-like "bursts" and "thunderings" it develops "expansive" eyelids (note those of the serpent) and ears like "a golden ascent winding round to the heavens of heavens" (37–38). This life existing in Urizen's "Abysses" with "lion or tyger or scorpion" (with colors approaching the serpent's gold and gems) could (we are told) open "at will" into Eternity, "But they refusd because their outward forms were in the Abyss" (74:1–2). The statement that this "dire Web" grows from Urizen's "Soul" suggests that soul and body are inseparable. The illustration diagrams this: serpent and woman, body and soul, are "adjoind" (34) not by moon bridge or iron trap but by human form: if the serpent bit his tail and shut his eyes they would again be in deepest hell. (But we see he has no fangs.)

As the narrative proceeds, we see Orc becoming this serpent; or we see, from another perspective, that Urizen's body-web is Orc, wound round his Tree in "scales that shine with gold & rubies" (80:27–28).

As for Narcissa in this design, her vigor and beauty bring vitality to the sleeping females of the previous drawing; the splendor of the phallic serpent, despite forked tongue (for we are still in the Abyss, in the wilderness where tygers roam) promises a future not ruled by a King.

Page 74

URIZEN "WARRING WITH MONSTERS"

"Thus Urizen in sorrows wanderd many a dreary way," vortex after divisive vortex, "Warring with monsters of the Deeps in his most hideous pilgrimage Till his bright hair scattered in snows, his skin barkd o'er with wrinkles" (74:9–11). We can imagine the snowy hair and the wrinkles, but we see no web nor monsters but only the potential Diogenes: "Still he with his globe of fire immense in his venturous hand" (35). Yet what his hand grasps is not the sun, not a globe but a whirling vortex!

We are to realize that Urizen is striding toward a fresh generative ambiguity, a vortex of vortices, "not bent from his own will," yet "By Providence divine conducted" (31–32). Creating vortices as he ascends and descends "thro' the Affrighted vales" (36) into the vale of human tears, he is surprised but able to comprehend that instead of meeting with human objects of pity and obedience he is approaching the voice of resistance to his oppression of Luvah and Vala. When he beholds "the world of Los" he hears "the howling of red Orc distincter & distincter" (39–40).

(In *Urizen* 25 he *is* carrying a globe, with spikes of radiation, having somehow found a handle to it.)

Page 75 (NT 27:35E)

"DARK GREW HIS GLOBE, REDDNING WITH MISTS" (5)

In Young's text, "midnight veil'd" the sun's face at Christ's passion on the cross, and the sun fled from the Creator's pain—or from the "enormous load of human guilt" that "bow'd his blessed head." Blake's sun-god weeps and bows *his* head, but his horses rage with Orc-like breath of flame. "I rage . . . Yet my fierce fires are better than thy snows," Orc will declare (79:1–2).

In Blake's text, Urizen is venturing into the vale of Urthona as he hears Orc and encounters the Spectre and Tharmas. They attack him with apocalyptic blasts. The fire-breathing horses' heads in the illustration can serve well as the "Four-winged heralds" who "mount the furious blasts & blow their trumps" (19). But the naked, weeping Apollo, suitable for Young's sun, can be accounted for in relation to Blake's text only ironically: Urizen backs off from the confrontation, "back many a mile Retiring, into his dire Webb" (25–26). He and the Spectre of Urthona both guide squadrons that "wheel" in the sky; the term alludes to their orbiting and suggests the wheels of chariots like Apollo's.

The wheeling daunts Urizen temporarily, partly because he recognizes the four horsemen "in arms Of Gold & silver, brass & iron," who lead those squadrons, as his own "mighty sons." One Zoa, Luvah, is still lying in the void of the East. Within that void the forces of Urthona and Tharmas, of construction and destruction, led by the trumpeting horses, can only prepare the rule of Jehovah, the "leprous" sixth eye of God, who will perfect "the Body of Death . . . in hypocritic holiness"— whereupon Jesus will come and die "willing" (115:49–50). The text of this Sixth Night ends with the crucifixion of "red Orc" by the blood-drinking Comets wheeling like scythed chariots at Urizen's command (75:29–31).

Page 76

A FORM "INTENDED NOT"

The apparently human form of this suspended figure seems to be losing a struggle with the monstrous, despite the hope of Urizen's redemption in Night of the Fifth. Though apparently standing on one foot and coming forward, holding out and up his/her hands, this "shape" we see has feet and hands that lack articulate form. In Night the Eighth the monstrous component will triumph as, to Urizen's terror and astonishment, "the battle take[s] a form Which he intended not, a Shadowy hermaphrodite" which the soldiers name Satan, a male hidden within a female (101:33–37). Note that the face is double, with a left profile "hidden within" a front face, the two faces sharing one of the eyes, and two kinks of hair beside the nose, near where the profile face would have its ear.

The helmet shape enclosing the front face suggests a warrior-body, more human than that of the iron man of page 75, whose "dread visage" is armed with "scales of iron" and whose skull has "iron spikes instead Of hair" (75:16–17). The helmet is topped by feathers, as in Blake's 10th and 11th designs for Gray's *Bard*. The breasts seem neither clearly male nor female. The sexual area (from what can be seen despite erasures) is neither simply male nor simply female: there may be two penises surrounding a vulva, or possibly one long penis reaching to the navel (or is that mostly hair?): this is War as hermaphroditic Satan.

As we turn to this page, it is easy to imagine that it prompts the gesture of horror made by the Apollo of the previous page. Whatever the specifics, Blake clearly tells us that the dominance of Urizenic deformity continues. In the last lines of Night the Sixth, Urizen is still rotating "the massy Globes" of our planetary lives in "vast excentric paths . . . at his dread command." Their wheels are torture instruments which reach "red Orc" and return "back to Urizen gorgd with blood." The squadrons of soldiers are still "weaving the dire Web . . . & preparing Urizen's path before him" (75:28–34).

De Luca remarks that "the figure has been drawn twice—the torso of a male, with slimmer hips, thighs, waist, broader chest, and flatter breasts, inside the figure of a female" (except for the chest!); but while we may *see* the female form superimposed over the male, *or* vice versa, it was clearly Blake's intention to indicate this duality from the start; we are not faced with a design begun with one figure in mind and changed to another (as in some of Blake's figures with alternate positions of the head or limbs).

NIGHT THE SEVENTH[1]

Page 77 (NT 27:7E, first state)

"LOS FELT THE ENVY IN HIS LIMBS" (27)

As this dark Night begins, Los hides behind a rock while Urizen descends to the Caves of Orc and proceeds, keeping a cautious distance, to set up his library, "brooding Envious over Orc" (19). Blake makes no pictorial effort to depict Orc's infernal "Universe of flaming fire," with its howling lions and roaming tigers, its "adamantine scales of justice Consuming in the raging lamps of mercy"— a process, prepared in page 71, that transforms Urizen's adamantine books—and its plow and harrow of ages wading through fields of gore while "the immortal seed is nourishd for the slaughter" (6–15). Instead, by employing a variant proof sheet of the *Night Thoughts* design used on page 49 (Night IV) Blake flashes our attention back to the family origins of jealousy.

The proof chosen is of an earlier state of the plate; birds have not yet been set in the sky, nor clouds; the tongue of the serpent is shaped like an arrow-head. The effect is suitably bleak. Yet in these caverns Orc's fires are not only transforming the bible of vengeance to the gospel of mercy, but "pulse after pulse" Orc's spirit is darting "high & higher to the shrine of Enitharmon" (21–22)—boding no immediate good, however, since Los feels toward the growing youth not pride but the same envy as Urizen, a blight "in his limbs" (27).

In Night the Fourth this picture could emphasize Los's acceptance of serpentine guilt and the Urizenic impulse to bind the family to the rock of sacrifice and war. Binding their organs of sense represented the original Oedipal structure, for Los and Enitharmon could give birth to Orc only when *all* the Zoas were divided. Now, in Night the Seventh, when Urizen is attempting to destroy the son (Orc, Luvah-Christ), we are able to read the serpent-entwined man as Orc as well as Los. At the same time we may see the woman as Enitharmon, guiding yet restraining the child in his play with the bird/phallus.

In both scenes, as textually defined, Los feels the blight of jealousy; in both, Tharmas, though fallen, intervenes. In Blake's myth, both scenes are analogues of states of existence. He calls the first Tirzah, the second Rahab—different yet similar forms of

Natural Religion and Moral Virtue, under memory of the stings of the serpent of good and evil. Christ will accept dying "beneath Tirzah & Rahab" (115:50), but since Los, in Night the Fourth, participated in the fall, that part of Orc which communes with Rahab as "Harlot of the Kings of Earth" will also be responsible for the corruption of Christianity, giving rise to a new "Babylon," a new form of "Natural Religion" (111:1–24).

[1]We have combined the pages often grouped as Seven A and Seven B. See Introduction.

Page 78

"SURE THOU ART BATHD IN RIVERS OF DELIGHT" (36)

Forced to abandon his "book of iron" to escape the labyrinthine roots of his own jealous logic (7–12), Urizen at length addresses Orc, moved by pity (he says) "to reveal myself before thee in a form of wisdom" (30–31). In a moment of true wisdom, cloaked by a sort of tongue-in-cheek camaraderie which belies it, Urizen suggests that Orc is able to "laugh at all these tortures" because he feeds on "visions of sweet bliss" in a sweet golden clime. The next moment he shifts to another hypothesis (potentially Christian, but also potentially more sadistically Urizenic): "Or is thy joy founded on torment which others bear for thee!?!" (32–41).

Adult, naked Orc, still chained on his back, is drawn to fill the bottom of the page, his eyes closed against any but visions of Expanses outside these caves. "Curse thy hoary brows," is his reply to Urizen. "What dost thou in this deep? Thy Pity I contemn; scatter thy snows elsewhere" (42–43). Blake tried each leg in various positions before settling on this quite springless accommodation to the rock, head dropped back. (Not using the pillow beyond his head—if it is that: it may be an earlier body position.) Can the heavy curls above and beside his head be simply hair—or are they buds of wings, recollections of those cupid wings in earlier Nights?[1]

(In the upper left margin is an erased drawing, with inscription, probably there before this proof sheet became a page of manuscript. When turned about, it can be seen as a drawing of two feet, with perhaps a small third foot, and the words" "B Blake / Catherine Blake / 76." The combined ages of William and Catherine Blake would have been 76 in 1797–98, a likely time for inscription of this proof.)

[1]The heavy shading in his genital area may cover another figure, which Butlin sees as kneeling with his head on the Orc-figure's loins.

Page 79 (NT 96:28E, trimmed)

STILL URIZEN SITS, CLOSED UP

Young's text for which the design was made exhorts one afraid of death to listen to "the silent address" that dead friends make to our hearts. They hover over us in expectation of the "revolution" which our hearts will undergo if we let the "thought of death" inspire us "like a god." For Young such revolution meant a longing for death which allows us to resume eternal life. For Blake the traditional ideas of death and life had undergone so energetic a revolution that, speaking of the dead, he would transform Jesus' saying, "Let the dead bury the dead," into the diabolic proverb: "Drive your cart and your plow over the bones of the dead" (*Marriage* 7).

For the confrontation and taunting of Urizen and Orc in pages 78–80, each could take turns in this scene as exhorter or exhorted. Urizen is ready to see his antagonist borne "down beneath the waves in stifling despair" (78:29), Orc to see the "rocks roll oer" Urizen (79:13). But Orc's is the more revolutionary irony, since it is he, not Urizen, whose "feet & hands are naild to the burning rock" yet Urizen who sits "closd up." "Thou art not chaind," observes Orc. "Why shouldst thou sit, cold grovelling demon of woe," why "fixd, obdurate, brooding, sit Writing thy books?" (1–11). Each, though it is said of Orc, turns "affection" (or "wisdom": first reading) "into fury & thought into abstraction" (80:47)—somewhat as Young's dead friend inspires him with the "thought of death." Yet the obdurate mourner of the picture, woebegone among tombstones and a wall that need not imprison him, more accurately suits Urizen, the tombstone and wall his stony books.

The accident, if such it be, of this leaf's being cut off to exclude the grave and briars and flowers in the full engraving and reduce the mourner to a stony diagram serves well the spirit of the text.

Returning closer to Young, the hovering figure, one of Young's "Angels sent on Errands full of Love," can be taken, Butlin suggests, "in ironic allusion to the ministrations of Urizen's daughters to the bound Orc, kneading the 'bread of sorrow'" (line 23).

Page 80

"O URIZEN, PRINCE OF LIGHT!"

Since this page of the manuscript has no illustration—except for a few pencil strokes including four curving lines that fall short of suggesting either a serpent or a garment or a wing—the reader is free to consider the aptness of the images in the engraving on the facing page, 81. Urizen is identified (by furious, wormlike Orc, "divided" by Urizen's hypocrisy) as properly the "Prince of Light" yet actually hostile to light and warmth, a cold "King of furious hail storms" (80:34–37). The engraving shows a Urizenic figure standing on fallen kings and holding a blazing sun in his right hand, yet menacing it with an iron dart held in his left.

(The leaf may have been cut off at the bottom to modify the design on page 79, or to cancel some drawing on page 80.)

Page 81 (NT 20:5E, first state)

"HOW THOU ART SHRUNK!" (29)

The engraved proof used for this page takes us back to the First Night of Young's poem, where the poet laments the "treason to divine decree" which has allowed "darts of agony" to pierce his heart. Young had failed to believe himself immortal and all material things subject to "Death! great proprietor of all." Death's role is "To tread out empire" and even, one day, to "pluck" the sun "from his sphere." Blake depicts Death as trampling on kings and preparing to pluck down the sun, even threatening to pierce it.

There is ironic counterpoint in the *Four Zoas* text of pages 80–81. Urizen is not described as reaching for the sun but, while he sits "envious brooding," as compelling Orc to "stretch out & up the mysterious tree," to "flame high in pride, & laugh to scorn the source of his deceit" (i.e. to despise "Urizen's light" and turn it "into flaming fire" 80:45–81:4). Orc does not recognize his deceit as Urizenic. Urizen does not know that his effort to "draw all human forms Into submission to his will" must have a "dread result" (80:50–81:6)—for the reader, a double entendre.

Orc does remember stealing Urizen's light ("& it became fire consuming"); perhaps he does know that Urizen is the "source of his deceit" (80:39–40,

50) and that he has only "sufferd him to Climb" to achieve dominion (81:5–6). It is Urizen the "wise" who, like the wits of Young's poem, knows not "the source" but thinks "himself the Sole author Of all his wandering Experiments in the horrible Abyss" (80:51, 81:1).

"How thou Art Shrunk!" (Los's exclamation to Enitharmon in this ambience) can apply to all the Zoas caught in the tree of Mystery.

The shrinking of Urizen's universe may also be seen as a symbol of the darkened relations between Los and Enitharmon, with Orc a Promethean in potentially human form. Urizen's showers of deceit and envy chill Los and Enitharmon. But Los's "broodings rush down to his feet, producing Eggs" which hatch and "burst forth upon the winds above the tree" (i.e. take wing) (8–9). Also, even while lying frozen on Los's knees, Enitharmon has moments "when her spirit returnd as ruddy as a morning when The ripe fruit blushes into joy" (16–17). Los, as if he were in Urizen's place ready to quench the sun, freezes silent at her sunshine. But even his lament is expressed in solar images: "thou in thrilling joy, in beaming summer loveliness . . . . thy grapes that burst in summer's vast Excess . . . Thy roses that expanded in the face of glowing morn" (25–33). His desire for her "beauty" is all drenched in sorrow at her "trembling" when he approaches (26–27). Death may dominate the picture, but the light is not really at its mercy.

Page 82

"BUT THE NEXT JOY OF THINE SHALL BE IN SWEET DELUSION" (35)

In Night the First we were told that Tharmas stretched "out his holy hand" and "Turnd round the circle of Destiny with tears & bitter sighs" (5:10–11); then that Enion, as she "loved & wept," labored nine days and nights (pregnant with the universe, as it were); that "on the tenth trembling morn the Circle of Destiny" was "complete" (5:22–24). In Night the Fourth the Saviour found the limits, naming them Satan and Adam, and "Then wondrously the Starry Wheels felt the divine hand" (56:19–23). (There is an echo here of the Ptolemaic primum mobile or tenth sphere.) At the end of Night the Sixth the "dismal squadrons of Urthona" slowly "o'erwheel" at Urizen's command (75:32–33). In the drawing of this page, is it Enitharmon (or her Urizenic shadow?) who grasps and perhaps turns the starry wheel—in streams of water and of air? (Note the turbulence between hoop and face and the water falling on the wheel.)

There are eight stars, in Blake's symbolism the eight "eyes of God," of which the seventh will be Jesus, the eighth the present reader. Elemental streams flow into the Circle, and Enitharmon's running/swimming body with the concentration of effort expressed in her eye and arms bears intimations of hope—and also of utter involvement that will catch her in the coming crash of the conflicting wheels of all the Zoas and Emanations of Man. Indeed, the coming of Christ will be enmeshed in priests' blessings and tyrants' usurpations of glory that will constitute a new kind of Natural Religion. (On page 104, where we shall see the Circle closer, the pushing will be even more strenuous but the stars will open as eyes. Finally, on page 128 in a new dream of Innocence we shall see it serving in the hand of a dancing woman, as a tambourine.)

In the poetry of this page a human song of love expresses the craving of Los, like any earthly Adam, for a female human, while Enitharmon, like any earthly Eve, divides the stream of her sexual energy between natural and elemental love. Some progression of the imagination results. Los, Enitharmon, and the Spectre—all portions of Urthona, source of Albion's power to create images—come together. They do so under the sapless "tree of Mystery"; yet visions result. The sap of the river of love might make it the tree of Life, even if a painful and poisonous transformation: "the tree . . . Began to blossom in fierce pain, shooting its writhing buds in throes of birth, & now, blossoms falling, shining fruit Appeard, of many colours & of various poisonous qualities" (16–21).

The left leg of the striding female was at first drawn in a less strenuous position, more immersed in the stream. At her ear there is a crude suggestion of an ark (as in *Jerusalem* 18 and 24) which is probably supposed to be a decoration on a helmet.

Page 83 (NT 94:27E)

"THAT SUBTERRANEAN WORLD, THAT LAND OF RUIN!" (YOUNG 54:4)

To illustrate Young's text, Blake engraved this stream of human forms emerging from the "subterranean world" of death and he personified Young's "darkness, brooding o'er unfinish'd fates With raven wing." Young's "thought" walks along the margin of the stream, "expatiating." Our dying friends, Young ponders, help us to "chase our

thoughtlessness, fear, pride, and guilt." (The foremost figure in the stream has an eye of fear, the next figure covers his ears in pride, the next two, with hands in prayer, confess guilt.)

Blake's text in page 83 is relevantly subterranean, and like Young's darkness the Spectre of Urthona is now perceived by the "Shadow of Enitharmon" as a "Shade" (like herself?), "horrible" yet seeking her love (82:37–38; 83:3). Adapting the picture, we can see her white shade approaching his dark shade; in the text, fallen, they exchange confused recollections of the world of Eternity. He remembers the "discordant" birth of Orc (82:34); she remembers a wall built round Beulah, Man falling with the birth of Urizen and then an Enormity called Luvah & Vala, then all Beulah falling, riven from its hinges. "Nor do I more remember till I stood Beside Los in the Cavern dark, enslavd to vegetative forms" (26–30). The forms emerging from the river, which emerges from darkness, suggest the human direction which this living wheel of destiny (if we remember the stream and wheel of page 82) may now flow in, with the walls of the dark cavern riven. The face and the wheel-embracing arms of the woman of page 82 were probably drawn to match the face and all-embracing arms of the woman who is swimming, with confidence, in this stream.

"Just as Los will be liberated only by acknowledging the Spectre in himself, the side of himself that serves rather than rules man and is in touch with the darker realities, so Enitharmon too must learn to love the lower side of Los before she can love him at his ultimate best." (Wilkie and Johnson p. 154.) The "dark" Urthona is needed to ensure enough time for love, the shadow of Enitharmon, to ensure enough space.

Page 84

"BUT MY EYES ARE ALWAYS UPON THEE" (38)

Blake's text continues the imagery of the stream issuing from darkness. The fallen Spectre, wooing the fallen Emanation with remembrance of the "mild fields of happy Eternity Where thou & I in undivided Essence walked about Imbodied" (4–6), recognizes the Fall as a separation. When there issued from the "infinite labyrinths of the heart & thro the nostrils" a stupefyingly fragrant and bright "female," he abruptly halted his work at the anvil preparing "spades & plowshares" and suddenly sank down "with cries of blood, issuing downward in the veins Which now my rivers were become . . . sunk along The goary tide even to the place of seed" (14–21).

In the drawing we see the Spectre, well aware of his limitations ("Thou knowest . . . that I am . . . a ravening, devouring lust") but able to "view futurity" in Enitharmon. Sunken, he is no longer sinking. At first both hands were drawn supporting his body from collapse into the tide; now he can reach up, seeing even the Tree as "this delightful Tree . . . given us for a Shelter from the tempests of Void & Solid Till once again the morn of ages shall renew upon us To reunite in those mild fields. . . . " He recognizes that his yearning for his counterpart distinguishes him from spectres of the dead: " . . . I am as the Spectre of the Living" (40). "Listen, O vision of Delight!" (12).

(It may or may not be meaningful that the drawing technique here is much more swirling and indistinct than otherwise similarly tentative designs, e.g. page 44 which is motivally comparable, and page 126. The treatment of the face, however, is something in the special effects department. As John Grant points out, a strong *vortex* draws us into the sketch-maw; the eyes, with beam-brows, are themselves vortex-derived, each made with a spiral stroke of the pencil—as were those mad "hairs" on the cheek of the hermaphrodite soldier in page 76.)

Page 85 (NT 153:42E)

"NOR COULD HIS EYES PERCEIVE THE CAUSE" (9–10)

Blake engraved this design to be the next to last plate in the 1797 Young, which ends with a goddess of Truth pointing both hands up, to the Christian triumph over Death. (A proof of that last page is used below, for page 113[109].) The reclining figure is the Socratic fool—his face resembles that of "Reason" on page 67—who views the Crucifixion as a dishonorable blot on Christ's scutcheon. "If angels tremble, 'tis at such a sight"—not at the sight of Christ's giving himself, but at the blindness of the wretch who cannot understand.

When Blake chose this proof for *The Four Zoas*, he intended to end Night the Seventh with it, concluding the Night with line 21, "Till many of the dead burst forth from the bottoms of their tombs." The only person in the text at this stage who bears any resemblance to the uncomprehending Socratic fool is Los himself, whose "fierce soul was terrifid At the shrieks of Enitharmon, at her tossings: nor could his eyes perceive The cause of her dire anguish, for she lay the image of Death" (8–10). The pair of angels are not mentioned, though in late additions to the text on this page Blake introduces "male forms without female counterparts" (19)—to whom we may contrast this pair of male and female (the Shadow of the Spectre and the Shade of Enitharmon?) intimately joined.

(In the reconstruction of text for the 1982 edition, edited by Erdman, Night the Seventh moves from 85:22 to 95:15 at this juncture.)

Page 86

"SHE SIGHS THEM FORTH UPON THE WIND" (99:24)

This verso page at first contained the drawing with no text and was evidently intended to serve as a full-page design standing between Nights Seventh and Eighth. The drawing, which we take to be of Enitharmon after the breaking of her heart's Gates, was probably made while Blake was writing "End of the Seventh Night" half way down page 85. (He wrote this first after line 21, but then erased it and added lines 22–31 as explanatory afterthought, writing again "The End of the Seventh Night.")

This is a moment of great reversal of direction in the humanizing of the four Zoas. The embrace of "the spirit of Enitharmon" and the spectre of "Her once lovd Lord" results, at one extreme, in the birth of Vala as the Whore of Revelation: "a wonder horrible, a Cloud, she grew & grew"—the magnification of error, a sign of the approach of a great storm. This bursts "the Gates of Enitharmon's heart with direful Crash" and causes "many of the dead" to "burst forth from the bottoms of their tombs, In male forms without female counterparts or Emanations" (85:1–19). Such male forms are "Cruel, and ravening with Enmity & Hatred & War" (20).

Closing the Night at this point, Blake may have drawn the picture on page 86 to offer a vision of the simultaneous contrary development: Enitharmon, with the gates removed from her heart ready to offer female counterparts that will transform these male forms from spectres of the dead to spectres of the living (see 84:40). But the ten lines he added when he moved down his finis line make explicit the change occurring in the Zoas, from death to life, from hatred and war to love and embracing:

But then the Spectre enterd Los's bosom.
  Every sigh & groan
Of Enitharmon bore Urthona's Spectre on
  its wings.

Obdurate, Los felt Pity. Enitharmon told the
tale
Of Urthona. Los embracd the Spectre, first
as a brother
Then as another Self; astonishd,
humanizing & in tears
In Self abasement Giving up his
Domineering lust.

(85:26–31)

Perhaps only at this point did Blake make his drawing on page 86, with half a dozen "spectres of the Dead" bursting from the bottoms of the grave, and Enitharmon on her knees offering them living nurture. Blake's leaving these forms in an extremely sketchy stage (compared to those given various human and humanoid forms in the title-page, page 1) makes the possibilities infinite. (After making this drawing, the poet continued to expand his text, but the lines crowded above and below the drawing and on to the next page simply amplify the positive open-hearted development, even to Los's repentant welcoming of "Reason's power"!)

On page 99 (once the page facing this picture) we learn that when the dead "descend thro' the Gate of Pity, The broken heart Gate of Enitharmon, She signs them forth upon the wind Of Golgonooza" (the city of Art), and there Los stands "recieving them . . . From out the War of Urizen & Tharmas" (99:22–100:1).

That her nipples and navel (and left thumbs) were drawn twice may not mean that Blake intended them to be double. As for the sketched forms in Enitharmon's shadow, what seem at first a standing and a sitting figure on each side may be more multiple than that; or the sitting figures, made from the original knees of the standing figures, may be meant to replace them. (The standing ones are covered by shading strokes; yet the one on her left remains distinct.)

The sitting figure beside Enitharmon's right thigh may be holding an infant, swaddled. The standing (or soaring?) figure toward which her face is turned has loops of hair which suggest Orc, though decidedly not "howling" as he was a moment ago (85:22) when put in the sinister charge of the "horrible" shadow of Vala. There is a sense, however, in which Enitharmon's story and Vala's are both conveyed in this picture; Vala's materialization under the tree of Death and Enitharmon's heart's opening which confirms the spectre's vision of "this delightful Tree" (84:1).

In what was once the facing page, 95[87], Enitharmon, Eve-like, urges Los to take and eat of "the fruit Of Urizen's Mysterious tree" (14–22), a sexual offer that can be taken as illustrated by this picture (suggestion of John Sutherland). The posture may be related to images of the "Mother of the Gods," according to Irene Chayes. Butlin sees "a representation of Charity, apparently unrelated to the text"; there is a drawing of Charity with infants at her breasts made by Blake in 1799 (Butlin, pl. 494). Hagstrum sees a resemblance to the traditional lactating Madonna.

Page 87 [95] (NT 64:20E)

"IF YE WILL BELIEVE . . ." (6)

This design was engraved for a page in Young which dwells on the mutuality of education: "Teaching, we learn; and giving, we retain The births of intellect; when dumb, forgot. Speech ventilates our intellectual fire." At first glance Blake's design seems ironic, seems to imply that teachers never learn. The seated elders—a Urizenic old man in a bat-winged chair and a silent maternal sybil seated like a flower in a stem of vegetation, a Vala figure—appear to be in full command of the teaching as a one-way process. Even when we realize that the foremost pupil is making a digital pun with her forefinger, both to count in imitation of the old man and to direct his attention to a youthful lyrist at the top of the text—whose face shows he is using *his* fingers to make music—we may doubt whether Age is learning anything from Youth. The cloud-borne young woman on the right has an enigmatic smile: she approves—but whether of the whole scene or only of the manifest "teaching" is hard to say.

The *Four Zoas* text which Blake inscribed on this proof expresses not enigmatic but contrary themes. In the first part (lines 1–14, later given a more terminal position when Blake inserted instructions to begin this Night with line 15) a sinister Vala is said to stretch "thro' all the worlds of Urizen's journey"; yet the benevolent Daughters of Beulah assert the mutual dynamic of education by writing in golden letters the words "If ye will believe, your Brother shall rise again" (6). (We shall see Lazarus again, on page 89). To suit this text, the young woman looking down must be a Daughter of Beulah; the lyrist must be seen as willing to believe in the bard's golden words and to be singing as well as playing.

Urizen, however, dominates the second portion of the text—a Urizen who has yet to learn the folly of imperial arrogance. Proclaiming himself "A God & not a Man, a Conqueror in triumphant glory," he compels all mankind to bow beneath his feet and to build a war economy: "Trades & Commerce, ships & armed vessels" (23–25). His only education for children is to have them "sold to trades of dire necessity, still laboring day & night till, all Their life extinct, they took the spectre form in dark despair" (26–28). He commands his Sons to "found a Center in the Deep." Urizen "laid the first Stone & all his myriads Builded a temple in the image of the human heart" (31–33). That sounds fine, but the ikon in the temple is still the human phallus of Urizen's secret temple in Night the Third (and see also the next page). His response to Christianity is to build upon it the structures of "a Religion of Chastity, forming a Commerce to sell Loves" (*Jerusalem* 69:34).

For this text the design can help us fight off despair, even while "the Universal Empire groans" (30), if we can interpret the ambiguous figure of the young woman on the cloud (whose ambiguity is like that of the kneeling woman in page 86) as appreciating the gesture of the girl she looks down on and as listening to the song and tune of the lutanist above: it is surely significant that she holds the hair back from her ear—with her finger pointing up, in close correspondence to the gesture of the wise pupil below.

Page 88 [96]

"THE HIDDEN WONDERS ALLEGORIC . . . OF SECRET LUST" (4–5)

Three cowled votaries abase themselves before a huge erect penis flanked by testicles. (The elbows of the second and third pair of praying arms are left to our imagination.) Urizen's manner of control of the human heart is described at considerable length in the text, but without this drawing the central image of the "allegoric" wonders and "secret lust" would be left also to our guessing. The hocus pocus of "whispered hymn & mumbling prayer," or priests and priestesses in "beastial" disguises, of "intoxicating fumes" which evidently subjugate Los and Tharmas and (in the next page) Orc completely, is here sharply exposed. (Some of us can see eyes, nose, and mouth on the head of the penis.) In epic language we are told that the central power put into the temple of Urizen is that "terrific orb" the sun, brought down by "immense machines . . . to the sound of instruments that

drownd the noise Of the hoarse wheels." When we see what the priests are offering for worship, we understand the sun's use in dividing "day & night in different orderd portions, The day for war, the night for secret religion" (5–18).

We see also the "allegoric" form of Los, now enslaved: "Los reard his mighty stature . . . his loins in fires of war," and of Tharmas' new perception of his son Los, as "crowned and inthrond" (19, 31). The only glimmer of hope (on the next page) is Enitharmon's refusal to put "any trust" in fierce, bloody Orc, or in his "glittering scales" and flaming crest (89:28–30). The appearance of Tharmas, laughing "furious among the Banners, clothed in blood," offering to supply bodily food both for Urizen's carnage and to "preserve" his son Los, "tho Enemies arise around . . . numberless" (28–32), demonstrates the common roots of instinctual energy whether "enslaved" for sacrifice and war or given as sustenance to the imagination. Humanity, we learn in this Night, is so entrapped in its long history (in the Hegelian sense) that only a Last Judgment within the flesh and souls, within Los and Enitharmon, can fully liberate the oppressed *and* the oppressors. If the Sun does shine in this secret temple, it is bringing to light the interchangeability between organized religions and between sexual and imperial egos and their victims. Without slaves, there would be no slavery. These bowing figures repeat the submissive posture of the parents in "A Little Boy Lost" (*Songs* 50) who kneel at the auto-da-fé of their own son.

And yet, on the facing page the reappearance of the Saviour, offering Resurrection to the fallen, to the spiritually dead, should assure us that we are approaching the historical event of Christ's walking this earth—simultaneously with the mythic event of the union of Orc/Luvah/Los/Jesus through the creative working of Los. The appearance here of an eyed penis should perhaps be taken to signify a contrary view to the pagan penis-worship of pages 39 to 42, a view of its human form that can see in its balmy drops the promise of a newborn child that will ensure Creative Life. Cannot the bowing figures be the Three Wise men?

Page 89 [97] (NT 148:40E, second state)

"LIFT UP, LIFT UP, O LOS!" (90 [98]:4)

Blake's earlier use of this engraving for page 45 came shortly after the depictions of love reduced to phallic sex (pages 39 to 42). Here it immediately follows the depiction of the phallic worship at the heart of universal hate. Nothing in the text implies this picture of a pitying Jesus calming the panting heart of a dejected but pleading poet, who welcomes the role of Lazarus. It is as though Blake the illuminator felt he must anticipate the cry at the center of Night the Eighth: "Come, Lord Jesus, come quickly!" (104:17), or the plea of Enitharmon, on the very next page (90[98]:4) urging Los to "Lift up" (as the poet here lifts arm and eyes) to wake "my watchman, for he sleepeth."

Enitharmon's desperation arises from the fear that Tharmas, "the God of waters in the wracking Elements," has fallen into a deadly policy of loving only "those who hate" and "rewarding with hate the Loving Soul" (36–37). Perhaps her uttering of that phrase is to be taken as powerful enough to invoke the true, loving God, even to inspire Tharmas and Los to lift up their eyes to Him.

Page 90 [98]

"THE PRESTER SERPENT RUNS ALONG THE RANKS" (22–23)

At the peak of the "War song" of all earthly things showing "their immortal energies in warlike desperation" (11), even "fruit trees humanizing" (10) and "the wooly sheep" walking "sullen . . . through the battle" (17–18), all "rending the heavens & earths & drinking blood in the hot battle" (to feed their hidden children in their "secret palaces") (12–14), religious sanction is offered by the Prester Serpent, pictured here with human face and cobra hood:

> Listen to the Priest of God, ye warriors!
> This Cowl upon my head he placed in
>   times of Everlasting
> And said "Go forth & guide my battles; like
>   the jointed spine
> Of Man I made thee, when I blotted Man
>   from life & light"
> (23–26)

If we consider the head as the commander, Urizen, we may take the three coils to be the other Zoas, reduced to headless articulations.

This is Blake's Antichrist, his Satanic contrary to the Human Form divine, or, to use the terms understood by Los when standing "on the Limit of Translucence," the spinal portion of the "Limit Twofold named Satan & Adam" (95[87]:11–12).

At one time Blake intended the Seventh Night to

end here, but then he rearranged it to enclose this climax within its coils. (He signals on Page 91 that the Night should continue there.) Butlin observes that the face of the Prester Serpent "mirrors, to a certain extent, that of Time in the engraving" on page 99—which was evidently the facing page when the Serpent was drawn.

Page 91 (NT 34:9E)

"STOP WE THE RISING OF THE GLORIOUS KING" (30)

"All men think all men mortal, but themselves," wrote Young. Blake's engraving depicts Young calmly reading even though wrapped in the graveyard briars that had recently enwrapped the body of his dearest friend, Philander. The chains around Young's ankle are shown, in this design's engraved sequel (used later for page 123), to be an extension of the briar which chains him and his music to a bleak earth, Young having been more successful than he supposed in keeping "the thought of death" alive. Even when he believes he is soaring, the poet cannot reach the stars as (he says) the lark's song can.

All Blake's Zoas, in Night the Seventh, have become obsessed with thoughts of death. And Blake's text directs our attention to the historical war, to the campaign of 1799 in which the British army joined the Continental powers against Napoleonic France. Even Orc now, the Zoa of "flaming youth," is bent on combat. It is not purely ironic, however, that he is identified by the "dragons of the North" as "the glorious King" and, in the text of the next page, "naild . . . to the tree" as Luvah/Christ, an "allegoric" repetition of the parental chaining to the rock.

In the astronomical symbolism of the text, Orc's "shoulders huge" appearing above the mountain/horizon (6–7) represent the rising of Orion (Albion), whose "shoulder" (the star Betelgeux) appears with the two dogs and two lions called Canis Minor, Canis Major, Leo Minor, and Leo). "The fiery dogs arise the shoulders huge appear. . . . The hairy shoulders rend the links; free are the wrists of fire. Red rage redounds he rouzd his lions from his forests black" (the "forests of the night") (9–18).[1]

Hopeful signs in the picture are the nightingale on the briar, the attentive look on Mrs. Midnight, the dark woman perched on Young's thigh—and the fact that Young is reading Milton or Homer and that his song, like theirs, is of "immortal man."[2]

The free-soaring emanations have, however, more hazards to contend with than their lithe bodies and scroll-like gowns might suggest. A white cloud covers the head of the bright spirit at top right; the dark ascending spirit below her has a dark cloud-mountain to climb; the descending spirit on the left is being rent on thorns! We must read the gestures of the spirit standing on Young's calf, then, as both pointing the way up and sounding the alarm. A dominant note of hope, nevertheless, is signified by the lark soaring above the text, above the title-word "Vala." If Young is bound down, Blake would bear witness that his song "Oft bursts . . . beyond the bounds of life."

When we turn to page 92, with a drawing obviously intended to reinterpret the symbolism of this engraving on its recto, we find the poet transformed from briar-bound reading, on the quiet grave, to inspired writing, immersed in the bloody stream.

[1]On the astronomical details, see Worrall, 1981.
[2]See comment, below, on page 123.

Page 92

"AND ALL THE ARTS OF LIFE THEY CHANGD" (21)

Blake's drawing on this page is a curious imitation and reversal of his engraved design on the recto. Birds and briar are gone. The poet, seen from the back, is not reading now but writing[1] (with a long-feathered quill visible over his shoulder) and sitting in a more strenuous position. The book and perhaps the poet himself are in or beside a stream, perhaps the gory river of the battle. In it up to her thighs is a stout naked woman, flanked on each side by huddling figures—or corpses. This is Vala as goddess (and victim) of war, Vala now among the slain, and now bitterly reproached: "Wilt thou now smile among the slain, when the wounded groan in the field?" (37)

The languid, soaring nymphs of the engraving are replaced by three naked and squat figures: two in the left margin canceled even before given complete form, and a third (derived from an inspiring figure in *NT* 490, notes Grant) floating just above the poet's head to call his and our attention emphatically to that concluding line of the text.

The message continues in the next page: "This is no warbling brook . . . but blood & wounds & dismal cries & clarions of war" (93:15). In these verses there seems to be no intermediate

spokesman between Blake and the spirit he addresses—though ultimately we are told that these words are sung by "the demons of the deep" (93:20):

> Now, now the Battle rages round thy tender
>   limbs, O Vala!
> Now smile among thy bitter tears, now put
>   on all thy beauty.
> Is not the wound of the sword Sweet & the
>   broken bone delightful?
>
>   (34–36)

Young's dark companion in the engraving (the spirit of melancholy and night and of the plaining Philomel) becomes Blake's "Melancholy Magdalen," Vala (93:1–2).

[1]Perhaps revising this "bloody" Night.

Page 93 (NT 99:29E)

"THEY RETURN WITH LAMENTATIONS, MOURNING &
WEEPING" (31)

Ultimately, to Vala's "Supreme delight" (29), Orc is transformed entirely into the phallic serpent "round the tree of Mystery" (24) (i.e. at the cneter of Urizen's secret religion) and her own members are "strewn thro' the Abyss" (22). "The form of Orc was gone; he reard his serpent bulk among The stars of Urizen in Power, rending the form of life Into a formless indefinite & strewing her on the Abyss Like clouds upon the winter sky" (25–28). Vala rejoices, but the "Warriors" mourn, disappointed (29).

In the engraving Blake shows us, as it were, the disgruntled warriors at the local tavern. The design was originally made to depict a group defined by Young as "wrecks of human hope," drinking not so much to forget death as to snatch "each gulp" before "death should snatch the bowl." Like Blake's warriors, they partake of the "want of thought" which Young and Blake know is death (see "The Fly"). Both Young's debauchees and Blake's bloody-backs (as British soldiers called themselves) live on borrowed time, having lost "the form of life" in any organized sense.

It is seldom noticed that Blake's famous lines,

> Unorganizd Innocence, An Impossibility
> Innocence dwells with Wisdom but never
>   with Ignorance,

often taken as unrelated to *The Four Zoas*, were

written, neatly and vertically (the first line in pencil, the second in ink, with a pencil line running into the text between paragraphs) alongside this account of the loss of human form, the collapse of war songs into "brute sounds" (34), and the breakdown of warriors. Are these blood-sodden brutes innocent victims, or, to use a Blakean epithet, "Ignorant hirelings"? They clutch their heads, where the deep trouble lies. They are fools, like Satan himself—or Solomon.

(In the lower left margin is the pencil sketch of a small, narrow foot or footprint, going up the page; below it a hand with fingers holding, possibly, a writing instrument. Grant suggests a sort of Blakean signature comparable to that in *Job* 14, where the central figures are a hand and a thumb, drawn to suggest a W and a B, Blake's initials.)[1]

[1] The story of this Night as Blake works over it seems to affect him very personally (see note 1 to page 92).

Page 94

"NEVER, NEVER WILL I ARISE, TILL HIM I LOVE IS LOOSD FROM THIS DARK CHAIN" (22–23)

The demons have clearly underestimated Vala. All the horrors and false hopes of the text seem to weigh upon her, as Blake shows her almost flattened beneath the manuscript lines that conclude by defining her as "the howling Melancholy." Butlin sees her as "falling beneath a heavy sky." At this point Tharmas, saying "I hear thy voice but not thy form see" (8), mistakes her for his lost Enion. And Blake draws her in a form recalling that of Enion on page 7. But here it is Vala, sinful Magdalen that she is, who persists in her loving search for the crucified Luvah. Note too that Tharmas, despite the perversity of his condemnation—"Vala, thy Sins have lost us heaven & bliss, Thou art our Curse"—has a similar stubborn objective: "and till I can bring love into the light, I never will depart from my great wrath" (24–26).

They nevertheless continue to torment themselves and each other. Perhaps neither shall manage to attain wisdom. But we are at once (as the narrative continues, on page 87[95])[1] comforted with "the Eternal Promise" which the daughters of Beulah write "on all their tombs & pillars & on every Urn: . . . 'If ye will believe, your Brother shall rise again,' In golden letters, ornamented with sweet labours of Love, Waiting with Patience for the fulfilment of the Promise Divine" (4–8).

The design on page 94 seems to be over a previous sketch of a different subject.

[1] Since Blake directed lines 15–33 of that page to be moved (hence our moving leaf 95–96 to position 87–88), he left the first 14 lines to be read as continuation of page 94; they were written when these were facing pages and are available as context for the picture on page 94.

Pages 95 [87], 96 [88], 97 [89], 98 [90] (proof of Edward and Elenor)

These pages are crowded with extensive manuscript additions begun in the middle of page 85, crowded above and below the picture of Vala on page 86, and continuing in the margins of 98[90]. Blake made no illustrations for them and probably considered these two leaves as appendages rather than new pages.

One slight exception may be the small sketch in the lower left corner of 97[89], in which a man in dueling posture thrusts his rapier at a skirted kneeling figure with arms praying for mercy. (See tracing.) This seems like marginal comment on the engraved picture of *Edward & Elenor* (1793) rather than an illumination for *The Four Zoas*. The two leaves made by cutting up a print of this old engraving do not represent a cutting in half; they differ from each other in both dimensions, the print being cut in such a way as to eliminate an inch and a half of the central scene of this history picture.[1] King Edward, murderer of Welsh bards, was one of Blake's villains. Blake may have intentionally sliced the paper to remove the scene of Queen Elenor's sucking poison from a wound made by an as-

Page 97. Marginal attack.

sassin's attempt to kill the king.

We cannot know what pictures Blake might have drawn in a less hurried and crowded draft of these concluding pages of Night the Seventh. We can, to avoid the impression that there is a serious thematic gap here, call attention to passages in the text which prepare the way for the apocalyptic occurrences of Night the Eighth. In page 107[115] the sweep of divine history culminates in the ambiguous image of a Christ who accepted a predestined sacrifice, who "Came & Died willing beneath Tirzah & Rahab" (50). In these unillustrated pages Los, having bested Urizen in vain, is willing to open other "Center[s] . . . within the brain . . . heart . . . loins"—accepting both the worlds Urizen created and the threefold world of Urthona (95[87]:3–9). Standing between the limits of Satan and Adam, he repeats with Enitharmon the eating of forbidden fruit in the Garden of Eden. He and she, with the Spectre as a protecting Cherub, discover that the Urizenic paradise was static, while the bright Universe of Urthona, now transformed into a comforting Spectre, enables Los to see that he must undergo another two thousand years of "Cares & Sorrows," of "self denial and bitter contrition," the Christian era, the previous four thousand years having already been "consumed" (27–28).

Enitharmon also foresees the descent of "the Lamb of God . . . to meet these Spectres of the Dead" (52–53), but as the bodily-female vehicle that furnishes flesh both for the carnage and the redemption she acts in terror as a virgin madonna who fears the dualism of bearing in her womb both a Son of God and a Son of Man. Her last words on page 95[87] are, in fact: "Such is our state, nor will the Son of God redeem us but destroy" (59).

An inscription by Blake above the picture on page 96[88] could be a comment on the *Edward & Elenor* picture but is more clearly appropriate to the text of the poem, seeming to predict what the text itself describes in Night the Eighth, the exploitation of the death of Jesus by the divided Christian churches which leads to a rebirth of Babylon or Deism "Calld Natural Religon" (111:22–24):

> The Christian Religion teaches that No Man is Indifferent to you but that every one is Either Your Friend or your enemy. He must necessarily be either the one or the other. And that he will be equally profitable both ways if you treat him as he deserves.

This implies the threat of Manichean dealings

with one's neighbor: he *must* be friend or foe. And it implies calculation on the part of the priest who obtains your confession, having offered forgiveness if you promise not to repeat your sin. He profits either way, whether you keep your promise or break it.

Page 98[90] ends the revolving circularity of the Seventh Night with gleams of visionary hope, dark shades of fear and terror, and lines of creativity crossing the clouds and tinctured by the colors of Enitharmon's "blushing love," until Los, like a new earthly father, a new Joseph, finding himself to be a father through the intervention of the Holy Spirit, sees Urizen in his hands as the infant image of the Son of God. Like Joseph,

> he wonderd that he felt love & not hate;
> His whole soul loved him; he beheld him an
>   infant,
> Lovely breathd from Enitharmon; he
>   trembled within himself.
>   (98[90]:35–67)

[1]Butlin's explanation, that Blake first wrote his text "consecutively" on the back of the print, then cut it in half and trimmed the halves to fit the ms, does not explain why Blake chose to cut out the center (as the position of the text permitted) instead of trimming off the wide, blank left margin.

NIGHT THE EIGHTH

Page 99 (NT 45:14E, second state)

"THE LIMIT OF CONTRACTION NOW WAS FIXD" (11)

The Eighth Night, next to the last, can fill with darkness and despair—and with intimations, indeed divine Visions, of the coming Dawn. Father Time's spanning gesture can appear to be an assertion of his power—or a measure of its limitations. "The Limit of Contraction now was fixd," according to the text, as an act of divine mercy. "Man began To wake upon the couch of Death"—an action marked by his sneezing "seven times" and reposing ("again") in "the saviour's arms" (11–14). He is now outside the "span" of mortal "time."

When Blake made this design for Young's poem, he was giving his own paradoxical version of Young's warning against the "false opticks" which give man a dual view of time, a view which fixates on the creeping terror of scythe and hourglass and keeps man's "soul . . . on the rack." In Young's vision, man is perverse in fearing "rest" as torture and in trusting "action" for all his joy. Blake's depiction of Time as winged but scarcely moving, aged but youthful, invites us to sieze his prominent forelock (to start the sneezing spell of waking = creating). No hurry, says the posture of the hour-sized spirit resting its head upon the hourglass; yet time seems to be running out. Once we, with Albion, are with Jesus, however, we know that life can never run out. In the final state of the engraving (of which this proof is an early version) there is no sand in the bottom of the glass and the top is almost full.[1]

[1]This was a working proof: note Blake's penciled circle around Time's big toe and his pencil sketch of an improved shape for the toe, nearby. The toe *was* modified in the final state of the engraving, and prominent veins were added to the underside of arms and leg. (Butlin ignores this evidence when he remarks that the pencil additions "are not necessarily by Blake.")

Page 100

"BUT URIZEN . . . " (26)

Urizen cannot read the clock aright. In "self deceit" he still fools himself into thinking that "futurity" is forever, a future of "Desperate remorse" that "swallows the present" and leaves only "quenchless rage" and dark dissimulation" in control (100:32; 101:26–32).

Blake's drawing shows a Urizen whose human survival is failing: his face is aging with rage; vestigial wings will not enable him to soar; and his legs though goatlike are so malformed—the right leg has no ankle—as to seem powerless to run or even to kick. We last saw him as a massive, toothy crocodile (on page 70), moving to devour his own creation, the state of generation and decay. Now he is a newly hatched chick, with battle hardened visage, glaring backward, so to speak—though whichever way he looks he will see only great flames that surround him like the petals of a fiery rose: "Sparkles of Dire affliction . . . round his frozen limbs" (27).

(Behind his rump but deleted by dark shading is an earlier conception in which this beast was apparently to be a quadruped.)

The text (pages 100–101) tells of the great joy which the light of Jesus in Human form spreads through "All Beulah" (100:12) and of the busy action of Los and Enitharmon in weaving bodies for "the Spectrous dead" (25) rescued from "the War of Urizen & Tharmas" (21–22).

The war is not yet over, but the births of Christ and the Shadowy Female are causing it to change. "Terrified & astonished," we are told, "Urizen beheld the battle take a form Which he intended not, a Shadowy hermaphrodite black & opake." The monster which we have identified as Urizen may as plausibly be viewed as this new abortion: "The Soldiers namd it Satan, but he was yet unformd & vast; Hermaphroditic it at length became" (101:33–36). The chicken form shows the individual smallness, but it is going to turn into a Congregation of Wicked Men (see 104:30) who sentence to death other wicked little men: examples, those who sentenced Jesus, communing with the political and religious powers who wanted to crucify him; the witch-hunters of Massachusetts; the Directory who empowered Napoleon.

Page 101 (NT 31:8E)

"HIS HURTLING HAND GAVE THE DIRE SIGNAL" (28)

Making this design to illuminate Young's aphorism, "The present moment terminates our sight," Blake depicted the blindness as Death's, not the infant's or the mother's.

It suits the situation of this page to let Urizen appear as blind Death signalling war against mother and child. Urizen is terrified to behold "a new Luvah" after the opening of the heart gates, "the lamb of God clothed in Luvah's robes" (1–2). It is fitting that while Urizen sees Orc as an augmenting "Serpent, wondrous" (8), devouring "the fruit of the mysterious tree . . . in raging hunger" (16–18), *we* see a human child loved by and kissing its mother, while its bright eye takes in the arrow's point. Blake is showing us another version of the form which the battle takes. Or he is showing us the human forms of Orc and the Shadowy Female a split second before the Urizenic signal transforms their love into a poisoned arrow or a serpent-sting of good and evil.

We have seen a somewhat different version of this family conflict before, in the Oedipal jealousy of Los at the kissing of Orc and Enitharmon (pages 60 and 64).

Page 102

"WHAT WORDS OF DREAD PIERCE MY FAINT EAR?" (29)

Despite the efforts of Los and Enitharmon in Golgonooza, the city of Art, to "humanize" (101:46) the participants in the dire battle, they keep reappearing in their "beastial state" and at the end of each battle are "No more erect" (2,9). Possibly Blake's drawing is meant to suggest the fallen human form "drawn out in length" and "weakend" by Urizen's "Engines of deceit" (9–15). Is there only one leg, one thigh, one arm?

As we read down the page, we can see the Shadowy Female here, after Urizen's lecturing from his "books of iron & brass" until she has absorbed his "enormous Sciences . . . ages after ages" (23–27). "O Urizen, Prince of Light," she says, "What words of Dread pierce my faint Ear? What falling snows around My feeble limbs infold my destind misery? I alone dare the lash abide . . ." (28–31).

The paper which was used for this page, the verso of the Death engraving, bears some faint impressions, in the top right corner, of images from another engraved plate (that of *Night Thoughts* 44).

When we turn to the next page, we see that the wretched human image here is a back view of the Youngian sinner on page 103.[1]

[1]Butlin calls attention to the striking resemblance of this figure, in page 102, to a figure behind Satan and turned away with eye shut, yet listening—while Satan agitates, in Blake's variant versions of "Satan Calling up his Legions" or "Satan Arousing the Rebel Angels".

Page 103 (NT 52:17E)

"TANGLED IN HIS OWN NET IN SORROW, LUST, REPENTANCE" (31)

(The engraved proof on which pages 103–04 were written was cut in half after being written upon, and then rejoined with an overlap that eliminated one line, traces of which can be seen, on this page.)

Young's "treacherous conscience!" is the veiled, heavily wrapped, angel-winged woman who takes notes of our sins (with inflexible, jointless fingers)—while we drink and smile and "dream gay dreams." Blake as Young's illustrator concurs in his severity, depicting "us" as a wine-bibber whom we can scarcely find attractive. For his own poem, however, this rigid prude serves well to represent Blake's Shadowy Female, which Vala has become, a prude so thoroughly indoctrinated in Urizen's tyrannous "Direful Web of Religion" (26) that she believes that only "those who sinned not" (10) can live. Vala has, from worshipping the Urizenic Christ/Orc/Serpent, become in effect the very substance of Urizen's beclouding web.

Beginning at the tree of Mystery, circling its root,
She spread herself thro' all the branches in the power of Orc,
A shapeless & indefinite cloud in tears . . .
Steeping the Direful Web . . . swagging heavy.

(23–26)

The result is a misplacing of every Center, a rotting of the true fruit by "hungry desire & lust" (28)—and the accumulation of such weight of guilt that the web entangles Urizen himself, bringing him down as it falls heavy.

Meanwhile Enitharmon and Los are busy forming an alternative image, Jerusalem, "a Universal female form" (38) created out of the salvaged Urizenic dead.

Page 104

"THE DIVINE VISION SEEN WITHIN" (3)

Enitharmon and Los, having created and named the universal female form "Jerusalem," can see "the Lamb of God within Jerusalem's Veil, The Divine Vision . . . within the inmost deep" of her bosom (this is Enitharmon's version: 1–4), can see "the Lamb of God . . . born of Fair Jerusalem" (Los's version: 32–34). Note that the art of Los and Enitharmon has transformed the veil of Vala, just shown in the grey and black clothes of Lady Conscience on page 103, into Jerusalem's gate of birth, the vagina. Los said: "I saw Pitying, the Lamb of God descend thro Jerusalem's gates" and "stood in fair Jerusalem to awake up into Eden the fallen Man" (31–34).

Because Los in Night VII had drawn a new line of thought and vision, in space and time, which Enitharmon now makes visible in the full color of the human form, the artist and his wife are no longer trapped in the illusory vision of Vala's "mystery." Seeing Jerusalem as liberty, and yet as the incarnation of femininity (1–10), enables them to accept the sacrifice of Jesus in its double aspect: under the Satanic, dishumanized form that cannot be redeemed (20–30) and as a Man "born on Earth" to "put off Mystery time after time" (33–34). In long historical terms they have put eyes in the spoke holes of "the wheel of Destiny," which we saw Enitharmon (or Enion) running with on page 82. She ran holding it as a hoop through which to direct the flowing energies of life. Now she is struggling to turn it, as a wheel.

In a canceled passage the Lamb, Jesus, was to summon all the Zoas to help her. "He stood in fair Jerusalem to awake up into Eden The fallen Man but first to rend the Veil of Mystery," i.e. to be born, "and then Call Urizen & Luvah & Tharmas & Urthona." But in revision Blake shifted the emphasis from the Incarnation (which Blake felt had to be qualified) to the Crucifixion, which puts more stress on the Spiritual and the death of the purely physical: "but first to Give his vegetated body To be cut off & separated that the Spiritual body may be Reveald" (36–38).

The urgency of Enitharmon's effort to shift this emphasis signifies the artists' awareness that "Night the Ninth . . . The Last Judgment" must come soon. "We now behold the Ends of Beulah," they say, in a double entendre. Jesus must hasten to assume "the dark Satanic body in the Virgin's womb," in order to put it off, for his Redemption is "Begun Already in Eternity. Come then, O Lamb of God! Come, Lord Jesus, come quickly!" (11–17).

At this point we may imagine Catherine Blake culling her file of *Night Thoughts* proofs. A scene of the final trumpeting is supplied for the next page (105[109]), and for the last eleven pages of Night the Eighth we are given four full-page portrayals of Jesus, three from the engraved proofs and one drawn afresh by William Blake, with a more mature and deep expression than in the engravings, for page 108[116].

Further context for the turning wheel is provided in the text that overflows onto page 105[113], unillustrated. A song of "Glory to the holy Lamb of God" (104:6) moves from recognition that Life Eternal depends alone upon the Universal hand, to admiration of the industry of the laborers at "Enitharmon's Looms and Los's Forges," whose efforts in the Mental War combat "the Spindles of Tirzah & Rahab and the Mills of Satan & Beelzeboul" by creating "terrific Passions & Affections" in "periods of Pulsative furor" (105:1–6). The wheel image is built up gradually. The spindle and reel of creativity busily supply the poor spectres of the dead, "Clothing their limbs With gifts & gold of Eden" (112–13). But the Satanic "Mills of resistless wheels . . . unwind the soft threads," and Vala's daughters, Rahab & Tirzah, reclothe the spectres with mantles of despair and veils of ignorance (17–21). It seems a hopeless contest. No wonder that Enitharmon pushes with all her might; no wonder that we cannot see motion in the wheel. Laboring in the mill like a slave, she cannot see the Eyes—but we can. And what happens is that the whore

Rahab cannot help seeing the Lamb of God—whereupon she imitates Penelope: "with her knife of flint she destroys her own work" (33). Thinking to destroy the Lamb, she has enabled him to put off the clothing of blood, to awake the sleeping humanity.

(Unerased lines of a previous sketch appear beneath the drawing of Enitharmon, producing some confusion.)

Page 105 [113]

There are no illustrations on this page, and the verses on it consist of additions to pages 104 and 110[106].

Pages 106 [114] (NT 1:31E, second state); 107 [115] (NT 121:34E, third state); 108 [116]

WALKING WITH THE SAVIOUR

The sequence of these three pictures of Jesus is firmly established by the textual sequence, which makes clear that Blake intended to defy convention by putting Christ's Resurrection first, then his Crucifixion, and then his walking the earth. He is with us now because his spiritual birth enables us to survive agonies of time and space and walk the earth with Jesus. In the mistaken arrangement of manuscript leaves made early in the twentieth century (and fixed by the present binding) the Last Judgment of Night the Ninth immediately followed these eschatological sign-posts. In the present arrangement (required by the manuscript evidence of Blake's intentions) there is room, in eight more pages, for Blake and his mythic persons to interpret and respond to the momentous presence of the Lamb of God and to approach Night the Ninth from a more desperate and more human—but therefore more humanly promising—perspective.[1]

In either arrangement the resurrected and the crucified Christ are on facing pages. The picture on page 106, of Christ rising from or descending to the earth and benignly parting the clouds to make the radiance of his nimbus (his anti-cloud) accessible to us all, was engraved to be the title-page of Young's concluding Night (in the four-Night sequence of 1797) with the cloud on the left kept open for the printed title, "The Christian Triumph," as the focal center of the page, indeed of Christ's body angles. Christ's look, however, regards and invites all humanity, while the attention of both kneeling attendants is clearly upon the earth, as they prepare to fold the winding sheet from which the naked Saviour demonstrates the body's freedom.

The unhealed wounds in feet and left breast (locus of the anguish of Los in page 48) remind us, as do the iron chains dangling from the ascending figure in page 2 (and in *America* 3), that slavery or crucifixion is not bypassed—but also assure us that Orc too shall become free.

The facing crown-of-thorns picture (107) bluntly reminds us again of the fiery intensity of the Passion and the grim blackness of the nails. (The differences from the proof of page 59 are slight and minor.) "Jesus came & died willing between Tirzah & Rahab" (107:50), Los explains in a speech from his anvil addressed to the Great Whore, i.e., Rahab, which he delivers "with tenderness & love not uninspird" (105:44). And if we tried to define the earnest gentleness of expression in the three faces of Christ in these three pages, we might satisfy the hints of the context best by accepting that not unWordsworthian language. The familiar message of the three pictures is that Christ is here, that fires may "inwrap the earthly globe, yet man is not consumd" (*America* 8:15), and that the saviour is with us always, parting the clouds.

The third picture, drawn in the *Four Zoas* manuscript at this point to fit the engraved Christs into the poem on its own terms, is also a link in the series of depictions of Los—who will be drawn, in the final design of this Night, p. 116[112], almost as large and strong and tall as this naked Man. (That this is an emblematic man, nevertheless, is indicated by a macabre detail: his body shows no stigmata, but his right foot, firmly on the earth, is shod with a curiously helmet-shaped or skull-shaped sandal—or it displays the bones of a skull-shaped tarsus—see facing page.)

The grand *discovery* of these pages, the text makes known, is the potential identity of Los and Christ; and it is expressed by Christ's discovery of himself *to others*, of his willingness to die—not, as the Bible tells, between criminal men, but between Tirzah and Rahab, who are sisters, in the eyes of accusers, with Mary ("Every Harlot was a Virgin once").[2] The discovery is the theme of Los's sermon on the anvil:

> Los wipd the sweat from his red brow &
>   thus began
> To the delusive female forms shining among
>   his furnaces:
> I am that shadowy Prophet who six
>   thousand years ago
> Fell from my station in the Eternal bosom. I
>   divided

> To multitude & my multitudes are children
>   of Care & Labour
> O Rahab I behold thee! I was once like thee
>   a Son
> Of Pride and I also have piercd the Lamb of
>   God in pride & wrath
> Hear me repeat my Generations that thou
>   mayst also repent.
>
>   (105[113]:46–53)

When we have heard the prophet's survey of his 6,000 years of division and generation, to match the ambiguities and mysteries of Rahab, whose "knife of flint" (105:33) was meant to destroy Jesus' redemptive power, and of her sisters or of the Daughters of Beulah—a sanctified aggregate of redeemed Magdalens who will worship his body "and anoint his feet" (105:37)[3] we may look again at the Ascension engraving and recognize in those kneeling human, though winged, forms, a woman at the left and a man at the right, the sexes sharing the revelation.

The threefold Rahab we shall see pictured on page 114[110]. Meanwhile we may read that:

> Rahab burning with pride & revenge
>   departed from Los;
> Los dropd a tear at her departure, but he
>   wiped it away in hope.
>
>   (108[116]:4–5)

Not to be overlooked as a striking mark of the unity of this poem is the identity, by contraries, of the naked bodies of Los in the "Rest before Labour" frontispiece (p. 2) and Christ in the Resurrection (p. 106[114]). Compare their leg positions, the curves of the bodies (one is reversed from the other almost as though traced and reversed by engraving), the match of cloven foot and nail-pierced feet, the passive muscular potential of Los, the active muscular labor of Christ. The importance? Night VIII displays the discovered identity of Los and Luvah/Jesus—by the Zoas and by the readers.

[1] Note that there are three proofs of the engraved picture of Jesus crowned with thorns and standing, with nailed hands and feet in vast flames (*NT* 121:3–4E)—each from a different state of the engraved plate. The first state was used for page 115[111], the second for page 59, the third for page 107[115]. The present arrangement puts the first state toward the end of this Night, followed only by the drawing of Los and Enitharmon standing on this earth (page 116[112]). This puts an almost angry Jesus, with great drops of blood (compare pages 48 and 50) under his crown of thorns, and a wrathful Enitharmon into the concluding pages.

(See commentary on p. 116.)

[2] "To the Accuser," 3.

[3] People's being able to see only his feet has been a recurrent problem. Remember page 16.

Page 109 [105] (NT 38:12E)

BOUND UPON THE STEMS OF VEGETATION (53)

The design Blake engraved for Young's need of an "Emblem of that which shall awake the dead" inspired the trumpeter drawn in the title page of this poem. In that drawing (page 1) Blake shows the dead very much alive, in animal and human, or almost human, forms. For the present nadir of human hope, the bare skeletal bones of this Emblem make the starkest point.

The text tells how the Lamb of God, slain in all the centuries of holocausts, was sentenced by the Synagogue of Satan (14), a false conclave, actually "multitudes of tyrant Men" (104:29) operating in collusion with a false "feminine counterpart," (109:11) employed Eve-like to frame a new Mystery "from fruit of Urizen's tree" (20). How Rahab, the "false Female," has daughters called Tirzah, whose "various divisions are calld The Daughters of Amalek Canaan & Moab"—note the threefold fission—"binding on the Stones Their victims & with knives tormenting them singing with tears Over their victims" (25–30). They attack and melt down and nail to the rock each of the inlets of the human form, eyes, nostrils, loins, tongue, ear. Our skeleton represents the bottom line of this circumscribing (49).

But all to no avail. The picture delineates a full, free, dancing human form who is blowing such a blast of reassurance as to cause the skeleton to hear without ears and to see with the dark shadows that are his eye-sockets, miraculously raising his face toward the bell of the trumpet. Legs and arms prepare to spring from the rent veil. To become what he beholds?

Page 110 [106]

"URIZEN SAT STONIED . . . FORGETFUL OF HIS OWN LAWS" (22–23)

Urizen's response to the trumpet call, i.e. to the news of the death of the Lamb, is a panic of characteristically hypocritical repentance—and a collapse of morale. Since Rahab brings him the news, "Rahab Who is Mystery, Babylon, the Great Mother of Harlots" (6), he imagines Death as a priestess of his own "secret holiness," a fatal, if "deadly dull," "delusion" (21).

Urizen sitting in his web of decietful
    Religion

Felt the female death a dull & numming
    stupor such as neer
Before assaulted the bright human form . . .
                                    (18–20)

He simultaneously fears the "horrors of Eternal death" and lusts after her, "Forgetful of his own Laws" of chastity. In short, he falls apart. In a parody of Christ's entombment and resurrection, his human body becomes "A form of Senseless Stone," his own tomb. And his desire (his attempt "to Embrace The Shadowy Female" without the use of his body) collapses into a bestial but impotent amphibian, a monster who "lashes the Abyss" and beats "the Desarts"—perhaps not in vain, for the "Desarts . . . shake their slumbers off" (45–47).

When Urizen, Zoa of the human brain, steps out of his skull (stops functioning rationally) he becomes scaled, falls "upon his belly," and "Lashes his tail in the wild deep": "No longer Erect, the King of Light" (parody of the fallen Satan). His "mouth wide opening, tongueless" (implying impotence) "his teeth a triple row, he strove to sieze the shadow in vain." Frustrated in both forms, stunned human and tongueless monster, he swims "in vain . . . around his stony form" (28–40). Since, as Blake explains, "life cannot be quenchd, Life exuded" (24).

Having shown us Urizen's crocodile form on page 70 (tongueless if not triple-dentured), Blake now shows us the human equivalent of lifeless body and impotent dream. (The facing engraved design of the sleeping poet and his swimming dream, may be recognized as the contrary symbolic model.) Urizen's "Stonied" (22) or sleeping human form, almost flat upon the ground, has its eyelid shut and its left arm pressing its side as though Urizen's last sensation had been a twinge in the groin. (Do the parallel marks above his left hand indicate a probe or a dagger? Can this be suicide?) (Some see, rather, the flabby folds of old age.)

A vision of two full-breasted naked women represents his dream of impotence. Standing one behind the other (the second is very shadowy: see detail figure) they assist one another in masturbation and pay no attention to Urizen—though his power over them is evident from their behavior.

Beyond their heads is a small face, possibly an infant's, but almost completely erased.[1]

[1] Below, an erased drawing of a man's profile, facing toward Urizen and away from the women, may or may not have some shadowy relation to this scene. (Butlin judges, on stylistic grounds, that this profile may not be by Blake; we have been unable to recover it photographically.)

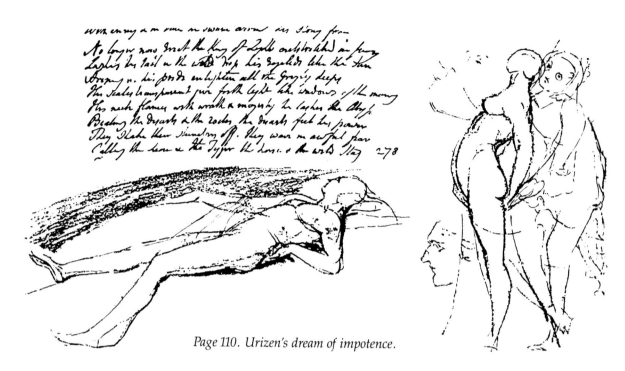

Page 110. Urizen's dream of impotence.

Page 111 [107] (NT 14:3E, second state)

*"LOS FELT THE STONY STUPOR & HIS HEAD
ROLLD . . ." (25)*

The other two Zoas besides Urizen and Luvah
(Christ) are also caught in the delusion of "a living
Death" in which "the nameless shadow" binds "all
Mortal things" (35–36). (Three persons are in-
volved, since Blake treats Urthona and his fallen or
Spectre form, Los, as different creatures.)

Then Tharmas & Urthona felt the stony
    stupor rise
Into their limbs. Urthona shot forth a Vast
    Fibrous form;
Tharmas like a pillar of sand rolld
    round . . .
An animated Pillar rolling round & round
    in incessant rage.

Los felt the stony stupor & his head rolld
    down beneath
Into the Abysses of his bosom; the vessels
    of his blood
Dart forth upon the wind in pipes, writhing
    about in the Abyss;
And Enitharmon pale & cold in milky juices
    flowd
Into a form of Vegetation, living, having a
    voice,
Moving in rootlike fibres, trembling in fear
    upon the Earth.
                                        (21–30)

The benign purpose in this making all mortal
things permanent is "that they may be put off Time
after time by the Divine Lamb who died for all"
(36–37).

The engraved design, made to interpret the
opening passages of Young's poem, in which the
poet contrasts his existence as "a worm" yet "a
God," a stranger at home lost in himself (whose
"reason reels") yet "a miracle" whose soul can tread
"fantastick measures . . . O'er fairy fields" while
his body sleeps, is wonderfully apt to Blake's pur-
pose in these zenith/nadir passages of his own
poem, opening into the final Night of Judgment.
The poet Young, sleeping on his open manuscript
volume with pen in hand—the pen that will write
the inspired parts—can stand for Los, stonied like
Urizen yet never putting down his creative hope.
Young's soul (which Blake depicts as masculine; it's
really after all Young himself) engages in six "fan-
tastick" actions while his body sleeps, and we may
read them in Young's sequence while numbering
them in the clockwise order of Blake's arrange-
ment: Young's soul (1) mourned along the gloom of
pathless woods (Blake has him exclaiming at what
he sees, not obviously mourning); (5) plunged
headlong down the craggy steep; (6) swam with
pain the mantled pool; (4) scaled the cliff; (2)
danced on hollow winds; and (3) danced with
antick shapes, wild natives of the brain—all actions
called for in Young's lines.)

All these fantasies contrast with the frustrated
falling, seizing, and swimming of Urizen, on page

110[106]. They suit the Los who has wiped a tear away in hope. We may imagine him (1) exploring the vegetative forest, hoping to recognize the "root-like" "Fibrous" forms of Urthona and Enitharmon; (2) soaring up out of the forest like Orc; (3) meeting and embracing Enitharmon in human form (see the last page of this Night); (4) combining security and freedom, on the cliff's edge; (5) trusting himself to the abyss (compare the leg positions of Los on page 2); and (6) swimming in the oceanic waters of instinctual parenthood, the seas of Tharmas. The garment of the sleeping poet exposes his feet as well as his head and arm, perhaps implying an open circle for the dance of creative fantasy.

Page 112 [108]

"LISTEN TO HER WHOSE MEMORY BEHOLDS YOUR ANCIENT DAYS" (20)

There can be no more sleep in this Night. In this page Ahania, and in the next Enion, Blake's great social critics, cry out in the language of street ballads and radical pamphlets to awake "all the children of Men" to see "the Divine vision" (5–7). With "her Eyes Toward Urizen," Ahania cries aloud to his numb skull, i.e. to "the Caverns of the Grave":

> Will you keep a flock of wolves & lead
> them, will you take the wintry blast
> For a covering to your limbs? . . .
> Will you seek pleasure from the festering
> wound or marry for a Wife
> The ancient Leprosy, that the King & Priest
> may still feast on your decay?
> And the grave mock & laugh at the plowd
> field, saying
> "I am the nourisher, thou the destroyer . . .
> I am a goddess & queen"?
> But listen to Ahania, O ye sons of the
> Murdered one.
>
> (9–19)

Some of the force of these outcries is the indirect gift of Tharmas, who "gave his Power to Los" and now rides "on high . . . furious thro the afflicted worlds"—trying to escape the voice of Ahania even while he shares her fury. (111:31; 112:1–4)

The regal bed she reclines on, the gesture of her left arm matching that of Urizen's on page 109, is a relic of better days. Cupid, sitting on Ahania's buttock but wingless and with no arrows left, seems to be unstringing his bow. He looks old; his hair must be a wig. She is ready for love, not war. "Looking for Urizen in vain, in vain seeking for morning,"

she laments that Albion, the Eternal Man, "sleeps in the Earth . . . nor feels the . . . hosts of heaven move in his body" (22–24). "Alas! that Man should come to this!" (32). Yet Albion's "faint groans" do "shake the caves & issue thro the desolate rocks," and the voices of the protestors are hopefully directed to his ears.

The contrast between sleeping bodies and waking souls in the preceding pages is continued in the contrast between the sleepy (if high-riding) evasive action of Tharmas, or the silence of Urizen, and the open-mouthed and angry summonses of their emanations, Ahania and Enion. Ahania on her couch is angry, but desperate. (If that strange object she is falling asleep upon was once the giant penis—and its shape and curves under her leg suggest that it may have been—it has been worn down into a sofa.)

Enion, recognizable in the engraving on the facing page as the woman named "Truth" in Young, rides the lightning and points upward with both hands. Her speech, in Blake's text, begins with the brave words: "Fear not, O poor, forsaken one."

Page 113 [109] (NT 156:43E)

"AWAKE, THE BRIDEGROOM COMETH!" (21)

Young's and Blake's purposes converge in their texts which are accompanied by this design. For Young the exhorting female is "Truth, eldest daughter of the Deity." She was of God's council when he "made the worlds" and is ready to serve "when he shall judge the worlds he made." At the trumpet's hour, "from her cavern in the soul's abyss . . . The goddess bursts in thunder and in flame."

Blake quite possibly had those two moments in mind, of creation and judgment, when he depicted the goddess as pointing upward with both hands. Also perhaps when he placed her left foot on the rock and her right foot in the fire. In *The Four Zoas* we are asked to recognize her as Enion, last seen blind and age-bent—just as Truth lay so long caverned "in the soul's abyss" (beneath Aetna) until the "heaven-commission'd hour"—now raised by her vision to this mature, beautiful, deadly-earnest human form. To Ahania's cry, Enion "replies from the Caverns of the Grave." What does she say?

> Fear not, O poor, forsaken one. O land of
> briars & thorns,
> Where once the Olive flourished & the
> Cedar spread his wings.

Once I waild desolate like thee . . . but
   soon
A voice came in the night, a midnight cry
   upon the mountains,
"Awake! the bridegroom cometh!" I awoke
   to sleep no more. . . .

                                (13–21)

Ahania's social satire had described the mocking triumph of the grave over the "plowd field." Enion transforms that irony to prophetic vision, letting "The furrowd field repl[y] to the grave": "Behold the time approaches fast that thou shalt be as a thing Forgotten; when one speaks of thee, he will not be believed" (28–30)—and so on. The crucial revelation being that "The Lamb of God has rent the Veil of Mystery" (114:1).

The combined strength of Ahania and Enion is implied in their communing, and in their matching expressions of speaking fear and speaking hope, both angry. The growth of Enion to full humanity appears in the more selflessly wrathful expression of her face, and in the size of her body, suitable for the bride of the Jesus we have been seeing in these pages.

The forward and upward momentum of the poetry in the concluding pages of this Night is reflected in the sequence of pictures. The horizontal water of the ocean in which Urizen swims to little gain, in page 110, flares up now into the vertical sea of flames that rise and support the upward movement of the body and arm of Truth. Although in the next page the element in which Rahab struggles may be water or air, or even vacancy, on the following page, 115, the flames rise again to consume the steely ikon of crucifixion and Mystery, though with impermanent effect.

In these pages, Blake's construction of his own epic upon an artful selection of the Young designs is impressively successful.

Page 114 [110]

"NO MORE SPIRIT REMAIND IN HER" (115:10)

We take this caption from the next page, for these facing pages function as a unit. It is Rahab, momentarily triumphing over all and taking Jerusalem captive, "A Willing Captive by delusive arts impelld To worship Urizen's Dragon form, to offer her own Children Upon the bloody Altar," who is pictured here (though Butlin guesses Ahania or Enion) already falling from her triumph. For

"when she saw the form of Ahania weeping" and "heard Enion's voice sound from the caverns of the Grave, No more spirit remaind in her" (115[111]):2–10). We have seen Rahab almost won over by Los, but turning in pride from her friend to her priest, Urizen. A stronger tie binds her to the other women. Yet perhaps the triple sisterhood indicated in the drawing is intended to be ambiguous. Do we see one woman with three heads, or three trial drawings for one head? Is the action of feet and arms flailing or swimming? (The second head has an arm bent for swimming.) Is that simply a breast, or a heart on the wrong side? (Compare page 52.) Rahab is losing heart as the triple Harlot. She is potentially united with the prophetic sisters in the present sequence.

"John Saw these things Reveald in Heaven On Patmos Isle" (115:4–5), Blake explains, and further comment is hardly necessary for a reader of Blake's text and the book of Revelation. The action of Los & Enitharmon, on hearing the dialogue of Ahania and Enion, is to take down the body from the Cross. In the last lines of the Night, another sinister attempt is being made to recycle "Mystery," all permitted by the will of God.

(Remnants of an earlier drawing appear above and between the woman's legs; the bottom of the sheet has been trimmed; and on a level with her right heel is the left profile of a man who probably does not belong in this poem. Compare the right profile on page 110[106].)

Page 115 [111] (NT 121:34E, first state)

"RAHAB TRIUMPHS OVER ALL" (1)

This third appearance of the engraved design of Christ crucified is like a third blast of the trumpet. "John Saw these things. . . ." And in this version of the design, the face of Jesus seems (in context at least) to verge upon impatience if not wrath, impatience presumably at the last-minute resumption of secret worship of his dead body.

. . . Los & Enitharmon took the Body of the
   Lamb
Down from the Cross & placd it in a
   Sepulcher which Los had hewn
For himself in the Rock of Eternity,
   trembling & in despair;
Jerusalem wept over the Sepulcher two
   thousand Years.

                        (114[110]:30–33)

We are told that Rahab's repentance is ambivalent, that her communing with Orc in secret almost caused the Synagogue of Satan to unite against Mystery, the religious whoredom she had represented. Actually, when "Satan divided against Satan revolvd in open Sanhedrim To burn Mystery with fire," like the clever parliamentarians they are they only divided the *motion,* first to burn Mystery, and then to "form another from her ashes," Phoenix like. When the "Ashes of Mystery began to animate, they calld it Deism . . . so now anew began Babylon again, in Infancy Calld Natural Religion" (19–24). But it is the end of the Eighth Night. As Blake wrote on the frontispiece of *Jerusalem,* "The long sufferings of God are not forever; there is a Judgment."

(This proof represents an early state of the plate, close to the details of the watercolor. In the second and third engraved states, represented by the proofs used for pages 59 and 111[115] respectively, the face is turned towards us, with both eyes visible, and is more gently accepting or reproachful; the drops of blood on the brow are few and barely show. In this version the drops of blood are prominent and many; there is a suggestion of bitterness in eye and mouth. In the context we may assume that Jesus is about to join the comments of Ahania and Enion.)

Page 116 [112]

"AND LOS & ENITHARMON BUILDED JERUSALEM WEEPING" (117:1)

The caption for this textless page we borrow from the first line of the next, the beginning of Night the Ninth. For these full-standing, naked, loving, contending, patient and impatient man and wife are Los and Enitharmon, and their building Jerusalem is what gets us out of this dark Night the Eighth. In drawing their bodies, Blake has made Los and Enitharmon as big as life and as fully human as the Jesus of page 108[116] walking on the same Earth. Their taking the body down from the cross and placing it in a sepulcher "which Los had hewn for himself" (114:31–32) may have enabled the Synagogue of Satan to reanimate the ashes of Mystery, but it also kept the prophet and his emanation together and in the company of Jerusalem, as a human form divine, and has now led to their building Jerusalem as a city.

In the designs thus far we have not been shown a male and a female body in this position or at-titude. The first full-page drawing of a male body, on page 66, was a back view; the second, on page 76, was drawn as somewhat monstrous in head and genitalia (now partly erased). The only large drawing of a female body, on page 86, shows her kneeling. We have seen a large design of Eve and Adam, in the engraved proof of page 67, but with vines hiding their nakedness. The engraved proofs of Narcissa and Truth (pages 76 and 113[109]) balance the engravings of Christ. Bodies of male and female together, in the smaller pictures, have been shown in jealous family or erotic group entanglements, often with figures of monstrous or indeterminate humanity. What we see at last is the image of two erect, adult figures, a man and woman in a humane togetherness at a moment of intense, shared crisis, with their bodies in the unison of uniting and dividing musical chords. The man's right leg, in final position after three trials, stretches behind the woman's knees, and his toes touch the toes of her left foot, bringing her forward—a position of progress, not stasis. (For Blake, in *Milton* at least, foot-touching is an incarnation movement.) But most hopeful are the man's loving and gentle movements of comfort and support. He holds her body against his and presses his fingers under her left breast, as though to feel and calm the terrific pulsations of her heart. With his right hand he seems ready to protect her shoulders from falling down (as many female shoulders have fallen, into the Urizenic vortexes in this poem).

Her body has no ambiguous outlines; the naval is well-marked and centered, also her nipples. But she has a terrible fear in her eyes, and great wrath (which his patience supports). In her eyes and mouth we sense a culmination of the wrathful expressions of Ahania and Enion, and of Jesus—and an anticipation of the cries of birth and groans of death to come in the human vintage and harvest of the coming Night. She fiercely tears her hair, a climactic gesture.[1]

---

[1]Butlin, thinking of this as a family picture, remembers page 62 and wonders at the absence of Orc: "On this scale he would have to be on the facing page." Hagstrum also sees an Orc implied here, and sees Los as trying to rescue Enitharmon from her Oedipal madness.

NIGHT THE NINTH
BEING THE LAST JUDGMENT

Page 117 (NT 76:23E)

"TERRIFIED AT NON EXISTENCE FOR SUCH THEY DEEMD THE DEATH OF THE BODY" (5–6)

The gentleness of this design (which in the *Night Thoughts* engravings follows on a facing page the design used below for pages 121 and 131) provides a serene resting place during the last moment of calm before the apocalypse. Los & Enitharmon weep under the illusion that "the Crucified body" is "still in the Sepulcher." So Jesus stands "beside them in the Spirit, Separating Their Spirit from their body" (2–5). Since nothing seems to happen, they ought to realize that they are here and now in the Spirit and have nothing to fear. If they could feel and see angels conveying them to a sweet golden clime, as in the design made for Young, they should be able to see Jesus beside them and take his hand. The design implies, in the wingless figure clutching his breast, an act of calming the flow of blood; Blake's text implies a contrary act of causing the blood to flow. This is the moment of stillness before passage from a "bloody" apocalypse to a "mental" apocalypse.

What happens now is that Los acts under the inspiration not of Young's message but of Blake's: the whole cultural tradition must be destroyed that retains—and again and again "reanimates"—the image of Christ crucified as its ikon of iron and stone, that enslaves energy in war and debases beauty as seduction and sin, the whole postlapsarian conception of the universe. Los seizes the Sun in his right hand and the Moon in his left and tears them down, "cracking the heavens across from immense to immense" (9). The trumpet speaks; heaven and earth shake; Kings lose "their robes & crowns, The poor smite their oppressors," freed slaves pursue naked warriors, and Enitharmon is "let loose on the troubled deep," wailing "shrill in the confusion" (10–25). The actions of Los and Enitharmon here flow directly from their stance in page 116.

Page 118

"THEIR BODIES . . . MINGLED WITH THE CONFUSION" (5–6)

This quiet bedroom scene presents a deeply res-

onating contrast to the cataclysm (the washing down) and the apocalypse (the opening up) presented in the poetry. Blake has so much going on in the revolutions and revelations of the text that he may seem to let the illuminations play a minor role; yet it is often a crucial one. Touching certain points in the vast choral drama, the drawings and engravings can remind us that (as Urizen finally learns) "futurity is in this moment" (121:22).

The *poet* can give us a panorama in three lines:

And all the while the trumpet sounds, from
     the clotted gore & from the hollow den
Start forth the trembling millions into
     flames of mental fire
Bathing their limbs in the bright visions of
     Eternity.

                                          (17–19)

And he can give us hearsay reports of the Lion and Leopard quoting the Eagle and Raven (30–38). The *artist* can halt the "fierce raving fire" to show us three whores on their king-size bed. Rahab, we may conjecture, is the one with the small jeweled crown. The one clutching Rahab's right arm, and pulling her down between her knees, may be Tirzah. The third may be Vala, changing from the Shadowy Female into the Vala of page 128, ready for the "lower Paradise" which Luvah is preparing for her (see below).

These three women seem quite absorbed "in a complicated but apparently enjoyable tangle that seems to bear no relationship to the families trembling at the Last Trump" (Butlin. We agree). But the text tells us that when they hear it they will "wail aloud in the wild flames" and "give themselves to Consummation" (6). Or it may be that we see them already "Bathing their limbs"—Blake quite approves of limbs, when freed of Mystery.[1] A scene we shall have no more of is the ikon of Christ crucified; pictorially we may sense that the very accumulation of such images toward the end of Night the Eighth has built up the pressure under which, "rivn link from link, the bursting Universe explodes" (122:26).

[1] Butlin well describes that which Blake first drew in this space but almost completely erased or covered as "what may be a completely distinct sketch of a draped figure kneeling, head on the ground on the right, and one arm raised in the air, jutting up into the right-hand margin and perhaps suggested by the extended arms of the figure in the engraving on the facing page."

PAGE 119 (NT 141:37E, second state)

"ON HIS ROCK LAY THE FADED HEAD OF THE ETERNAL
MAN" (28)

Blake's use of this engraving for page 61, in Night the Fifth, emphasized the importance of looking at the earthly globe with a new vision.

Here the message is more complex. If there is "Universal Confusion" (24) we might suppose that the earth is a very insignificant part of the explosion of worlds throughout "the wide Universe" (16). And when we are told that Albion, "the Eternal Man," lies on a rock "Beyond this Universal Confusion, beyond the remotest Pole" (24–28)—but is now lifting "the blue lamps of his Eyes," and crying "with heavenly voice, Bowing his head over the consuming Universe" (30–31)—we need to be reminded forcibly that the whole conflict is taking place inside the Imagination of Man, inside the brain of Albion, who is beginning to realize that he must come down out of the clouds and come to life right there (pointing finger) where he lives—in Babylonian London, which *could be* Jerusalem.

The preceding passage explains how it is that Albion is at last coming to: "And when all Tyranny was cut off from the face of the Earth . . . The flames . . . Began to Enter the Holy City . . . living flames, winged with intellect And Reason: round the Earth they marched in order, flame by flame" (14–20). The awakening of "the trembling millions into flames of mental fire" *is* the lifting of the eyes of the Eternal Man,. (22)

As we were promised on page 117, these are the flames of a mental, not a physical apocalypse.

(Blake redrew in pencil, on the engraving, the extended leg and foot, shortening the man's leg by about two inches, in scale. Perhaps he was matching the leg of the figure first drawn, and partly erased, on page 118.)

Page 120

"AS THE PERSON SO IS HIS LIFE PROPORTIOND" (31)

Albion is weak but determined no longer "to give up all my powers To indolence" (6–7). The first of his powers he calls upon is Urizen, sleeping somewhere "in cold abstraction" but properly "Prince of Light." Urizen cannot even answer, at first, because he has become that tongueless

Dragon of the deeps. Albion commands the Dragon to "lie down before my feet" and rise as Urizen, whom he blames for deforming the "beautiful proportions Of life & person, for as the Person so is his life proportiond" (28–31). Before his fall, Urizen's proportions were kept human by his collaboration with "bright Ahania," his Emanation, who danced and sang while he sang and played the harp (15–16).

When Urizen shakes the "snows from off his Shoulders" in the next page, Ahania comes like dancing May—though with such "excess of Joy" that she falls "down dead at the feet of Urizen Outstretchd a smiling corse" (121:27–38).

The drawing of a naked female body, half risen but with back turned, and resting head in right arm (upon the rock) supplies a pantomimic image of Ahania just before awaking. A matching image on page 122 shows her again after her joyous rising and her collapse momentarily ("Smiling") into a corpse.

Above the resting figure on page 120 are sketched the bench marks of Urizen's abstraction (see Blake's "Ancient of Days" frontispiece to *Europe*): fingers and compasses constructing "deformed" proportions. (The compasses and fingers in *Europe* are opened to a right angle, 90°; these are spread to 110°.) Another set of measuring instruments is sketched just under Ahania's left hip and perhaps on it: one pair of small callipers opened at 90°, another at 75°. (Bentley and Butlin see these as the torso and legs of a nude woman: perhaps here too the mechanical and the human are proportioning each other.) But we are entering The Last Judgment, which "is an overwhelming of Bad Art & Science" (*VLJ*: E565). Only the appropriate use of Urizen's tools in the hands of a good artist, of Los (who has begun using his hands: 117:6), can delineate the true living proportions of humanity.

The design on page 120 clearly recalls the one on page 102, a reversal of the engraved picture of 103. The reclining figure on the facing page, 121, shares the motif of weariness with the design on 120 but more completely serves as a contrary to that on page 108—which it may have suggested. The sexual identities of these naked figures, all related perhaps to that (sexless) fallen angel reclining behind Satan in Blake's painting of "Satan Calling up his Legions" (Butlin 536.1 and 662—first version dating ca. 1800–1805), may be intentionally ambiguous. The figures in the engravings (pages 103 and 121) appear more male than female, those in the drawings of pages 112 and 120 seem more female than male; we all query the sex of the figure on page 102.

What may seem to be an indifference on Blake's part to sexual indications in these final drawings, however, may rather be an intended ambiguity—to remind us that liberated "Humanity knows not of Sex" (*Jerusalem* 44:33). The contrast to the heavy emphasis on sex in the earlier Nights is surely deliberate. Blake has firmly shown us, on page 116, a fully grown man and woman. Now, in the mental flames, the distinction is out of place, and out of time.

Page 121 (NT 71:22E, second state)

"THAT LINE OF BLOOD . . ." (120:50)

Young's death-bed consignment of sleeping Man to another world (*NT* 71:22E), with his dearest friend bidding farewell instead of welcome, is marked as error by a broken line of ink or paint the color of dried blood, across the chest of the reclining figure. (Applied to the proof by a straight-edged surface, it may have been a defect already in the paper but hardly unnoticed by Blake, or a half or fully intentional act by him.)[1]

The text on this page begins with Urizen's anxious resolve to "reassume the human" in exchange for his disproportioned "Scaly form." In a world redeemed from Error, this is immediately possible ("for lo, futurity is in this moment"); Urizen shakes off his snows and "glorious, bright, Exulting in his joy," he rises "into the heavens in naked majesty, In radiant Youth" (1–32). The engraving and its original sequel (used above for page 117) can be taken straight to illustrate such a dying and rising into the heavens. But the whole force of the speech by Albion, to which Urizen's resurrection is a fully conscious response, works more deeply than that. Albion's speech culminates in the declaration that "Sin, Even Rahab, is redeemd in blood & fury & jealousy," redeemed "from Error's power" by "That line of blood that strechd across the windows of the morning" (120:49–51). Rahab's communing "with Orc in secret" and hiding him "with the flax" is the gesture that is equated to the biblical harlot Rahab's stretching a scarlet thread in the window where she hid the spies of the prophet Joshua (Los). The bloody line on the engraved proof can be seen to mark exactly the moment when one sees or does not see through the "windows of the morning." If the line was present in the proof, by accident, before Blake wrote on this leaf, it may have inspired

his writing. It seems only remotely possible that he put it in to illustrate his text. Either way, he was redeeming the plate "from Error's power."

Rahab and her sisters have been seen on a couch that mocks this one, on page 118. De Luca suggests that the engraving of "three ambiguously sexed figures guarding over someone on a couch of death corresponds nicely with 121:40–41": "The three daughters of Urizen guard Ahanias Death couch . . .". Though the couched figure in *Night Thoughts* is male, "yet it may have presented itself to Blake as a reasonable visual approximation."

[1]Whether it is ink, paint, or some kind of stain is not known. Andrew Lincoln defines it as "very dark brown dried blood/rust colour, with a faint brown halo." Three tiny flecks appear in the left margin, about half way down, and a spot is visible beside the second "f" in "feet of Urizen" (fourth line from the bottom). Another proof of this design, lacking the line of blood—so Blake had a choice—he used for page 131.

(Spottings of the same material appear on page 117, on the body on the right and down the left margin, of no possible relevance.)

Page 122

"ALL THESE ELEMENTS . . . SHALL REFLOURISH" (5–6)

The renovated Urizen's happiness makes his wife Ahania'a happiness too much to bear.

> Ahania rose in joy—
> Excess of Joy is worse than grief—her heart
>   beat high; her blood
> Burst its bright Vessels. She fell down dead
>   at the feet of Urizen
>
> (121:35–37)

"The times revolve," explains Albion; "the time is coming when all these delights shall be renewd & all these Elements that now consume Shall reflourish" (122:4–6). Judgment Day is a misnomer; a week would be too short; this is seed time; wait for spring and summer, for "bright Ahania" to "awake . . . A glorious Vision to thine Eyes, a Self renewing Vision" (6–7). The whole human family, and "every species," need to enter the active life, "every one of the dead" first appearing "as he had livd before" (36–71). On page 120 Ahania was burying her face; now she is ready to arise from the deserts of one-dimensional vision.

The drawing synthesizes the past and present in the incarnate image of a female form, the vehicle which has given life and death to all—the whole troops of "Fathers & Friends, Mothers & Infants, Kings & Warriors, Priests & chaind Captives": (39–

40). She is emblematically stretched between two hills; the picture itself lies still. The deaths and regenerations of the poetry will revolve as the Zoas arise and unite with their emanations; the "black mound" and "sandy desert" will echo with the delights of fourfold vision. The human Albion will assume the bright vocality of Ahania indicated in the beautiful proportions of her body.

Page 123 (NT 35:10E)

"THE PRISONER ANSWERS . . . YOUR HIPOCRISY SHALL AVAIL YOU NOUGHT" (30–32)

Blake engraved this design to express the poet Young's wish to attain the "rage divine" of Homer, or Milton, or Pope ("Man . . . he sung—immortal man I sing"). Though a "Pris'ner of darkness," he would "call the stars to listen." Blake shows the poet-prisoner chained to the grave and its briars, though able to see the heavens and with his left foot free—Blake's way of granting validity to the line marked for illustration: "Oft bursts my song beyond the bounds of life."

The chained poet's gesture of helplessness, however, appears absurdly inappropriate to the *Four Zoas* text on this page, the theme of which is Albion's *attainment* of a vision of the "Incomprehensible," a vision of Jerusalem and of Christ's cloud of blood "descending from Jerusalem with power and great Glory" (27–37). In this context a poet's claim of helplessness would be foolish or hypocritical. Blake's truth-embracing "Prisoner" has burst his "cords & heavy chains" and scorns such posturing. Blake as poet does not call on the stars, but he can hear that "One Planet calls to another & one star enquires of another, 'What flames are these . . . ?'" (16–17).

This pictured poet, awake but chained and not using his lyre, is a negative contrast to the resting poet of page 2, who will soar free at the "End of the Dream" on page 139.

Page 124

"THEN BRIGHT AHANIA SHALL AWAKE FROM DEATH." (122:6)

If we argue backward from plate 28 of *Jerusalem*, a later conception, we should conclude that the naked woman in the flower in this drawing must be Vala (or even Jerusalem "assimilating in one

with Vala, The Lilly of Havilah" J19:41–42). But this has no place in the present story, and we would be wiser to see Ahania here. She was promised to Urizen (by Albion) as a "glorious Vision to thine Eyes, a Self renewing Vision" in the "spring" and "summer" (122:6–8). And soon, "Lo, like the harvest Moon, Ahania cast off her death clothes" (she comes in wearing them, in the shadowy drawing at the right of the page). "She folded them up in care" and "Bathd in the clear spring of the rock, then from her darksom cave Issud in majesty divine" (125:26–29). We may imagine the bottom of the page flowing in clear spring water; her floral majesty is exhibited on the lily.

Who is the old man wearing a frock coat and leaning on a crutch, whom she greets with a touch on the forehead? (Blake at first drew the man's head bowed too low for communication, but then lifted it, to glance at Ahania.) This is Urizen, ready to fling aside his crutch. In the text his response is put in hyperbolic language: "Urizen rose up from his couch On wings of tenfold joy, clapping his hands, his feet, his radiant wings In the immense" (125:32–33). But he also promptly must sit down again; he and his sons have been sitting "down to rest" after a hard day's harvesting: "And bright Ahania took her seat by Urizen in songs & joy" (22, 35). The drawing presents us, symbolically, with their first encounter; their sitting by each other on the "Couches of Beulah" is not depicted realistically.[1]

[1] The kneeling nude figure in the left margin above Urizen seems to have no arms or head: a trial sketch of some sort.

Page 125 (NT 58:18E)

"THE FLAMES REFUSD" (38)

As the Fallen Man awakes to a "Vision of God" (124:1) he recognizes the four Zoas as "four Wonders of the Almighty, Incomprehensible . . . named Life's in Eternity, Four Starry Universes going forward from Eternity to Eternity" (123:36–39). But in the living context of the planting and gathering of "the human harvest," the Zoas must each abandon his desire to be a heaven-dwelling God above all. "You shall forget your former state," explains the Regenerate Man to Luvah and Vala; "return, O Love, in peace, Into your place, the place of seed, not in the brain or heart" (126:7–8). Zoas may be gods, but if they "combine against Man, Setting their Dominion above The Human form Divine," they have to be thrown out of the "heavens of Human Imagination" to go through a reorganizing process, "ages on ages," till they learn human cooperation as "Servants to the infinite & Eternal of the Human form" (9–17).

The same respect for the Human form has not quite been grasped by the Regenerate Man himself, however. Even in this joyous moment of redemption, the Eternal Man sits moping upon the couches of Beulah, "Sorrowful that he could not put off his new risen body In mental flames" (125:36–38). The flames refuse, for his body "was redeemd to be permanent" (39). In Blake's engraved design, the poet of Young is being given (not by Young but by the engraver) the same lesson. He has asked about his heavenly future and summons his "past hours" to tell him "what report they bore to heaven." We may easily read these sylph-like "hours" as human forms of "mental flames." We can see that the hours dutifuly prepare a full report—and that the present hour, delivering the report, "refuses" to let him misunderstand what use it might be. He is about to take his inspiration from Memory instead of Imagination!

The brilliant, silent message of Blake's design is that the report comes, not from some extraterrestrial domain but from the poet's own brain, from which the sylphs arise, writing down his own words to be returned to him as circular communications. This is an image of solipsism in a more human form than the ouroboros but a delusion, nevertheless, he must be shaken out of.[1]

---

[1] Butlin sees "a peaceful scene showing past hours bringing experience to the poet, [which] may have been selected by Blake in ironic contrast to his account of the souls flying 'Howling & Wailing . . . from Urizen's strong hands' " [i.e. hand: 125:5].
  We are grateful to John E. Grant and Mary Lynn Johnson for rescuing us from an early misreading of this design.

Pages 126 and 127 (NT 45:15E)

"YON SUN SHALL WAX OLD & DECAY, BUT THOU SHALT EVER FLOURISH" (127:25)

These facing pages, with a very difficult drawing on page 126 but a very clear development of the narrative on page 127, are best taken together.

In the narrative, Luvah and Vala, no longer "flaming Demon & Demoness of Smoke," are turned over by the "Regenerate Man" to Urizen for instruction (126:3–5). Accepting his lecture of obedience to the Human form Divine, they reverse the Expulsion from the Garden—not without some risk. Walking "from the hands of Urizen" they en-ter "the Gates of Dark Urthona," moving from the pastoral impossibilities of the reason to the vital but often dark realities of the imagination, "in the shadows of Vala's Garden," where they see no more "the terrible confusion of the wracking universe" yet find, as in the Garden of Eden, tempting "impressions of Despair" as well as of Hope, "for ever" vegetating there (18–25). There is irony in the prophetic note that "thus their ancient golden age renewd" (29).

Luvah hovers invisble "in bright clouds," and at first Vala looks for him 'out there,' thinking that his mild voice, which calls her forth "from the grass," comes from the bright Sun, to which she must run at once to find her lover. It is, indeed, Luvah's "creating voice," but its creature, the sun, is mortal. If the Sun is her maker, then she will die like the grass. "The fruit shall ripen & fall down," explains Luvah, "But thou shalt still survive" (127:26–27). She accepts the good news in a liberal spirit:

> Hah! shall I still survive! whence came that
>   sweet & comforting voice?
> And whence that voice of sorrow? O sun
>   thou art nothing now to me
> Go on thy course rejoicing & let us both
>   rejoice together.
> I walk among his flocks & hear the bleating
>   of his lambs;
> O that I could behold his face & follow his
>   pure feet!
>
>   (28–32)

Vala has learned the lesson that Thel, whose "Cloud" was a potential Luvah/Jesus, never learned. She and the sun can be merry companions; no bowing down like Ahania's to Urizen.

The design on page 127, a giant figure of Time past, winged but striding heavily on a bare earth, smooth headed, with no forelock to grasp, his instep scarred with burns of some hellish grill, can represent the perishing nature of the existence that is Vala's if she worships the Sun as her "maker" and can only "sigh for immortality" (17–18).[1]

The drawing on page 126 appears to allude, in part, to the story of Vala's shifting perceptions of the sun. (The giant whose head and shoulders we see at bottom right may be Albion still sorrowing as he watches developments; the shepherd with crook, who strides toward his or Vala's flock—roughly sketched—anticipates the text of page 129.) In the left margin is an Apollonian image that suits Vala's idea of the sun as of "majestic" form and brightness, an exaggeratedly muscular torso per-

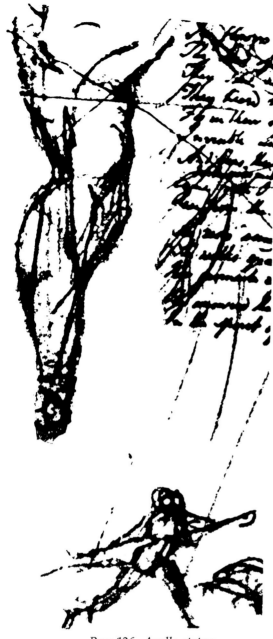

Page 126. Giant Sun.

The heavily drawn circles of the striding Sun enclose the word "reorganize" (126:15) perhaps to translate the central theme of this Night.

[1] For a helpful discussion of the conflicting voices and of Vala's learning "to distinguish herself from the material world" and "the role she is to play in it . . . by observing the nature of lambs (which are subject to her will), and the contrasting nature of birds (which are not)" see Andrew Lincoln, "Blake's 'Lower Paradise'" in *BRH*, 1981.

[2] Compare the eyes of "Pestilence" in two sketches of about 1805 (Butlin 443r and 443v).

Page 126. Apollo statue.

haps shrinking to mere light; head and arms almost gone, feet never developed. A contrasting image of the sun as a great brute with fierce eyes[2] that nearly burn holes in the text is drawn with alternative sets of limbs, one making him a giant strider with long, kneeless legs (fierce sun rays that pierce the shepherd and the Albion figure), the other with a left leg bent at the knee and flung back across the right margin and a right leg stamping down at the base of the Apollo image. (The Sun's legs in this position imitate—in mocking reversal—the legs of fleeting Time on page 127.) The Sun's arms seem to be swirling about, but his right hand, in the top left margin, grasps a spear the barb of which enters the vanishing left arm of Apollo. (Conceivably an allusion to time's destruction of the left arm of the famous Apollo Belvedere.)

Page 128

VALA "IN LOWER PARADISE" (30)

Rise up, O Sun, most glorious minister &
   light of day.
Flow on, ye gentle airs, & bear the voice of
   my rejoicing.
Wave, freshly clear waters flowing around
   the tender grass.
And thou, sweet smelling ground, put forth
   thy life in fruits & flowers.
Follow me, O my flocks & hear me sing my
   rapturous Song.
   . . . . . .
My Luvah here hath placd me in a Sweet &
   pleasant Land

> Here will I build myself a house &
>   here I'll call on his name.
> Here I'll return when I am weary &
>   take my pleasant rest.
>
> So spoke the Sinless Soul & laid her
>   head on the downy fleece
> Of a curld Ram who stretchd himself
>   in sleep beside his mistress
> And soft sleep fell upon her eyelids in
>   the silent noon of day.
>
> Then Luvah passed by & saw the
>   sinless Soul
> And said, "Let a pleasant house arise
>   to be the dwelling place
> Of this immortal Spirit growing in
>   lower Paradise."
>
> (4–30)

Blake's drawing replaces the "curld Ram" (26) with a silken pillow and clothes Vala, to her dream's content, in the translucent dress of a dancing Babylonian woman, decked in pearls and bracelets, turbaned, and holding a tambourine whose circle and bangles strikingly repeat the motif of those Wheels of Destiny depicted in pages 82 and 104! At her feet are a girl (blindfolded or with a hat over her eyes) and a boy, playing at some game that combines hand wrestling with exchange of marbles. Can this be, in some premonitory sense, a miniature representation of the great wrestling match of page 137 or a transitional stage between the "sweet delights of amorous play" (137:2) and the transforming of passion into love?

Above the sleeping Vala sits another elegant woman, somewhat bejeweled and finely coiffed, playing a flute, beside a lyre-player of whom we can see only the backs of head and body. Above them, faintly drawn, are suggestions of more players or singers—perhaps a whole chamber orchestra.

The figure of Vala is drawn with great care; her skin is touched with spots of brown, pink, and blue watercolor, and around her body is a blue wash. Around her waist is the diaphanous "golden girdle" which she ungirds and girds before and after her bath (129:13; 130:1).

The contrast of pastoral reality (shepherdess and ram) to palatial dream (dancing woman and orchestra) is not satiric but a promise of the civilized glory that awaits "the Sinless Soul" (25) for whom two thousand years of slavery have not been. In the fallen world such accoutrement might connote whoredom. In the "lower Paradise" which Luvah

prepares for her, with pillars and walls "as white as ivory" and the grass "pavd with pavement as of pearl" (30–32), courtly music and dancing are meet. On the interchangeability of humble and royal dwellings, it may help to recall Blake's sentiment in a letter of September 1800 upon the Blakes' moving into a seashore cottage in a pastoral setting which delighted him as palatial: "Our Cottage is more beautiful than I thought it & also more convenient, for tho Small it is well proportiond & if I should ever build a Palace it would be only My Cottage Enlarged."

Finally it may be noted that Vala's slippered feet are drawn in such a curious position as to remind us of the cloven right foot of the poet on page 2 who rests before the labor of this poem; when Vala awakes there will surely be fine singing and dancing to that music.

Page 129 (NT 68:21E)

"MY LUVAH SMILD" (1)

To illuminate Young's discussion of the fragility of friendship, "friendship delicate as dear, Of tender violations apt to die," Blake designed this vision of the proffered friendship of the good Samaritan, showing the stripped and wounded traveler hesitant to receive comfort from a stranger—whose cup bears a serpent and whom Blake depicts as Jesus himself (teller of the parable). On page 45, in Night III, a related scene of Christ's healing friendship was applied to Tharmas bellowing inconsolably for the loss of Enion.

Tharmas is again the subject. Vala's ability, in her sleep, to see "my Luvah like a spirit stand in the bright air" (128:35–129:3) results in her eyes' being "opend to the world of waters"—where she sees "Tharmas sitting upon the rocks beside the wavy sea" and hears "his mournful voice" still wailing for Enion (129:16–19). In the spirit of Luvah she manages, with much maternal diplomacy, to bring the shy Enion and the gloomy Tharmas together, restoring them to pastoral innocence:

> Thou, little Boy, art Tharmas & thou, bright
>   Girl, Enion.
> How are ye thus renewd & brought into
>   the Gardens of Vala!
>
> (130:7–8)

The comments of Wilkie and Johnson (1978, pp. 227–29) are excellently nuanced, e.g.: "Passion, especially sexuality, is no longer to be considered a hidden activity mysteriously reserved for adults; the very notion that innocence and passion are antithetical has been outgrown, and Vala no longer tries to appropriate for herself the sexual joys of others or to proclaim herself the exclusive deity of sexuality. If wisdom doth live with children round her knees—a Wordsworthian paraphrase for what Albion has taught Urizen earlier—so doth passion."

The other figures in the background, the priest and the Levite who passed by on the other side, suggest human seeds "driven" when sown by Urizen onto "unproducing sands" and "hardend rocks" (125:11).

The hesitancy of Tharmas and Enion is matched by that of the traveler to whom Christ's cup, egg-shaped and serpent-adorned, seems to offer the duality of life and death. In the great harvesting, the Human Odors who sing round the wine presses of Luvah (page 136) have not yet separated out the dregs; Enion has yet to "cast off" her "death clothes & Embrace Tharmas" (132:22).

Page 130

"AWAKE, THARMAS, AWAKE! AWAKE! THOU CHILD OF DEWY TEARS" (18)

The design drawn on this page cannot apply realistically to any of the persons on this or the adjacent pages, which are all concerned with the restoration of Tharmas and Enion to loving childhood, by the suasion and example of the reunited Vala and Luvah. But at the end of that drama of Innocence, summarized by the lines,

Thus in Eternal Childhood straying among
    Vala's flocks,
In infant sorrow & joy alternate Enion &
    Tharmas playd

(131:16–17)

we are reminded that these children are but "the shadows of Tharmas & of Enion in Vala's world" (131:19), the world of redeemed Nature. Thus the aroused mummy pictured here can well be Tharmas in the adult world of Urthona. We saw Tharmas half drowning in his waters on page 44, then saved by the touch of the Saviour on page 45. Here he seems half sunk into the grave, his chin and chest still wrapped in cerements. And lines beneath the shading indicate perhaps a more skeletal leg. But (we hear on the facing page) "Times are Ended," according to the adult Urizen (131:31).

It is not simply Tharmas, of course, who experiences this rite of awakening, but Albion on the way to recover full human embodiment.

Page 131 (NT 71:22E, first state)

"THUS WERE THE SLEEPERS ENTERTAIND UPON THE COUCHES OF BEULAH" (21)

The drawing on page 130 is so obviously placed as a parallel to the engraving of page 131 that we are clearly invited to recognize dear doubting Tharmas (cf. "Doubting stood Tharmas in the solemn darkness" 48:21) in the unsmiling figure on the couch of death. But then who are the others? The two soaring spirits are, of course, Vala and Luvah, who have rescued Tharmas from his doubts. But the anxious friend? In the context of this page it is Urizen. Having announced the end of Times, he has "pourd his light" to "exhale the spirits of Luvah & Vala thro the atmosphere," whose clouds then "dissipate or sink into the Seas of Tharmas," presumably leaving him on dry land for a moment.

On page 121, with the first use of this engraving, Eternal friendship was ensured by Urizen's miraculous discovery that Futurity is in this moment. On the present page friendship and futurity are secured through Albion's renewal and organization in innocence of his mighty paternal and maternal Zoas.

Page 132

"THE CLOUDS FALL OFF FROM MY WET BROW" (20)

On the morning after the feast of the human harvest, with wine "servd round by the flames of Luvah," Enion rose "like a gentle light" and saw that it was springtime:

"The clouds fall off from my wet brow, the
    dust from my cold limbs.
Into the Sea of Tharmas, Soon renewd, a
    Golden Moth,
I shall cast off my death clothes & Embrace
    Tharmas again:
For Lo! the winter melted away upon the
    distant hills!"

(20–23)

The drawing gives a quite literal rendition of Enion's "wet brow" with moisture streaming from her whole face as she bends lovingly, in lovely human form, over poor Tharmas still stiff from the winter freeze. Her legs are still under water, but at her presence,

> Joy thrilld thro all the Furious form of
>   Tharmas: humanizing,
> Mild, he Embracd her whom he
>   sought. . . .
>
>   (36–37)

The apocalyptic events that constitute this happy climax are represented by two giant figures drawn right over the text. One, a giant harvester, stands astride the bowed body of Tharmas, with his back toward us (as we see from the inward pointing left foot) and with his elbows raised and his hands wielding what may look like a broad sword (Bentley) but ought to be, according to the text, either a sickle or scythe (1–5) or (more visually convincing) a flail (135:32), the harvest implements wielded in succession (since Times are Ended, the acts can be simultaneous) by Urizen, who still wears at his left side the "bright girdle" from which he sowed the human seed (125:3–4) and who begins now to reap "the wide Universe" (132:7).[1]

Above his raised elbows hovers a horizontal human cloud with huddled legs (one foot protrud-

ing into the left margin), wide open mouth and eyes, and three darts of lightning that descend not very menacingly toward Enion and Tharmas. This is the Whirlwind that rises at dawn (13–14) and serves as Tharmas' threshing collaborator (134:3, 138:4). In this page the sequence is, first, "a whirlwind . . . in the Center & in the Whirlwind a shriek" (Blake's drawing indicates both whirl and shriek), and then "in the Shriek a rattling of bones," and finally the dolorous groan from which Enion rises in tears to embrace Tharmas humanizing.[2]

The threshing begins in the text at the end of page 133 and continues in 134. Graphically the scything of humans by "Time" (in the Young engraving; by Urizen now) on page 135 makes the theme most explicit. We can see that the Urizenic figure trampling on crowned kings on page 133 is cooperating both in the action of Los in pulling down the sun (at the start of the Night) and in the action of Tharmas in winnowing "Kings & Councellors & Giant Warriors" on page 134. (His dart, in page 133, also seems to have been a model for the lightning darts of the Whirlwind here.)

[1] The standing giant seems to have a coat with short tails, though just possibly we are meant to see his genitalia from behind. He holds his weapon or implement with two hands; so the object at his waist is probably Urizen's sack of seeds, not a shield.

[2] For sketches of a similar air-borne giant with emphatic eyes and mouth, see Blake's studies for his "Pestilence: The Death of the First-Born" ca. 1805 (Butlin 443 recto and verso).

Page 132. Giant Harvester.

Page 133 (NT 20:5E, second state)

"GO DOWN, YE KINGS & COUNCELLORS & GIANT WARRIORS!" (134:7)

In a speech at the harvest Feast, a "golden feast" where "Many Eternal Men sat," the therapy for man's tendency to be a worm is patiently explained. "Man is a Worm . . . Forsaking Brotherhood & Universal love in selfish clay, Folding the pure wings of his mind, seeking the places dark." When he gets sufficiently closed in on himself, "we cast him like a Seed into the Earth . . . every morn We visit him, covering . . . the immortal seed . . . till divided all In families we see our shadows born, & thence we know That Man subsists by Brotherhood & Universal Love. We fall on one another's necks, more closely we embrace, Not for ourselves but for the Eternal family . . ." (11–24).

The morning after *this* feast, Urizen goes to work with flail in hand on the threshing floor. "And all Nations were threshed out & the stars threshd from their husks" (134:1). The transformation of what "Nations" are—and of what we think they are—is involved as well as the replacing of our dead ideas of sun and moon and stars. The engraving (for Young's "Death! great proprietor of all! 'tis thine To tread out empire, and to quench the stars") functioned as ironic counterpoint to the text of page 81, but used here it serves as a positive illumination. Tharmas recognizes in this threshing of empire the end of Mystery:

> Art thou she that made the nations drunk
>   with the cup of Religion?
> Go down, ye Kings & Councellors & Giant
>   Warriors! . . .
> Go down with horse & Chariots &
>   Trumpets of hoarse war!
>
> (134:6–9)

The design suggests that getting rid of crowned kings and of sun worship are simultaneous tasks of reorganization.

Page 134

"HIS CROWN OF THORNS FELL FROM HIS HEAD."
(135:23)

> "Attempting to be more than Man, We
>   become less," said Luvah
> As he arose from the bright feast drunk
>   with the wine of ages.
> His crown of thorns fell from his head; he
>   hung his living Lyre
> Behind the seat of the Eternal Man & took
>   his way . . .
> . . . to the Vineyards bright.
>
> (135:21–25)

If a Zoa has learned this, *for* every "Eternal Man," and the Zoa cheerfully leaves the feast (he will be back; his Lyre remains alive) to work as the servant of Man, then the artist is ready to show us that each of these "Four Mighty Ones . . . in every

Page 134. Totem of Luvah.

Man" (3:4) is not, by itself, really a complete human form.

Some such thinking may have led Blake to adorn these festive concluding pages with some drawings depicting Zoas in quiet, unambitious, and unterrified or unterrifying states of contentment. Iconography of crucifixion is no longer necessary to be worn by Luvah (either to serve Mystery or to assist Prophecy). We have seen Urizen in a bird-animalman form on page 100, but not a viable form, and miserable in flames. Here (on page 134) is Luvah (it may be) in a rather delicately balanced emblematic combination of human, bird, and phallic serpent, and yet a servant of Man—with a human rider, a cupid without need of bow or arrow, who holds a very thin switch in his left hand but a goblet of wine in his right. (Compare the cup held by the dancing woman in the facing page, 135.) If we look back at the armed Cupid on the phallic serpent of page 4, we are amazed at the transformation. This is no longer the raging Orcan phallus, but one tamed into a humanized Luvah, who is love but not without passion. This gentle Zoa may more happily remind us of the serpents bearing children in *The Book of Thel*, page 6, and *America a Prophecy*, page 11.

Rose Zimbardo suggests that this creature looks like the half-bird, half-woman Harpy of Greek legend, humanized and no longer snatching food from others but enjoying wine at the final harvest feast.

Page 135 (NT 49:16E)

"HOWLING FELL THE CLUSTERS OF HUMAN FAMILIES"
(36–37)

All "the Legions of Mystery" (34) are being swept from the stage of human history. An appropriate illustration comes from the design illustrating Young's theme that Time was born with creation and hurries in order to return quickly to "his ancient rest." Blake depicts the scythe of Time as mowing down priest, warrior, and crowned king (who lie flattened) and as about to reap clusters of human families. The distinction is prophetic, since priests and kings are finished but families are to be regenerated. Young's view, that Time is in love with Eternity, may seem Urizenic—Blake's view is that "Eternity is in love with the productions of time" (*Marriage of Heaven and Hell* 7). But in the context of *The Four Zoas* we cannot mistake the theme—that the entire mental structure of Empire must be

transformed into the innocence of Brotherhood in a continuing "intellectual War," replacing the "war of swords" (see the last lines of the poem).

In this service, it is proper that Time be seen without his forelock, which was an invitation to opportunism, as with his great scythe he serves among Urizen's sons.

Page 136

"URTHONA . . . IN ALL HIS REGENERATE POWER"
(137:34)

Urizen, after his harvesting, is only once more referred to, when "Dark Urthona" takes "the Corn out of the Stores of Urizen" and grinds it "in his rumbling Mills" (138:1–2). Urizen may be the "Miller of Eternity," as we are told in Blake's *Milton* (3:42–43), but he has to be "made subservient to the Great Harvest, That he may go to his own Place, Prince of the Starry Wheels." He cannot be permitted to distort the mental economy by hoarding or exploiting the grain he reaps and stores. It must be Urthona who makes the bread, as he collaborates with Luvah and Tharmas in the rest of this Night. It is the Imagination, with Love and native Instinct, that makes human use and distribution of the stores of Reason.

We deduce that this seraphic portrait, of a creature that is all head and wings, is Blake's emblem of the Zoa Urthona as servant of the Human Brotherhood: wise, kindly, quiet but ever alert. The three tiers of wings associate him with the six-winged Seraphim seen by Isaiah: doubtless "with twain he [could] fly!"; with twain he *could* cover his face (but chooses not to); but the twain which might cover "his feet" seem to be holding a "live coal" such as was taken from the altar and laid upon the mouth of the prophet Isaiah (6:4–7).

The small human figure seated between the top wings is given no distinctive features but is writing in a small open book at his left side.[1] We should consider whether this rider and the wine-bearing rider on the emblem of Luvah on page 134 are not new, innocent versions of the cupid rider of fornication seen in the earlier Nights, his transformation being marked by his unstringing his bow, having run out of arrows when last seen (on page 108). He is now writing poetry. He too has become the servant instead of the tormentor of mankind.

Only the Imagination, only Urthona with that generous wide look, is able to see "all the idle weeds That creep about the obscure places" as hav-

With Mirth & Joy. Urthona, limping from
his fall, on Tharmas leand.

(7–8)

Page 136. Blake riding and writing.

ing "various limbs Naked in all their beauty" and
"dancing round the Wine Presses" (37–39). Only a
visionary can recognize in "the tender maggot" an
"emblem of Immortality" (32). His spirit presides
over this page. And it allows us to see, in the
anonymous author who has replaced Cupid in the
rider's position, William Blake himself.[2]

[1] There are also two small faces in the hair and near the eyes
of the central face: that of a bird on the left, that of a beast on
the right—images derived perhaps from the eagle and lion
faces of the creatures seen by the prophet Ezekiel (1:10).

[2] This figure bears some similarity to the scribe at the right
of the Devil in *Marriage* 10, who has been compared to the
prophet Daniel in a sketch by Blake based on Adam Ghisi's
copy of a detail in Michelangelo's Sistine frescoes. See Jenijoy
La Belle, "Blake's Visions and Re-visions of Michelangelo,"
p. 20 in *Blake in His Time,* ed. Robert N. Essick and Donald
Pearce (Indiana University Press, 1978). The Daniel designs are
reproduced in plates 25–26.

Page 137 (NT 145:39E)

"FOR WE WRESTLE . . . AGAINST SPIRITUAL WICKEDNESS"

The muscular Zoas in this picture must be Thar-
mas and Urthona, fullest *bodied* of the Zoas,
wrestlers of Samson-like power, wrestling (with
the collaboration of Luvah and Urizen) *for* "flesh
and blood." (We quote the King James translation
of the New Testament Greek inscribed on page 3.)
And the text supports this identification, for it is
here that the Eternal Man gives to Tharmas and
Urthona their assignments at the wine presses:

Then Tharmas & Urthona rose from the
Golden feast, satiated

Indeed, we may deduce that Urthona got "his fall"
in this match. Both are athletic types, Urthona with
"his hammer" and Tharmas with his ornamented
"Shepherd's crook" (9); for the crook, see page 126.

(On the engraved proof Blake carefully com-
pleted with his pencil the boxed-out body lines,
before inscribing verses in the text-box. The pen-
ciled variations on Time's big toe in page 99 were a
different matter, trial changes made on an un-
finished state of the plate, long before use of the
proof in the *Vala* manuscript.)

Urizen is nowhere around; Luvah has been
treading the human grapes with his "sons &
daughters" until they have become "quite ex-
hausted." They have drunk the new wine and be-
gun "to torment one another and to tread The
weak" (18–21). Luvah and Vala sleep "on the floor
o'erwearied." The two stouter Zoas, with their nu-
merous sons, go to work separating the lees, put-
ting Luvah "for dung on the ground," and loading
"all the waggons of heaven"—though first they
have had to form suitable "heavens, of sweetest
woods, of gold & silver & ivory, Of glass & precious
stones" (22–26). When Luvah and Vala come to, the
Man casts them "wailing into the world of shad-
ows" until the return of spring.

The "Human Wine" is (or are) delighted with the
new environment. They stand "wondering in all
their delightful Expanses," to which the world of
fire, air, earth, water must now take a subsidiary
relationship. "The Elements subside, the heavens
roll on with vocal harmony" ("rolld" in ms). Los,
we might say, is now in his Element; human ap-
proval at the imagination's new world (achieved
together with bodily vitality) has come to this, that
"Los who is Urthona rose in all his regenerate
power" and the sea "that rolld & foamd with
darkness & the shadows of death"—Tharmas's ele-
ment—now coming under Urthona's guidance
has to "vomit out" all its bad habits. Even the
floods are happy about this: "All the floods lift up
their hands, Singing & shouting to the Man; they
bow their hoary heads And murmuring in their
channels flow & circle round his feet" (28–38).

Looking back at the regenerate wrestlers, we re-
alize that Urthona must be the winner, not by
throwing Tharmas but by assisting in their mutual
demonstration of great powers put to benevolent
uses.

When we turn to consider what text of Young's inspired the original engraving, we are struck by how mutually beneficial the collaborative wrestling of Blake with Young could sometimes be! This wrestling emblem came quite near the end of the 1797 edition of Young; Blake uses it now even closer to the end—of *The Four Zoas* and of the Last Judgment, silently implying that the very length of the human struggle is a consequence of its precarious balance and fearful symmetry.

Like Los coming into his full powers, Young at this point in his poem expresses a strong sense of his playing the right music for "heaven's orchestra." He dismisses the tender-hearted and the rationalists who "Think . . . my song too turbulent," who would prefer "Reason alone," without "passions." Such reasoners would rather lose heaven's blessing than "wrestle . . . with heaven" to obtain it. The terms are slightly different—although Blake's stormy Tharmas represents much of what Young calls "the passions"—but simply as an illustration for Young, the picture indicates the poet's creative will (Urthona) wrestling not for a fall but for a blessing from heaven (from the Man), with the turbulence and warmth of passion (Tharmas, with Luvah's warmth, which we have seen Vala use to arouse him). "On such a theme," says Young, "Passion is reason, transport temper . . .".

In Blake's text, on this page, the "Human Wine" who had been engaging in "the sports of love & . . . the sweet delights of amorous play" while listening "to the luring songs of Luvah" (1–3), but to sadistic effect such as exhibited in the sexual wrestling groups of Night the Third, can now applaud the poet's success in forcing all cruelties to be "Vomited out."

Page 138

"THE GREY HOAR FROST . . . AND HIS PALE WIFE, THE AGED SNOW . . . WATCH OVER THE FIRES" (9–10)

After the winnowing of the grain by Urizen and Tharmas, it is stored in the stores of Urizen, then ground in the Mills of Urthona, powered by the storms of Tharmas: "Thunders, Earthquakes, Fires, Water floods," who "rejoice to one another" with voices that "shake the Abyss" (2–8). And then it is made into bread.

> They build the Ovens of Urthona. Nature in
>   darkness groans,
> And Men are bound to sullen
>   contemplations in the night.

> Restless they turn on beds of sorrow, in
>   their inmost brain
> Feeling the crushing Wheels; they rise; they
>   write the bitter words
> Of Stern Philosophy & knead the bread of
>   knowledge with tears & groans.
>
> (11–16)

Philosophical poetry requires all the psychic equivalents of seasonal maturation. "Such are the works of Dark Urthona," works of slow agony in the dark as well as rejoicing that illuminates the abyss.

>   Tharmas sifted the corn,
> Urthona made the Bread of Ages & he
>   placed it
> In golden & in silver baskets in heavens of
>   precious stone,

a characteristic description of Blake's desiderata for his works in Illuminated Printing.

> And then took his repose, in Winter, in the
>   night of Time.
>
> (16–19)

All the Zoas, then, except perhaps stormy Tharmas and cold Urizen, rest after as well as "before Labour" (see the frontispiece, page 2).

Where, in this season, is Enitharmon? In the simple drawing for this page, made as it were even as the artist's hand chilled, she is depicted as "the aged Snow," wife of Frost (9–10): Enitharmon as mother of hibernation. (Compare her portrait on page 50, reuniting with Los.) The wife of Dark Urthona comes back to the realm of the Earth-Owner or Imagination, where all images are forged. We may also recognize in this reclining figure the Vala who presided in the first page of text (page 3), whose regenerative function is not to preside but to assist: Nature the servant of Humanity.[1]

It will soon be fully declared (129:5–10) that while, separately, Los the Spectre of Urthona has been a "delusive Phantom" and Enitharmon his separated Emanation, their union enables Urthona to rise "in all his ancient strength." The rising Urthona is, in effect, Imagination and Fertility united. The inner fertility of snow, supplied to a cornfield barren after harvest and then frozen by winter, prepares soil for the grain that will come. Fertility and Imagination, joined in one as a liberated Eve and Adam, now inherit the Earth.

The rest of the poem, only thirty lines more, is a Chorus of prophetic joy. In short, the "bitter words" written in "sullen contemplations in the night," are very sweet to the ear. Blake is offering the prophetic experience of Saint John, in mirror reversal. In Revelation, chapter 10, the "little book" which a mighty angel directs the prophet to eat "shall make thy belly bitter, but it shall be in thy mouth sweet as honey." John found this to be true. The words were sweet as honey in his mouth, but as soon as he had eaten, his belly felt bitter. The bread of Urthona and Enitharmon is made of bitter words, but when it is eaten "Man walks forth from midst of the fires; the evil is all consumd" (22). There are many ways to eat a book of prophesy, and we can turn the pain it gives us into a fertile joy.

[1] We see her in very similar plight and spirit in *Jerusalem* 93, where she sits in a sulfur bath in the "furnaces of affliction."

Page 139

"END OF THE DREAM" (11)

The Sun arises from his dewy bed . . .
Urthona is arisen in his strength, no longer now
Divided from Enitharmon, no longer the Spectre Los.
Where is the Spectre of Prophecy? Where the delusive Phantom?
Departed, & Urthona rises from the ruinous walls
In all his ancient strength, to form the golden armour of science
For intellectual War. The war of swords departed, now
The dark Religions are departed & sweet Science reigns.
           End of The Dream
                              (1–11)

The nightmare is over, but the labor has just begun—for Blake the production of his great Illuminated Books, *Milton* and *Jerusalem*. No longer restless in the night with the sense of mankind's loss (Los) of paradise, he can now prepare the wise habitation of the Earth. In the final drawing, a contrary to the "Rest before Labour" picture of page 2, Urthona stands tiptoe upon the Earth, arising in strength without chains or blindfold, with no cloven foot—although there is a slight cleft in the earth-touching left foot—and worse yet, with only a divided mitten in place of fingers for the right hand; yet that hand is led by a (golden) string going right up off the page (a fine crease in the

paper, there when Blake used it for proofing and apt to his present purpose).[1]

Some see this figure as feminine, a reappearance of the small soaring figure beside the title in page 3. Other indications suggest masculine; the text already quoted, however, insists that we identify this human form as neither masculine nor feminine nor spectral phantom, but as the unity of Enitharmon and Urthona, purged of the hermaphroditic Spectre and of the "Female Will" (see Blake's *Vision of the Last Judgment*, page 85).

[1] The thread up the page may be accidental—or it may be a notice that the leading string of Cupid is now in the author's control. As for the very carefully drawn anus, it reminds us that "the body is permanent": this is no wraith or "soul." Neither here nor in page 2 is the poet about to leave this Earth.

CODA

Page 140 (NT 6:1E, penultimate state)

This press proof of the 1797 title-page for the first Night of Young's poem might be simply dismissed as the verso of the leaf of paper Blake happened to use for his final page of *The Four Zoas*; he could hardly use it elsewhere in the manuscript, since the proof was made after the printer had filled the central space. Yet we have seen with what economy and ingenuity Blake managed to relate the motifs in his own poem to those in the designs he had engraved for Young's. It takes little ingenuity on our part to read the title of Young's "Night the First, on Life, Death and Immortality" as a summary of what both Young's poem and Blake's, different as they are, have been all about.[1]

If Blake's vision of Young's "Death" suggests the tyrant power of Urizen's efforts to control "Futurity," a personification of the Wheel of Destiny *without* eyes or windows open to Eternity, Blake so erases the visual distinction between souls and bodies as to vindicate the Chorus on page 138: "How is it we have walkd thro fires & yet are not consumd?" Putting aside his bow and arrow (which in other pictures he handles like a short spear) Death conducts a transition from Life to Immortality that may perpetuate "The dark Religions"—but not after we have come with Blake through the "Dream" of "sweet Science" (139:10).

The family seem rightly to sense that this Death makes no threat to their "Sinless Souls" (to compare their domestic pastoral with Vala's in Night IX). These, we may opine, are not Kings and Councillors but a family building the city of Art. The mother's weaving is assisted by the youngest child, who holds the curved handle of her distaff (designed by Blake as a miniature of Death's wooden bow, which has no bowstring).[2] His sister, perhaps as young as he, is reading the book on their mother's knee—compare the boy and girl at a nurse's knee in the title-page of *Songs of Innocence*. At her feet sits an older boy with his back indifferently against the huge left foot of Death; he is busy writing something we can almost read. Older children, young adults, exhibit the closeness of Los and Enitharmon in page 116 but are serenely occupied with a lyre. The female holds the instrument and the male fingers its strings—balancing the adjacent collaboration of boy and mother. The carpentry in this scene is most economical, for the wooden frame of the lyre seems to come from the same shop as the distaff and the great bow.

The most striking contrast to active figures in *The Four Zoas* appears in the passivity of the female Soul who stands in the palm of Death. No leaping up (in her first position), no dynamic soaring (in her faint threshold position), no joyous welcome from the horizontal and almost needlessly winged sisters at the top. All implied movement is to be done by wires, or magnets, as if "Immortality" (unlike "Eternity") involved no Active Life at all.[3] Readers of Young in Blake's edition are struck with Blake's unconventional renderings, if not always critical reversals, of Young's motifs. Readers of *The Four Zoas* may see (using their imaginations to animate the bodies and lineaments) "all things . . . changd" (138:40) against a marble statue of Urizen in his "stonied" human form.

[1] Vincent De Luca agrees: "By making the first page of Young's work the last page of his own, Blake suggests that *The Four Zoas* moves in a counter direction from Young's poem. Back to back on the same leaf are the designations 'Night the First' and 'End of the Dream.' By using this proof where he does Blake suggests that the two works are contraries, one moving toward the installment of orthodoxy, the other towards a triumphant humanism."

[2] One might wish to read the line marking a fold of the garment as a bowstring, but Blake gives it no independence. One might like to see the boy holding a scroll, but this object is tubular; for the shapes of scrolls being held in hand, see page 125. One may well say, however, that the suggestion of a scroll in this object foreshadows texts to come.

[3] John Grant suggests, however, that the resurrection of a woman here was chosen to balance the resurrection of a man on page 2.

APPENDIX

Pages 141–45

Only one of these five pages of manuscript fragments now bound into *The Four Zoas* contains any drawing, the one numbered 144.

Page 144 contains part of two lines that occur also in a deleted passage in page 7. The Spectre (of Tharmas) is accusing Enion, "Thou sinful Woman," of darkening in his presence. A simple drawing, partly canceled by scribbling, depicts a woman with twisted torso (Eve? Enion?) sitting on her heels, seen from behind, encircled by a snake (the Spectre?) with three coils on the ground and two lifting the snake's head (presumably) close to the woman's left cheek. Her hands appear to support his upper coils. Compare the Prester Serpent of page 90[98].

(Consider this form as a stage in the serpent:beast:spectre development of pages 7 and 143.)

Butlin suggests that this figure, "partly in the midst of serpentine coils, partly terminating in such coils," is an alternative (or preliminary?) illustration of the words "Half Woman & half Serpent" on page 7.

Indexes

Name Index to the Introduction and Bibliography

Index to the Commentary

THE NUMBERS GIVEN ARE THOSE OF BLAKE'S MANUSCRIPT pages, as referred to in our Commentary. An italic numeral signifies that the page is on a *Night Thoughts* proof.

This index of images and names in our Com-mentary includes only those design details that are mentioned there. It also includes allusions to other works of Blake and works of other artists, also to scholars whose works are identified in the Bibli-ography section.

roots, bulbous, 30; exposed, 6. *See also* trees
ropes, twisted, 15, 24. *See also* cords; nets
rump, seeming pregnant, 32

saddle, 21
Saint Domittila, catacomb of, 4
Saint John, 138; Greek text of, 4
Samaritan, good, 44, *129*
Samson, *137*
sandal, helmet-shaped, 108; skull-shaped, 108
Satan, *55, 76, 93,* 100, 102; dividing in open Sanhedrim, *115. See also* Antichrist
"Satan Arousing the Rebel angels," 120
"Satan Calling up his Legions," 120
satyr, 2
Saviour, 45, 66, 130. *See also* Christ; Jesus
scale, of Reason, *69*
scars, *127*
Schotz, Myra Glazer, 2
scissors, 9
scourge, 15
scroll, *65, 140;* of Destiny, 43. *See also* gown
scrotum, 39, 41. *See also* genitals; penis, testicles
scythe, 72, 132; of Time, *135*
sea, 50; bottom, *67;* serpent, 21
seeds, 30, 32; sack of, 132
semen, 41
Sendak, Maurice, 70
Sense, *67*
senses crystallized into organs, 52
seraph, *136. See also* angel(s)
Seraphim, 136
serpent, 12, *77;* as gate, *73;* bearing children, 134; coiling, 1, 10, 12; half-human, 7, 22; half-woman, 141–45; in sea, 4; on cup, *129;* phallic, 4, *73;* serpent-horn, 13, 14, 22; shape, *49;* with human face, 90; with Satanic head, 4; three female heads, 14; triangular head, 1, 4, 6; two heads, 12; whispering, *49. See also* Prester Serpent; snake
serpent-beast-spectre development, 7, 143, 144
sex, anal approach, 32; chaotic potential, 5; dividing of sexes, 41; phallic sex, 89; sexual union, as metamorphosis, 26; sexual struggle, 6. *See also* coitus; rape
sexual ambiguity, 120. *See also* hermaphrodite
shadow of smoke, 44
Shadowy Female, *101, 102, 103*
shadowy outline, 31
sheep, 90. *See also* shepherd
sheephook, 15, 64. *See also* crook
shellelagh, 15
Shelley, P. B., 21
shells, 44
shepherd, 126
ship's mast and rigging, 38
shriek, 132
sickle, 132
Silenus figure, 38. *See also* satyr
sinner, 102
Sister Cities, 14, 17
sisters, winged, *140*
skeleton, dancing, *109*
sleep, creative, 2
slippers, 128
smoke, 44
snail shells, 44
snake, 144. *See also* Prester Serpent; serpent
snow, *43,* 54, 58; snow, 138
soaring, 1, 2
Socratic fool, *85*
sofa, 112
soldier, hermaphrodite, 84
Solomon, *93*
Songs of Experience, 8, 36; *Songs of Innocence,* 8, *140*

soul, dancing, *111;* in Death's palm, *140;* hurled down, *111;* scaling cliff, *111;* swimming, *111*
Southcott, Johanna, 58
spanning gesture, *63, 64, 73, 99. See also* gesture(s)
spear, *57,* 126
spectre as bat-winged genital, 26. *See also* bat-wings
sperm, drops of, 41
spider king, 15
spikes, 44
spirits, as musical notes, 14; bright, *91;* dark, *91;* following whirlwind, 14; "hour-sized," *99;* shaking rain from moon, 14; soaring, *131*
sponges, 42
spurs, 40
star(s), *55, 73, 82, 91*
statue, broken, 30; human, 44; of Urizen, *140*
steel, *59*
stem of vegetation, *87*
stone, books, *79;* doorway, *67;* head, 19, 20, 21; figure turning to, 4, *57*
Stothard, Thomas, 38
stream, *83,* 92; of air, *82;* bloody, *91. See also* water
strider, 126
striding, *73, 127*
string, *31, 38, 39,* 40, 42, 112, 136, 139, *140. See also* cords; nets; ropes
sulking infants, 8
sun(s), 15, 29, 47, 66, 80, 88, 132; as brute, 126; as person, 126; carried on shoulder, 2; cut down, 44; giant, spearing Apollo figure, 126; striding, 126; with fierce eyes, 126. *See also* Apollo
Sunflower, *47, 55*
sunlight, 2, 126. *See also* sun(s)
Sutherland, John, 86
swan, serpent-like, 7
swimmers, 66, 67, *83,* 114
switch, 134
swooping figure, 18
sword, broad, 132; phallic, 12; winged, 12
sybil, *87*
sylphs, 38, *125*
Synagogue of Satan, 109

tabernacle between breasts, 44; at vulva, 44
taboo, 40
talon(s), 37; motif, 38; of Urizen, 60
tambourine, 128; as Circle of Destiny, 82, *83*
tarsus, 106–8
teacher, *87. See also* instruction
teeth, triple row, 110
Tell, William, parody of, 21
temple, Urizen's, *87*
testicles, 26, 88. *See also* genitals; penis; scrotum
Tharmas, as Apollo, *47;* on couch of death, *131;* in his crystal form, *45;* as Demon of Waters, 4, 13, *45;* drowning, 130; emerging from smoke, 44; evasive action of, 112; hands buried in face, 5; intervening, 46, *77;* pensive, 5; preventive deluge, 46; reading, 5; restored to childhood, 130; sexual struggle with Enion, 6, 48; sleeping, 6; stiff with cold, 132; striding between waves, 46; winnowing, 132; wounded traveler, *129;* wrestling, *137;* Zoa of touch, 4
There is No Natural Religion, 49
thigh, hand on, 55
thong, 9
thorns, 62. *See also* Crucifixion
"thought," walking, *83*
three-headed, 14; three-faced, 17
threshing, 133

threshold, Gothic, *67*
thumbs, 86
Thunder, demon, *65;* god, 62
"Till thou dost injure the distrest," 70
Time, 126, *135;* as giant, *127;* big toe of, *137;* scything humans, 132, *135;* striding, *127;* winged, *127*
Tirzah, 77; as whore, 118; on couch, *121*
Titian, 3
toadstool, 32
toe(s), hidden, *57;* holding net, 29; reshaped, *99, 137;* of Time, *137;* touching, 116
tolling bell, 72
tomb, 1, *63;* tombstones, *79. See also* graves
tongue, darting, 1; forked, *73;* serpent's, arrowhead-like, *77*
tongueless monster, 110
tool, 120
torso, 126; as wave, 46; female, 24, 30, 120; twisted, 2, 144
totem, 40
"To the Accuser," 106–8
touch. *See* Tharmas
tradition, classical, 4, 41
Translucence, Limit of, 63
traveler, wounded, *129*
tree, 66, 84; as Urizen, *73;* double, 6, 8; Family, 60; leg-like, 72; of mystery, Urizenic, 72; trunk(s), 10, 72
Tree of Life, 8
triangles, in foot, 23
triangular head of serpent, 1, 4, 6, 12
triptich, of chapel, 44
triumph, over Death, *85*
trumpet, 1, 14, *109,* 118
trumpeter(s), 1, 13, *109;* trumpeting, final, 1, 2, 66, 104, *115, 117,* 118
"Truth," *113,* 116; as woman, 112; goddess of, *85;* pointing, *85*
turban, 32, 128
turbulence, 82
twins, 8

umbilical attachment, 9
urinating, 21, 31, 35
Urizen, aged, *67,* 100; as angel, 12; as anxious friend, *131;* as bird-animal-man, 134; as blind Death, *101;* as crocodile, 70; as Death, 53, *140;* as harvester, 132; as headless tree, *73;* as Jehovah, *43;* as mourner, *79;* as pyramid-builder, 24; as reason, 11; as serpent, 12, *73;* as serpent's head, 90; as stone head, 21; cutting down sun, 15, 64; falling, *111;* at feast, 13; holding vortex, 74; hovering, 12; his plight, 70; reclining, 120; seizing, *111;* sleeping, 37, *109,* 110; swimming, *111, 113;* with Ahania, 37; with crutch, 124
Urizenic figure, trampling kings, 132
Urizen's three daughters, 72; his youngest daughter, 68
urn, of a sybil, *67*
Urthona, Spectre of, arising, 39; as angel, 136; donor of time, 71; emblem, servant of Human Brotherhood, 136; fallen, into stream, 84; limping, 2, *137;* resting, 2; on tiptoe, 139; wrestling, *137*

vagina, 4, *41, 104. See also* vulva(s)
Vala, as Belinda, 39; as victim of war, 92; in coitus with Luvah, 40; emerging from smoke, 44; at feast, 13; flattened, 94; in flower, 124; half of two-headed figure, 17; headless, 24; huddled, 31; measuring penis, 42; metamorphosis of, 26; prone, 40; reaching for Albion, 41; reclining, 3, 138; recognizing Luvah, 16; sleeping, 128; soaring, *131;*

The Manuscript of
The Four Zoas

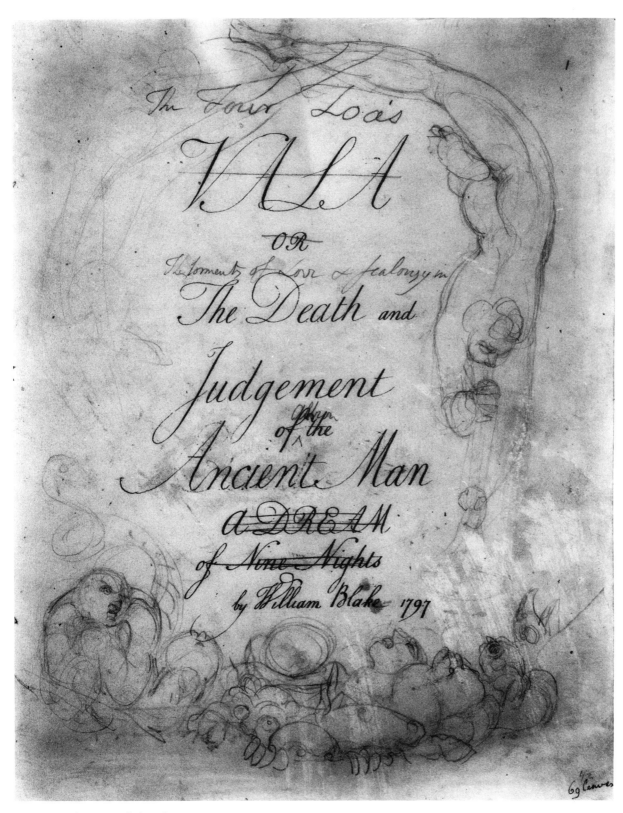

Page 1. Night I. Pencil drawing.

Page 2. Night I. Pencil drawing.

ΟΤΙ ΟΥΚ ΕΣΤΙΝ ημιν η παλη προς αιμα και σαρκα. αλλα προς τας αρχας,
προς τας εξεσιας, προς τας κοσμοκρατορας τε σκοτες τε αιωνος τετε. προς
τα πνευματικα της πονηριας εν τοις επουρανιοις. ΕΦΕΣ: VI Κεφ. 12

VALA

Night the First

The Song of the Aged Mother which shook the heavens with wrath
~~Hearing the march of long resounding strong heroic Verse~~
~~Marshalld in order for the day of Intellectual Battle~~
The heavens quake: the earth was moved & shudderd & the mountains
With all their woods, the streams & valleys: waild in dismal fear

Four Mighty Ones are in every Man; a Perfect Unity
Cannot Exist. but from the Universal Brotherhood of Eden
The Universal Man. To Whom be Glory Evermore Amen

Los was the fourth immortal starry one, & in the Earth
Of a bright Universe. Empery attended day & night
Days & nights of revolving joy, Urthona was his name

John XVII c. 21 & 22 & 23

John 1 c. 14 v
και εσκηνωσεν
εν ημιν

*Page 3, Night I. Pencil and ink drawing with brown, blue,
gray, and black watercolor washes. (See color plate below.)*

Page 4. Night I. Pencil and ink drawing with blue, gray, pink, brown, and black washes. (See color plate, below.)

Page 5. Night I. Pencil and ink drawing with blue, gray, pink, brown, and black washes. (See color plate below.)

Page 6. Night I. Pencil and ink drawing with blue, gray, pink, brown, and black washes.

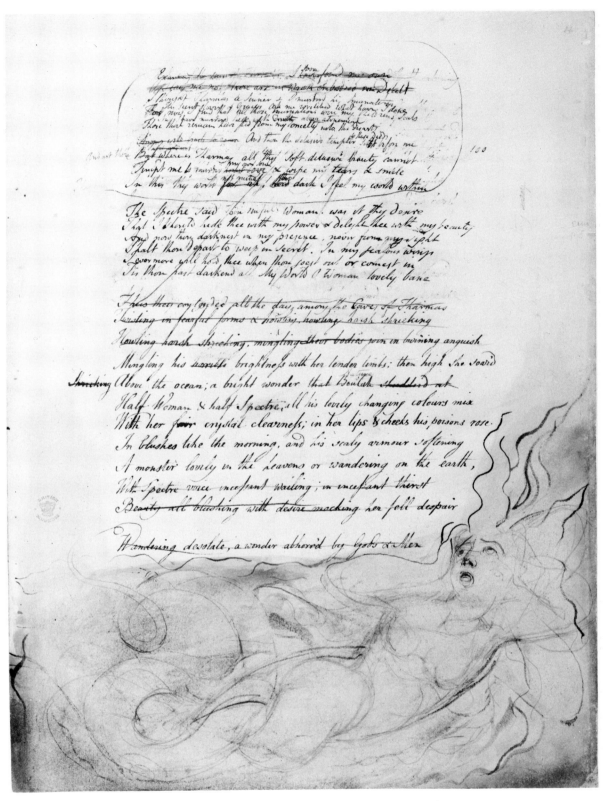

The Spectre said Thou lovely Woman. was it thy desire
That I should hide thee with my power & delight thee with my beauty
And now thou darkness in my presence. never from my sight
Shalt thou depart to weep in secret. In my jealous wings
I evermore will hold thee when thou goest out or comest in
Tis thou hast darkend all My World O Woman lovely bane

Thus they enjoyd all the day, among the Caves of Tharmas
twisting in fearful forms & howling harsh shrieking

Howling harsh shrieking. mingling their bodies join in burning anguish

Mingling his horrible brightness with her tender limbs; then high She soard

Above the ocean; a bright wonder that Beulah shudderd at

Half Woman & half Spectre; all his lovely changing colours mix

With her fair crystal clearness; in her lips & cheeks his poisons rose.

In blushes like the morning, and his scaly armour softening

A monster lovely in the heavens or wandering on the earth,

With Spectre voice incessant wailing; in incessant thirst

Beauty all blushing with desire mocking her fell despair

Wandering desolate, a wonder abhorr'd by Gods & Men

Page 7. Night I. Pencil and chalk drawing with blue and gray washes, and ink.

121

Page 8. Night I. Pencil and chalk drawing with gray wash.

Page 9. Night I. Pencil and chalk drawing.

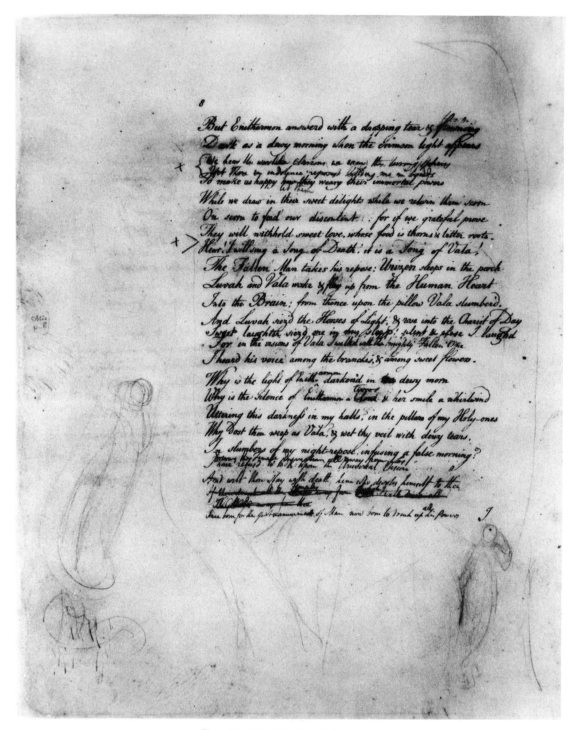

8

But Enitharmon answerd with a dropping tear [illegible]

Dark as a dewy morning when the crimson light appears

We hear the woollen clarions, we crave the [illegible]

[illegible] there in indolence reposd lulling me on [illegible]

To make us happy how they weary their immortal powers

While we draw in their sweet delights while we return them scorn

On scorn to feed our discontent : for if we grateful prove

They will withhold sweet love, whose food is thorns & bitter roots.

Hear! I will sing a Song of Death! it is a Song of Vala!

The Fallen Man takes his repose: Urizen sleeps in the porch

Luvah and Vala woke & flew up from the Human Heart

Into the Brain; from thence upon the pillow Vala slumberd.

And Luvah siezd the Horses of Light, & rose into the Chariot of Day

Sweet laughter siezd me in my sleep! silent & close I laughd

For in the visions of Vala I walked with the mighty Fallen One

I heard his voice among the branches, & among sweet flowers.

Why is the light of [illegible] darkend in this dewy morn

Why is the Silence of Enitharmon [illegible] & her smile a whirlwind

Uttering this darkness in my halls, in the pillars of my Holy-ones

Why dost thou weep as Vala, & wet thy veil with dewy tears.

In slumbers of my night-repose, infusing a false morning?

[illegible two crossed-out lines]

And wilt thou still [illegible] call him who devotes himself to thee

[illegible crossed-out line]

Free born for the [illegible] of Man now born to [illegible]

J

Page 10. Night I. Pencil drawing.

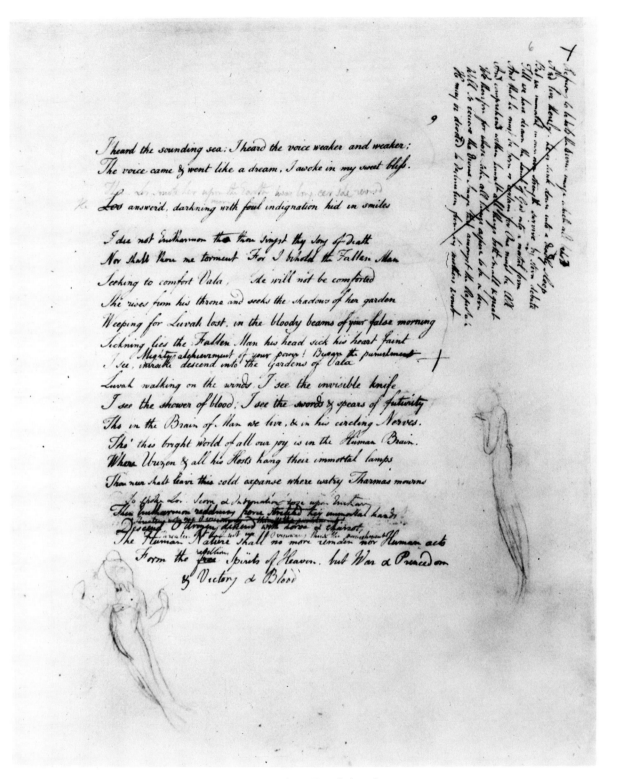

I heard the sounding sea: I heard the voice weaker and weaker;
The voice came & went like a dream, I awoke in my sweet bliss.

Los answerd, darkning with foul indignation hid in smiles

I die not Enitharmon tho thou singst thy Song of death
Nor shalt thou me torment For I behold the Fallen Man
Seeking to comfort Vala,   she will not be comforted
She rises from his throne and seeks the shadows of her garden
Weeping for Luvah lost. in the bloody beams of your false morning
Sickning lies the Fallen Man his head sick his heart faint
     Mighty atchievement of your power! Beware the punishment
I see, invisible descend into the Gardens of Vala
Luvah walking on the winds, I see the invisible knife
I see the shower of blood: I see the swords & spears of futurity
Tho in the Brain of Man we live, & in his circling Nerves.
Tho' this bright world of all our joy is in the Human Brain.
Where Urizen & all his Hosts hang their immortal lamps
Thou never shalt leave this cold expanse where watry Tharmas mourns

So spoke Los. Scorn & Indignation rose upon Enitharmon
Then Enitharmon reddning fierce stretchd her immortal hands
Descend O Urizen descend with horse & chariots
The Human Nature shall no more remain nor Human acts
Form the free Spirits of Heaven. but War & Princedom
          & Victory & Blood

Page 11. Night I. Pencil drawing.

125

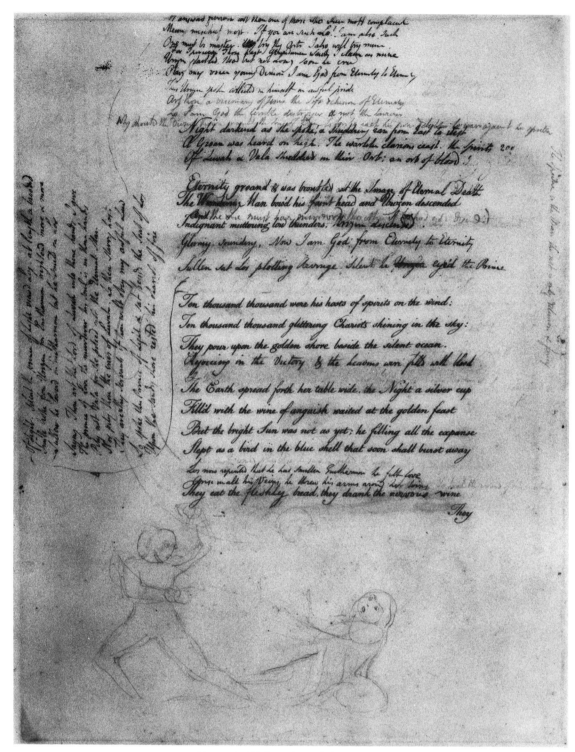

Night darkend as she spoke a shuddering ran from East to West
A Groan was heard on high. The warlike clarions ceast. the spirits
Of Luvah & Vala shudderd in their Orb: an orb of blood!

Eternity groand & was troubled at the Image of Eternal Death
The Wandering Man bow'd his faint head and Urizen descended
And the dire ...
Indignant muttering low thunders. Urizen descending

Gloomy sounding, Now I am God; from Eternity to Eternity

Sullen sat Los plotting Revenge. Silent he eyed the Prince

Ten thousand thousand were his hosts of spirits on the wind:

Ten thousand thousand glittering Chariots shining in the sky:

They pour upon the golden shore beside the silent ocean.

Rejoicing in the Victory & the heavens were filld with blood

The Earth spread forth her table wide. the Night a silver cup

Filld with the wine of anguish waited at the golden feast

But the bright Sun was not as yet: he filling all the expanse

Slept as a bird in the blue shell that soon shall burst away

Los now repented that he had smitten Enitharmon he felt love
Arose in all his Veins, he threw his arms around her loins
They eat the fleshly bread, they drank the nervous wine

They

Page 12. Night I. Pencil drawing.

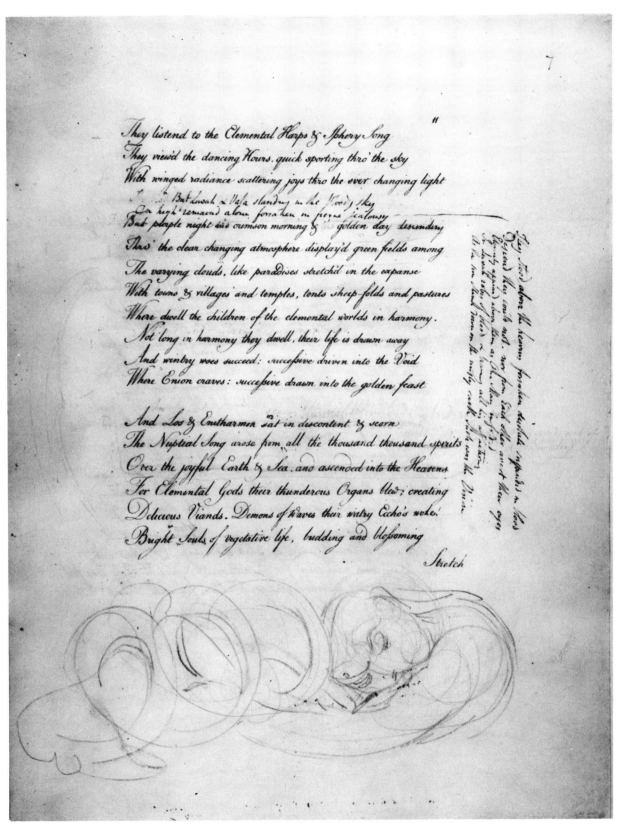

They listend to the Elemental Harps & Sphery Song

They viewd the dancing Hours. quick sporting thro' the sky

With winged radiance scattering joys thro the ever. changing light

But Luvah & Vala standing in the clouds sky

On high remaind alone forsaken in fierce jealousy

But purple night and crimson morning & the golden day descending

Thro' the clear changing atmosphere display'd green fields among

The varying clouds, like paradises stretch'd in the expanse

With towns & villages and temples, tents sheep-folds and pastures

Where dwell the children of the elemental worlds in harmony.

Not long in harmony they dwell, their life is drawn away

And wintry woes succeed: successive driven into the Void

Where Enion craves: successive drawn into the golden feast

And Los & Enitharmon sat in discontent & scorn

The Nuptial Song arose from all the thousand thousand spirits

Over the joyful Earth & Sea, and ascended into the Heavens

For Elemental Gods their thunderous Organs blew; creating

Delicious Viands. Demons of Waves their watry Eccho's woke.

Bright Souls of vegetative life, budding and blossoming

Stretch

Page 13. Night I. Pencil and chalk drawing.

12

Stretch their immortal hands to smite the gold & silver Wires

And with immortal Voice soft warbling fill all Earth & Heaven.

With doubling Voices & loud Horns wound round sounding

Cavernous dwellers filld the enormous Revelry, Responsing,

And Spirits of flaming fire on high, governd the mighty Song! 250

And this the Song sung at the ~~Feast~~ of Lord Urithamon

The Mountain calld out to the Mountain. Awake O Brother Mountain
Let us refuse the Plow & Spade, the heavy Roller & spiked
Harrow. burn all these Corn fields. throw down all these fences
Flattend on Human blood & drunk with wine of life is better far

Than all the labours of the harvest & the vintage. See the river
Red with the blood of Men. swells lustful round my rocky knees
My clouds are not the clouds of verdant fields & groves of fruit
But Clouds of Human Souls. my nostrils drink the lives of Men

The Villages Lament. they faint outstretchd upon the plain
Wailing runs round the Valleys from the Mill & from the Barn
But most the polishd Palaces ~~dark~~ silent bow with dread
Hiding their books & pictures. underneath the dens of Earth

The Cities send to one another Saying My Sons are Mad
With wine of Cruelty. Let us plat a scourge O Sister City
Children are nourishd for the Slaughter; once the Child was fed
With Milk; but wherefore now are Children fed with Blood

Page 14. Night I. Pencil and chalk drawing with chalk shading.

128

(a separate sheet. It cannot be placed on its sequel numbering.) 719 40 . . . .
513 48
1904

The Horse is of more value than the Man. The Tyger fierce
Laughs at the Human form the Lion mocks & thirsts for blood
They cry O Spider spread thy web! Enlarge thy bones & filld
With marrow sinews & flesh Exalt thyself attain a voice
Call to thy dark armd hosts. for all the Sons of Men muster together
To desolate their cities! Man shall be no more! Awake O Hosts
The bow string sang upon the hills. Luvah & Vala ride
Triumphant in the bloody sky. & the human form is no more

The listning Stars heard, & the first beam of the morning started back
He cried out to his Father, depart! depart! but sudden Siezd
And clad in Steel. & his Horse proudly neighd; he smelt the battle
Afar off. Rushing back, reddning with rage the Mighty Father

Siezd his bright Sheephook: Studded with gems & gold, he swung it round
His head shrill sounding in the Sky, down rushd the Sun with noise
Of war. The Mountains fled away they sought a place beneath
Vala remaind in desarts of dark Solitude. nor Sun nor Moon

By night nor day to comfort her, she labourd in thick Smoke
Tharmas endurd not; he fled howling. then a barren waste sunk down
Conglobing in the dark confusion, Mean time Los was born
And Enitharmon! Hark I hear the hammers of Los

Page 15. Night I. Pencil drawing, with gray-brown to gray tints.

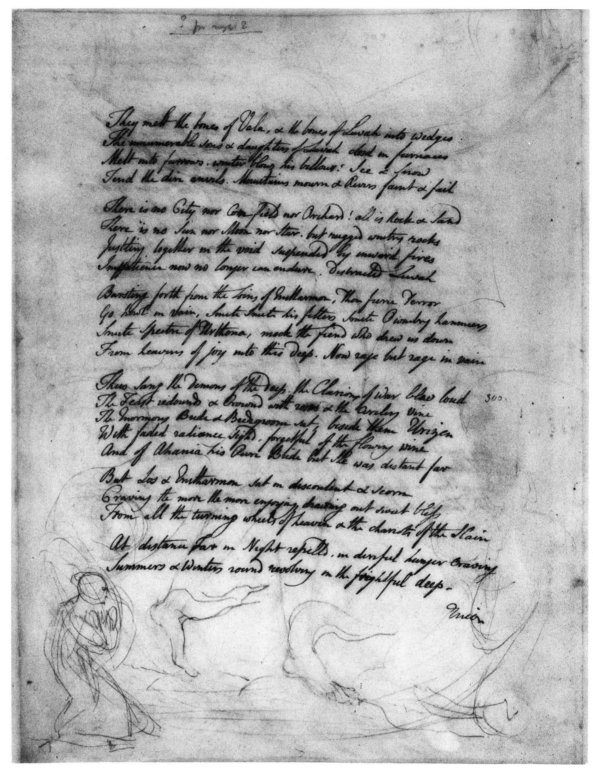

Page 16. Night I. Pencil drawing.

Οτι ουκ εστιν ημιν η παλη προς αιμα και σαρκα, αλλα προς τας αρχας,
προς τας εξεσιας, προς τας κοσμοκρατορας τ̃ σκοτ̃ς τ̃ αιωνος τ̃τ̃, προς
τα πνευματικα της πονηριας εν τοις επουρανιοις.

Εφεσ: 5 Κεφ. 12

VALA

Night the First

1 The Song of the Aged Mother which shook the heavens with wrath
2 Hearing the march of long resounding strong heroic Verse
3 Marshalld in order for the day of Intellectual Battle
6 The heavens quake: the earth was moved & shudderd & the mountains
7 With all their woods, the streams & valleys: waild in dismal fear
4
5

4 Four Mighty Ones are in every Man: a Perfect Unity
Cannot Exist. but from the Universal Brotherhood of Eden
The Universal Man. To Whom be Glory Evermore Amen

John XVII c. 21 m 22 m 23

John I c. 14 v
και εσκηνωσεν
εν ημιν

Los was the fourth immortal starry one, & in the Earth
Of a bright Universe. Empery attended day & night
Days & nights of revolving joy, Urthona was his name

In

Page 3. Night I. Pencil and ink drawing with brown, blue,
gray, and black watercolor washes.

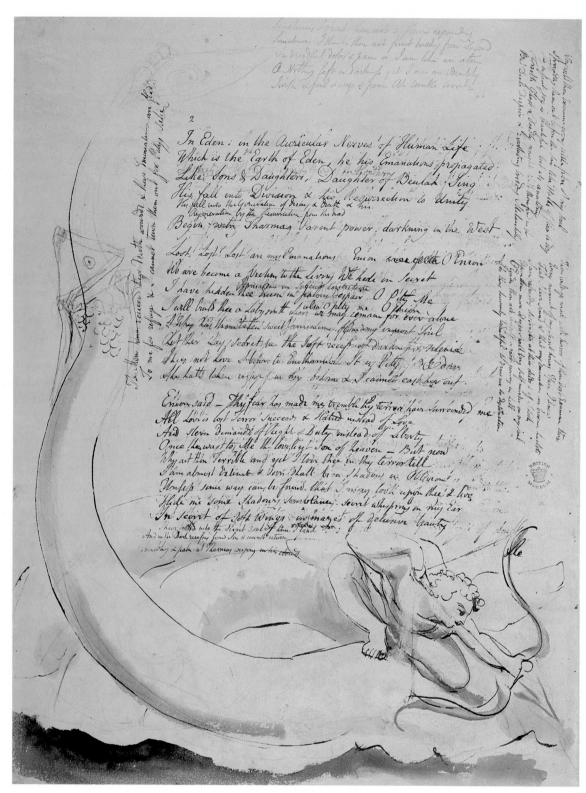

Page 4. Night I. Pencil and ink drawing with blue, gray, pink, brown, and black watercolor washes.

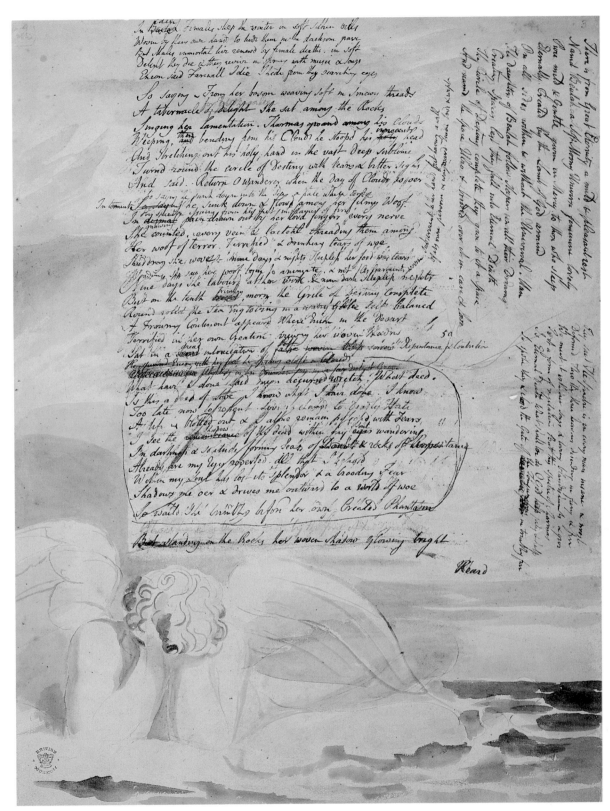

Page 5. Night I. Pencil and ink drawing with blue, gray, pink, brown, and black washes.

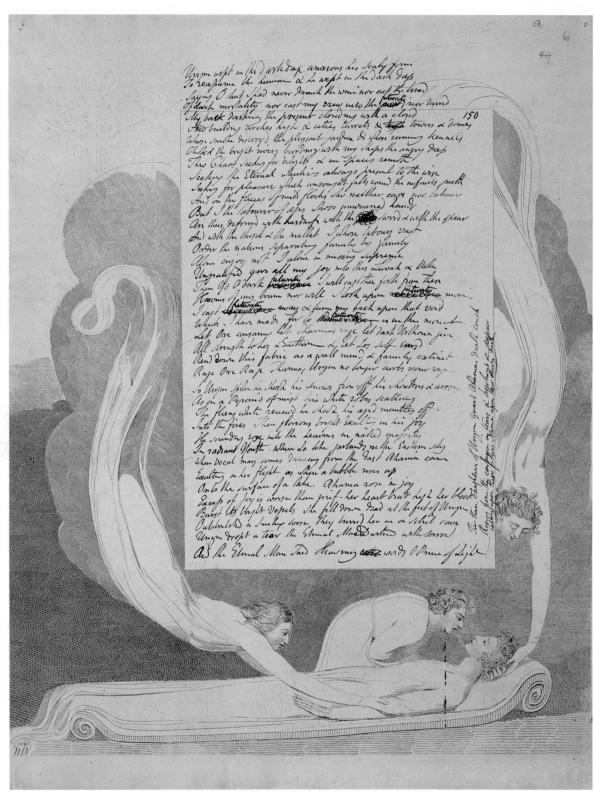

Page 121. Night IX. Proof: NT 71:22E, second state; streak across chest of reclining figure, dull red.

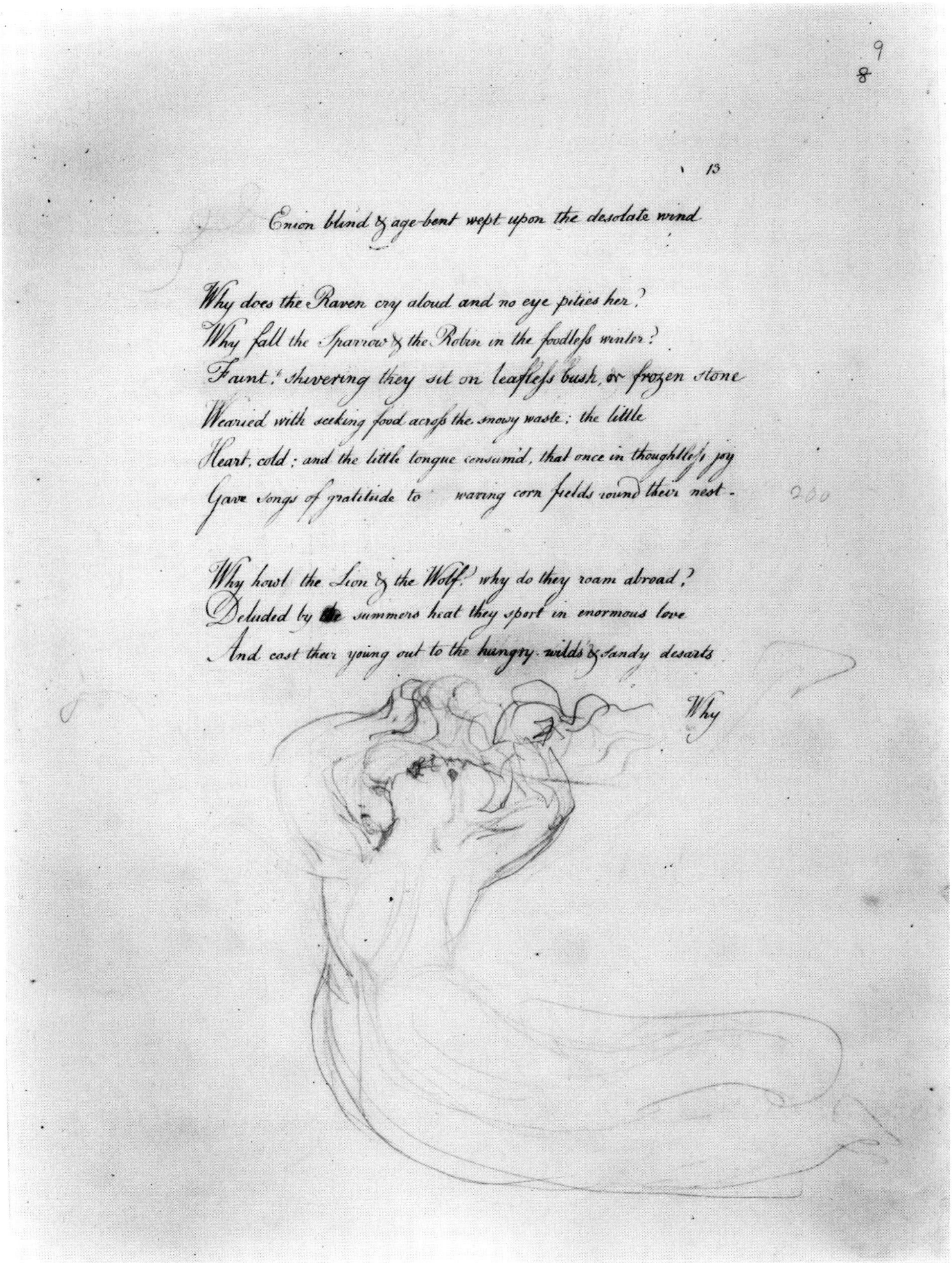

13

Enion blind & age-bent wept upon the desolate wind

Why does the Raven cry aloud and no eye pities her?
Why fall the Sparrow & the Robin in the foodless winter?
Faint. shivering they sit on leafless bush, or frozen stone
Wearied with seeking food across the snowy waste: the little
Heart. cold: and the little tongue consum'd, that once in thoughtless joy
Gave songs of gratitude to   waving corn fields round their nest.

Why howl the Lion & the Wolf? why do they roam abroad?
Deluded by the summers heat they sport in enormous love
And cast their young out to the hungry wilds & sandy desarts

Why

Page 17. Night I. Pencil and chalk drawing.

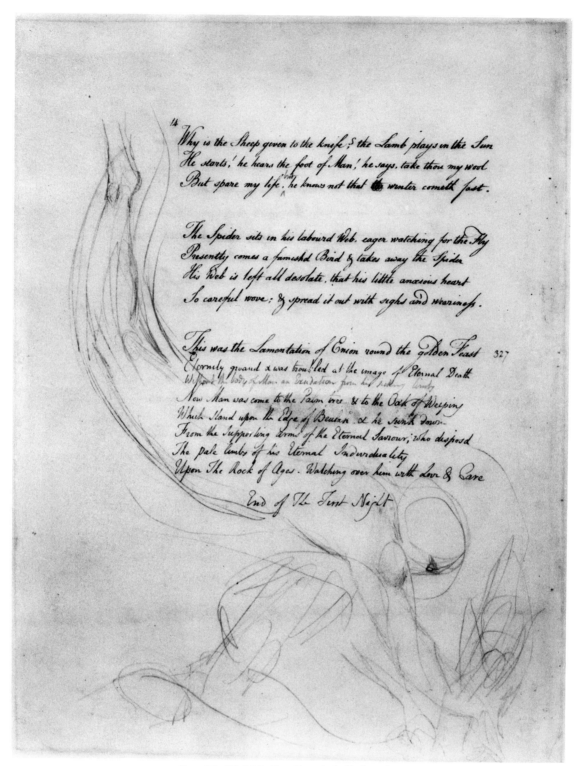

14

Why is the Sheep given to the knife? the Lamb plays in the Sun
He starts! he hears the foot of Man! he says. take thou my wool
But spare my life, he knows not that winter cometh fast.

The Spider sits in his labourd Web. eager watching for the Fly
Presently comes a famishd Bird & takes away the Spider
His Web is left all desolate. that his little anxious heart
So careful wove: & spread it out with sighs and weariness.

This was the Lamentation of Enion round the golden Feast   327
Eternity groand & was troubled at the image of Eternal Death
Within the body of Man an Emanation from his sleeping limbs
Now Man was come to the Palm tree & to the Oak of Weeping
Which stand upon the Edge of Beulah & he sunk down
From the supporting Arms of the Eternal Saviour; who disposd
The pale limbs of his Eternal Individuality
Upon The Rock of Ages. Watching over him with Love & Care

    End of The First Night

Page 18. Night I. Pencil and chalk drawing.

Then those in Great Eternity met in the Council of God
As one Man for contracting their Exalted Senses
They behold Multitude or Expanding they behold as one
As One Man all the Universal Family & that One Man
They call Jesus the Christ & they in him & he in them
Live in Perfect harmony in Eden the land of life
Consulting as One Man above the Mountain of Snowdon Sublime

For messengers from Beulah come in tears & darkning clouds
Saying Shiloh is in ruins our brother is sick Albion he
Whom thou lovest is sick he wanders from his house of Eternity
The daughters of Beulah terrified have closd the Gate of the Tongue
Luvah & Urizen contend in war around the holy tent

So spoke the Ambassadors from Beulah & with solemn mourning
They were introducd to the Divine presence & they kneeled down
In Conway Vale then recounting the Wars of Death Eternal

The Eternal Man wept in the holy tent Our Brother in Eternity
Even Albion whom thou lovest wept in pain his family
Slept round on hills & valleys in the regions of his love
But Urizen awoke & Luvah woke & thus conferrd

Thou Luvah said the Prince of Light behold our Sons & Daughters
Reposd on beds. let them sleep on, do thou alone depart
Into thy wished kingdom where in Majesty & Power
We may erect a throne. deep in the North I place my lot
Thou in the South listen attentive. In silent of this night
I will infold the Eternal tent in clouds opake while thou
Siezing the chariots of the morning. Go outfleeting ride
Afar into the Zenith high bending thy furious course
Southward with half the tents of men inclosd in clouds
Of Tharmas & Urthona I remaining in porches of the brain
Will lay my sceptre on Jerusalem the Emanation
In all her sons & on thy sons O Luvah & on mine
Till dawn was wont to wake them then my trumpet sounding loud
Ravishd away in night my strong command shall be obeyd
For I have placd my centinels in Stations each tenth man
Is bought & sold & in dim night my Word shall be their law

Page 19[21]. Night I. Pencil drawing.

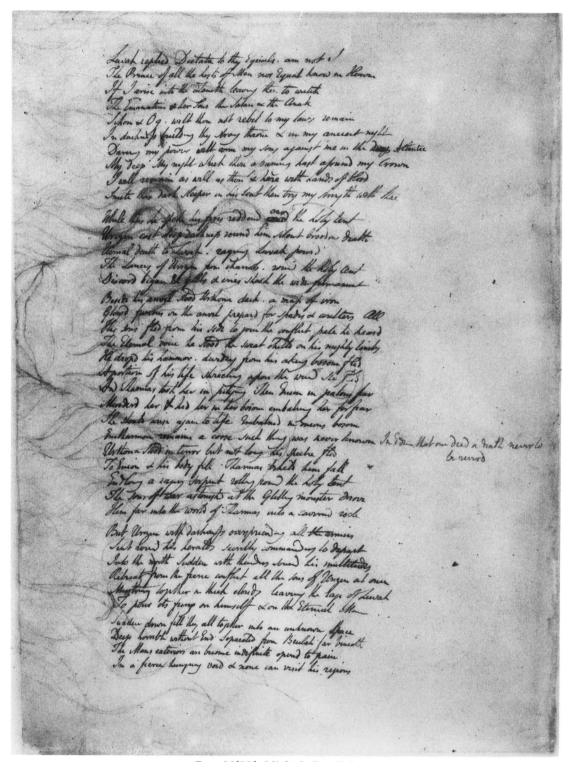

Luvah replied Dictate to thy Equals. am not I
The Prince of all the hosts of Men nor Equal know in Heaven
If I arise into the Zenith leaving thee to watch
The Emanation & her Sons the Satan & the Anak
Sihon & Og. wilt thou not rebel to my laws remain
In darkness building thy strong throne & in my ancient night
Darkning my power will arm my sons against me in the [deep] Atlantic
My Deep thy night which thou a damning hast apprond my Crown
I will remain as well as thou & here with lands of blood
Smite thou dark Keeper on his tent then try my strength with thee

While thus he spoke his fires reddend oer the holy tent
Urizen cast deep darkness round him silent brooding death
Eternal death to Luvah. raging Luvah pourd
The Lances of Urizen from chariots. round the Holy Tent
Discord began & yells & cries shook the wide firmament
Beside his anvil stood Urthona dark. a mass of iron
Glowd furious on the anvil prepard for spades & coulters All
The Sons fled from his side to join the conflict pale he heard
The Eternal voice he stood the sweat chilld on his mighty limbs
He dropd his hammer. dividing from his aking bosom fled
A portion of his life shrieking upon the wind She fled
And Tharmas took her in pitying Then Enion in jealous fear
Murderd her & hid her in his bosom embalming her for fear
She should arise again to life Embalmd in Enions bosom
Enitharmon remains a corse Such thing was never known   In Eden that one deed a death never to
Urthona stood in terror but not long his spectre fled   be revivd
To Enion & his body fell. Tharmas beheld him fall
Endlong a raging serpent rolling round the Holy tent
The Sons of war astonishd at the Glittering monster drove
Him far into the world of Tharmas into a cavernd rock

But Urizen with darkness overspreading all the armies
Sent round his heralds secretly commanding to depart
Into the north Sudden with thunders sound his multitudes
Retreat from the fierce conflict all the sons of Urizen at once
Mustering together in thick clouds leaving the rage of Luvah
To pour its fury on himself & on the Eternal Man
Sudden down fell they all together into an unknown Space
Deep horrible without End Separated from Beulah far beneath
The Mans exterior are become indefinite opend to pain
In a fierce hungring void & none can visit his regions

Page 20[22]. Night I. Pencil drawing.

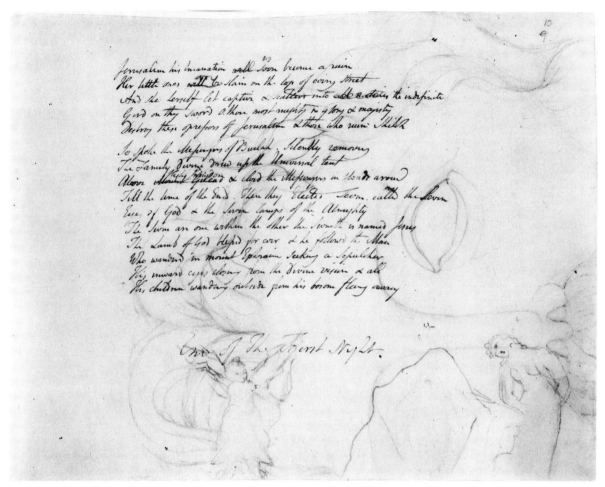

Page 21[19]. Night I. Pencil drawing.

135

Page 22[20]. Night I. Pencil and chalk drawing; pink detail.

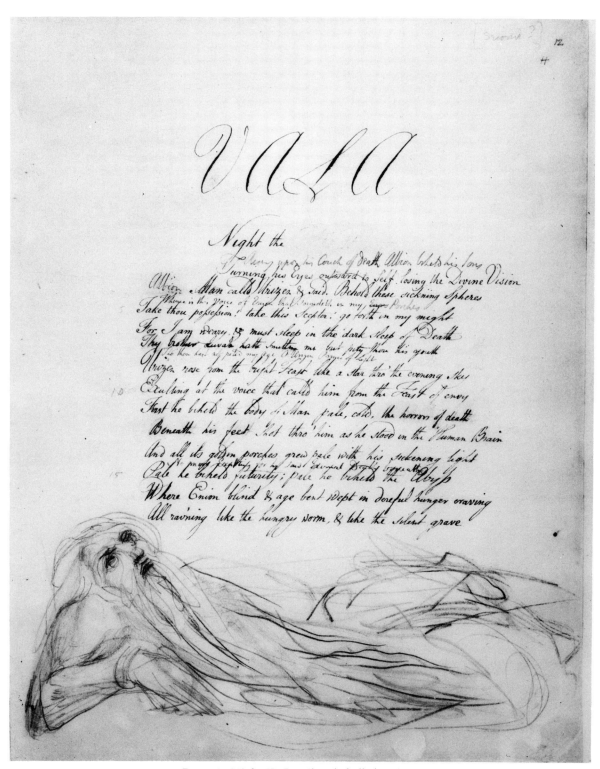

VALA

Night the

Rising upon his Couch of Death Albion beheld his Sons
Turning his Eyes outward to Self. losing the Divine Vision

Albion. Man calld Urizen & said. Behold these sickning Spheres
Whence is this voice of Enion that soundeth in my Porches
Take thou possession! take this Scepter! go forth in my might
For I am weary. & must sleep in the dark sleep of Death
Thy brother Luvah hath smitten me but pity thou his youth
Tho thou hast repelld my Age O Urizen Prince of Light

Urizen rose from the bright Feast like a star thro' the evening sky
Exulting at the voice that calld him from the Feast of envy
First he beheld the body of Man pale, cold. the horror of death
Beneath his feet Shot thro' him as he stood in the Human Brain
And all its gothic porches grew pale with his sickening light
No pitying tears for one of such Eternal Beings opposed to Infinity
Pale he beheld futurity; pale he beheld the Abyss
Where Enion blind & age bent wept in direful hunger craving
All raving like the hungry worm, & like the silent grave

Page 23. Night II. Pencil and chalk drawing.

Mighty was the draught of Voidness to draw Existence in

Terrific Urizen strode above. in fear & pale dismay
He saw the indefinite space beneath & his soul shrunk with horror
His feet upon the verge of Non Existence: his voice went forth

Luvah & Vala trembling & shrinking. beheld the great Work master
And heard his Word! Divide ye bands influence by influence
Build we a Bower for heavens darling in the grizly deep
Build we the Mundane Shell around the Rock of Albion
The Bands of Heaven flew thro the air singing & howling to Urizen
Some fixd the anvil, some the loom erected, some the plow
And harrow formd & framd the harness of silver & ivory
The golden compasses, the quadrant & the rule & balance
They erected the furnaces, they formd the anvils of gold beaten in mills
Where winter beats incessant; fixing them firm on their base
The bellows began to blow & the Lions of Urizen stood round the anvil

Page 24. Night II. Pencil and chalk drawing.

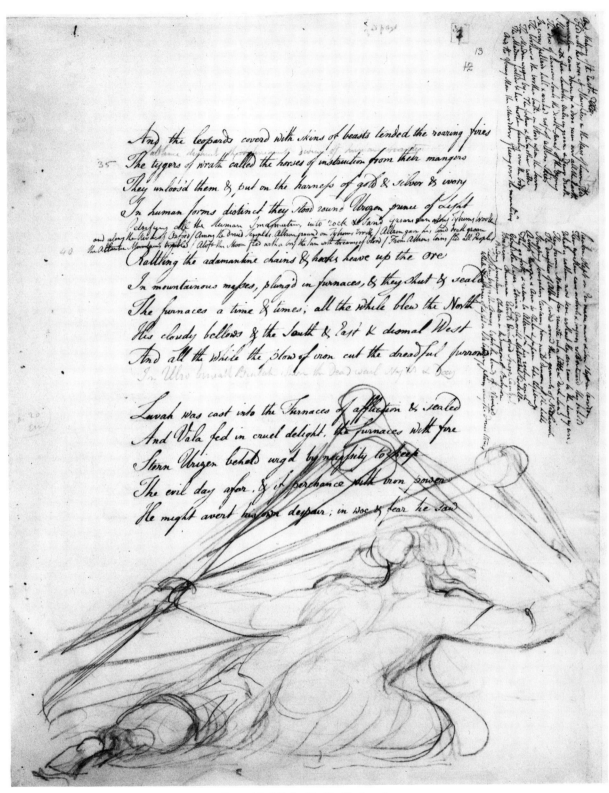

And the leopards coverd with skins of beasts tended the roaring fires

35   The tygers of wrath called the horses of instruction from their mangers

They unloos'd them &, put on the harness of gold & silver & ivory

In human forms distinct they stood round Urizen prince of Light

40   Rattling the adamantine chains & hooks heave up the ore

In mountainous masses, plung'd in furnaces, & they shut & seald

The furnaces a time & times; all the while blew the North

His cloudy bellows & the South & East & dismal West

And all the while the plow of iron cut the dreadful furrows

Luvah was cast into the Furnaces of affliction & sealed

And Vala fed in cruel delight, the furnaces with fire

Stern Urizen beheld urg'd by necessity to keep

The evil day afar, & if perchance with iron power

He might avert his own despair; in woe & fear he saw

Page 25. Night II. Chalk drawing.

Vala incircle round the furnaces where Luvah was clos'd
In joy she heard his howlings, & forgot he was her Luvah
With whom she walkd in bliss, in times of innocence & youth

Hear ye the voice of Luvah from the furnaces of Urizen

If I indeed am Valas King & ye O Sons of Men
The workmanship of Luvahs hands; in times of Everlasting
When I calld forth the Earth-worm from the cold & dark obscure
I nurturd her I fed her with my rains & dews, she grew
A scaled Serpent, yet I fed her tho' she hated me
Day after day she fed upon the mountains in Luvahs sight   50
I brought her thro' the Wilderness, a dry & thirsty land
And I commanded springs to rise for her in the black desart
Till she became a Dragon winged bright & poisonous
I opend all the floodgates of the heavens to quench her thirst

And

Page 26. Night II. Pencil and chalk drawing.

And I commanded the Great deep to hide her in his hand

Till she became a little weeping Infant a span long

I carried her in my bosom as a man carries a lamb

I loved her I gave her all my soul & my delight

I hid her in soft gardens & in secret bowers of summer

Weaving mazes of delight along the sunny paradise

Inextricable labyrinths, She bore me sons & daughters

And they have taken her away & hid her from my sight

They have surrounded me with walls of iron & brass, O Lamb

Of God clothed in slavery garments little knowest thou

Of death Eternal that we all go to Eternal Death

To our Primeval Chaos in fortuitous concourse of incoherent

Discordant principles of Love & Hate I suffer affliction

Because I love for I was love but hatred awakes in me

The Ray of Urizen who was Faith & Certainty is changd to Doubt

The hand of Urizen is upon me because I blotted out

That Human delusion to deliver all the Sons of God

From bondage of the Human form, O first born Son of Light

O Urizen my enemy I weep for thy Stern ambition

But weep in vain O when will you return Vala the wanderer

Page 27. Night II. Pencil and chalk drawing.

These were the words of Luvah patient in afflictions
Reasoning from the loins in the unreal forms of Uros night

And when Luvah age after age was quite melted with woe
The fires of Vala faded like a Shadow cold & pale
An evanescent shadow. last she fell a heap of Ashes
Beneath the furnaces a woful heap in living death

Then were the furnaces unseald with Spades & pickaxes
Roaring let out the fluid, the molten metal ran in channels
Cut by the plow of ages held in Urizens strong hand
In many a valley, for the Bulls of Luvah dragd the Plow

Then siezd the Lions of Urizen their work, & heated in the forge
Roar the bright masses, thundring beat the hammers, many a pyramid
Is formd & thrown down thundring into the deeps of Non Entity
Heated red hot they hizzing rend their way down many a league
Till resting. each his center finds; suspended there they stand
Casting their sparkles dire abroad, into the dismal deep
For measurd out in ordered spaces the Sons of Urizen
With compasses divide the deep; they the strong scales erect

         That

With trembling horror pale aghast the Children of Man
Stood on the unfemale Earth & saw these visions in the air
In waters & in Earth beneath they cried to one another
What are we terrors to one another Some Oliktion therefore
Was this wide woeful spread all abroad. we for wide wrath to roam
But many stood silent & buried in their families
And many said We see no Vision in the darksom air
Measure the course of that sulphur orb that lights the length day
Set Stations on this breeding Earth & let us buy & sell
Others arose & schisms Erected forming Instruments
To measure out the course of heaven. Stern Urizen beheld
In woe his brethren & his Sons in darkning woe lamenting
Upon the winds in clouds involvd Uttering his voice in thunders
Commanding all the work with care & power & severity

Page 28. Night II. Pencil and chalk drawing.

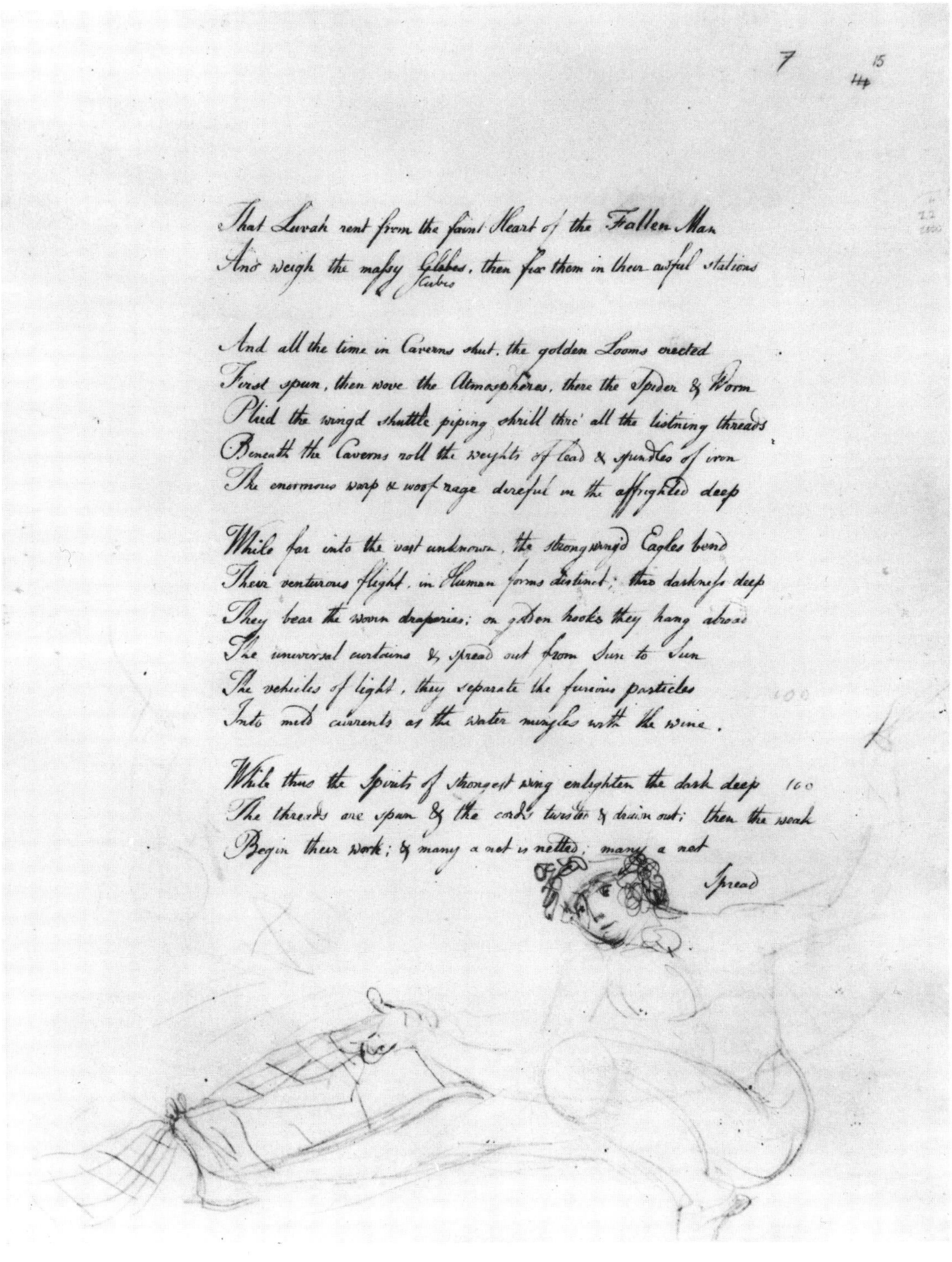

That Luvah rent from the faint Heart of the Fallen Man
And weigh the massy Globes. then fix them in their awful stations
Cubes

And all the time in Caverns shut. the golden Looms erected
First spun, then wove the Atmospheres, there the Spider & Worm
Plied the wingd shuttle piping shrill thro' all the listning threads
Beneath the Caverns roll the weights of lead & spindles of iron
The enormous warp & woof rage direful in the affrighted deep

While far into the vast unknown, the strong wingd Eagles bend
Their venturous flight. in Human forms distinct; thro darkness deep
They bear the woven draperies; on golden hooks they hang abroad
The universal curtains & spread out from Sun to Sun
The vehicles of light, they separate the furious particles
Into mild currents as the water mingles with the wine.

While thus the Spirits of Strongest wing enlighten the dark deep 160
The threads are spun & the cords twisted & drawn out; then the weak
Begin their work; & many a net is netted; many a net

Spread

Page 29. Night II. Pencil and chalk drawing.

143

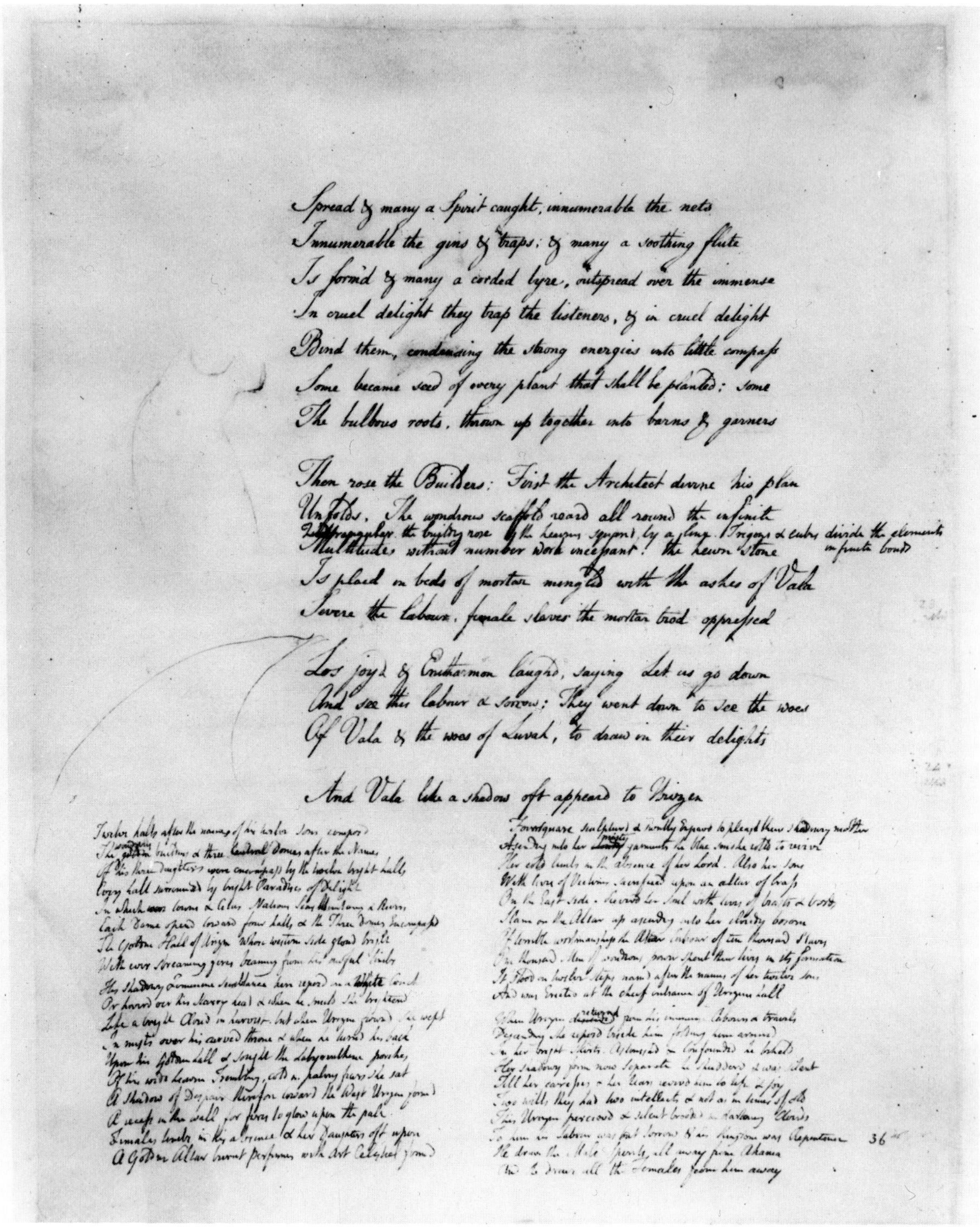

Spread & many a Spirit caught, innumerable the nets

Innumerable the gins & traps; & many a soothing flute

Is form'd & many a corded lyre, outspread over the immense

In cruel delight they trap the listeners, & in cruel delight

Bind them, condensing the strong energies into little compass

Some became seed of every plant that shall be planted: some

The bulbous roots, thrown up together into barns & garners

Then rose the Builders: First the Architect divine his plan
Unfolds. The wondrous scaffold reard all round the infinite
Quadrangular the building rose the heavens squared by a line. Trigons & cubes divide the elements
Multitudes without number work incessant! the hewn Stone   in fourite bonds
Is plaid on beds of mortar mongled with the ashes of Vala
Severe the labour, female slaves the mortar trod oppressed

Los joyd & Enitharmon laughd, saying Let us go down
And see this labour & sorrow; They went down to see the woes
Of Vala & the woes of Luvah, to draw in their delights

And Vala like a shadow oft appeard to Urizen

Twelve halls after the names of his twelve Sons compose
The wondrous building & three Central domes after the Name
Of his three daughters were encompass by the twelve bright halls
Every hall surrounded by bright Paradise of Delight
In which were towns & Cities Nations Seas Mountains & Rivers
Each Dome open toward four halls & the Three Domes Encompassd
The Golden Hall of Urizen whose western Side glowd bright
With ever Streaming gems streaming from his awful Limbs
His Shadowy Feminine Semblance here reposd on a white Couch
Or hoverd over his Starry head & when he smild She brighend
Like a bright Cloud in harvest. but when Urizen groand She wept
In mists over his carved throne & when he turnd his back
Upon his Golden hall & sought the Labyrinthian porches
Of his wide heaven Trembling, cold a pale aguish fever Seizd
A Shadow of Despair therefore toward the West Urizen formd
A recess in the wall for fires to glow upon the pale
Females locks in the aurora & her daughters oft upon
A Golden Altar burnt perfumes with Art Celestial formd

Foursquare sculpturd & sweetly inspird to please their Shadowy mother
Ascending into her cloudy garments the Wise woven with to revive
Her cold Limbs in the absence of her Lord. Also her Sons
With lives of Victims Sacrificd upon an altar of brass
On the East side. Reverd he Saw with eyes of pity & love
Slain on the Altar up ascending into her cloudy bosom
Of terrible workmanship the Altar labour of ten thousand Slaves
One thousand Men of wondrous power spent their lives in its formation
It stood on twelve steps namd after the names of her twelve Sons
And was Erected at the chief entrance of Urizens hall
When Urizen return'd from his immense Labours & travels
Descending She reposd beside him folding him around
In her bright Skirts. Astonishd & Confounded he beheld
Her shadowy form now Separate he Shudderd & was Silent
Till her caress & her tears reviv'd him to life & joy
Two wills they had two intellects & not as in times of old
Then Urizen perceivd & silent brooded in darkning Clouds
To him in Sevens was put Sorrows & in Kingdoms was Repentance
He down the Mile sternly, all away from him Shame
And to draw all the Females from him away

36

Page 30. Night II. Pencil drawing.

144

The King of Light beheld her mourning among the Brick kilns compelld
To labour night & day among the fires, her lamenting voice
Is heard when silent night returns & the labourers take their rest

O Lord wilt thou not look upon our sore afflictions
Among these flames incessant labouring, our hard masters laugh
At all our sorrow. We are made to turn the wheel for water
To carry the heavy basket on our scorched shoulders, to sift
The sand & ashes, & to mix the clay with tears & repentance
The times are now returnd upon us, we have given ourselves
To scorn and now are scorned by the slaves of our enemies
Our beauty is coverd over with clay & ashes, & our backs
Furrowd with whips, & our flesh bruised with the heavy basket
Forgive us O thou piteous one whom we have offended, forgive
The weak remaining Shadow of Vala that returns in sorrow to thee.

Thus she lamented day & night, compelld to labour & sorrow
Luvah in vain her lamentations heard; in vain his love
Brought him in various forms before her still she knew him not

Page 31. Night II. Chalk drawing with gray and brown washes.

145

Still she despisd him, calling on his name & knowing him not
Still hating still professing love, still labouring in the smoke

And Los & Enitharmon joyd, they drank in Tenfols joy   To come in
From all the sorrow of Beulah by the labours of Urizen
And Enitharmon joyd Plotting to rend the secret cloud
To plant diversions in the Soul of Urizen & Ahania

For infinitely beautiful the wondrous work arose
In sorrow & care, a Golden World whose porches round the heavens
And pillard halls & rooms receivd the eternal wandering stars
A wondrous golden Building; many a window many a door
And many a division let in & out into the vast unknown
Circled in infinite orb immoveable, within its walls & ceilings
The heavens were closd and spirits mournd their bondage night & day
And the Divine Vision appeard in Luvahs robes of blood
They was the Morn

Sorrowing   went the Planters forth to plant, the Sowers to sow   150
They dug the channels for the rivers, & they pourd abroad
The

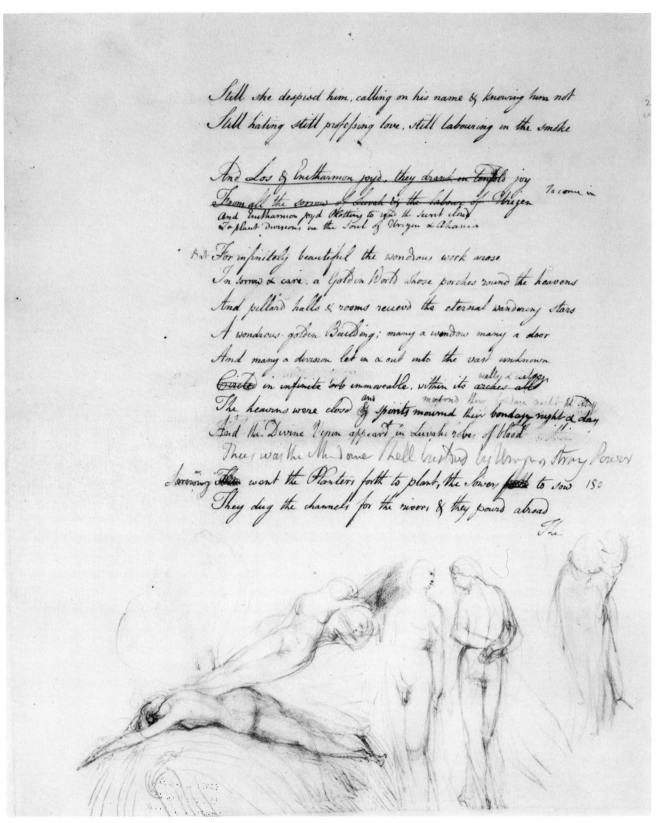

Page 32. Night II. Pencil and chalk drawing.

The seas & lakes, they reard the mountains & the rocks & hills

On broad pavilions, on pillard roofs & porches & high towers

In beauteous order, thence arose soft clouds & exhalations

Wandring even to the sunny orbs of light & heat

For many a window ornamented with sweet ornaments

Lookd out into the worlds of Tharmas, where in ceaseless torrents

His billows roll where monsters wander in the foamy paths

On clouds the Sons of Urizen beheld Heaven walled round

They weighd & orderd all & Urizen comforted saw

The wondrous work flow forth like visible out of the invisible

For the Divine Lamb Even Jesus who is the Divine Vision

Permitted all lest Man should fall into Eternal Death

For when Luvah sunk down himself put on the robes of blood

Lest the state calld Luvah should cease. & the Divine Vision

Walked in robes of blood till he who slept should awake

These were the Stars of heaven created like a golden chain

To bind the Body of Man to heaven from falling into the Abyss

Each took his Station, & his course began with sorrow & care

3 Travelling in silent majesty along their orderd ways
   In right lined paths outmeasurd by proportions of number weight
   And measure. mathematic motion wondrous. along the deep
   In fiery pyramid. or Cube. or ornamented pillar square
   Of fire. far shing. travelling along even to its destind end
   Then falling down. a terrible space recoving in winter dire
   Its wasted strength. it back returns upon a nether course
   Till fired with ardour fresh recruited in its humble season
   It rises up on high all summer till its wraind course
   Turns into autumn. such the period of many worlds
   Other triangular right angled course maintain. others obtuse
   Acute. in simple paths. but others move
   In intricate ways biquadrate. Trapeziums Rhombs Rhomboids
   Parallelograms. triple & quadruple. polygonic
   In their amazing hard subdued course in the vast deep

2 × In sum of tens & fifties, hundreds, thousands, numberd all
      Accordg to their various powers Subordinate to Urizen
      And to his sons in their degrees & to his beauteous daughters

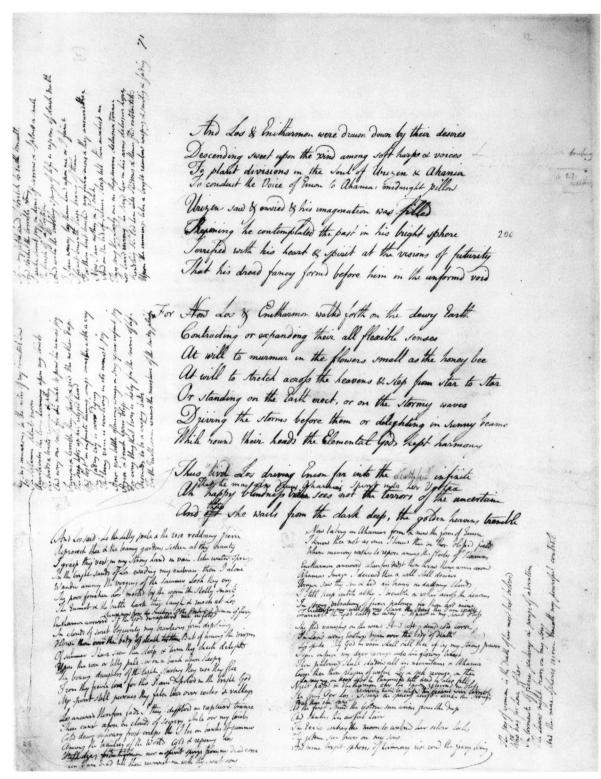

And Los & Enitharmon were drawn down by their desires
Descending sweet upon the wind among soft harps & voices
To plant divisions in the Soul of Urizen & Ahania
To conduct the Voice of Enion to Ahania's midnight pillow

Urizen saw & envied & his imagination was filled
Repining he contemplated the past in his bright sphere   200
Terrified with his heart & spirit at the visions of futurity
That his dread fancy formd before him in the unformd void

For now Los & Enitharmon walkd forth on the dewy Earth
Contracting or expanding their all flexible senses
At will to murmur in the flowers small as the honey bee
At will to stretch across the heavens & step from star to star
Or standing on the Earth erect, or on the stormy waves
Driving the storms before them or delighting in sunny beams
While round their heads the Elemental Gods kept harmony

Thus livd Los driving Enion far into the deathful infinite
An happy blindness sees not the terrors of the uncertain
And she wails from the dark deep, the golden heavens tremble

Page 34. Night II.

I am made to sow the thistle for wheat; the nettle for a nourishing dainty
I have planted a false oath in the earth, it has brought forth a poison tree
I have chosen the serpent for a councellor & the dog
For a schoolmaster to my children
I have blotted out from light & living the dove & nightingale
And I have caused the earth worm to beg from door to door
I have taught the thief a secret path into the house of the just
I have taught pale artifice to spread his nets upon the morning
My heavens are brass my earth is iron, my moon a clod of clay
My sun a pestilence burning at noon & a vapour of death in night

What is the price of Experience do men buy it for a song
Or wisdom for a dance in the street? No it is bought with the price
Of all that a man hath his house his wife his children
Wisdom is sold in the desolate market where none come to buy
And in the withered field where the farmer plows for bread in vain

It is an easy thing to triumph in the summers sun
And in the vintage & to sing on the waggon loaded with corn
It is an easy thing to talk of patience to the afflicted
To speak the laws of prudence to the houseless wanderer

Page 35. Night II. Pencil and chalk drawing.

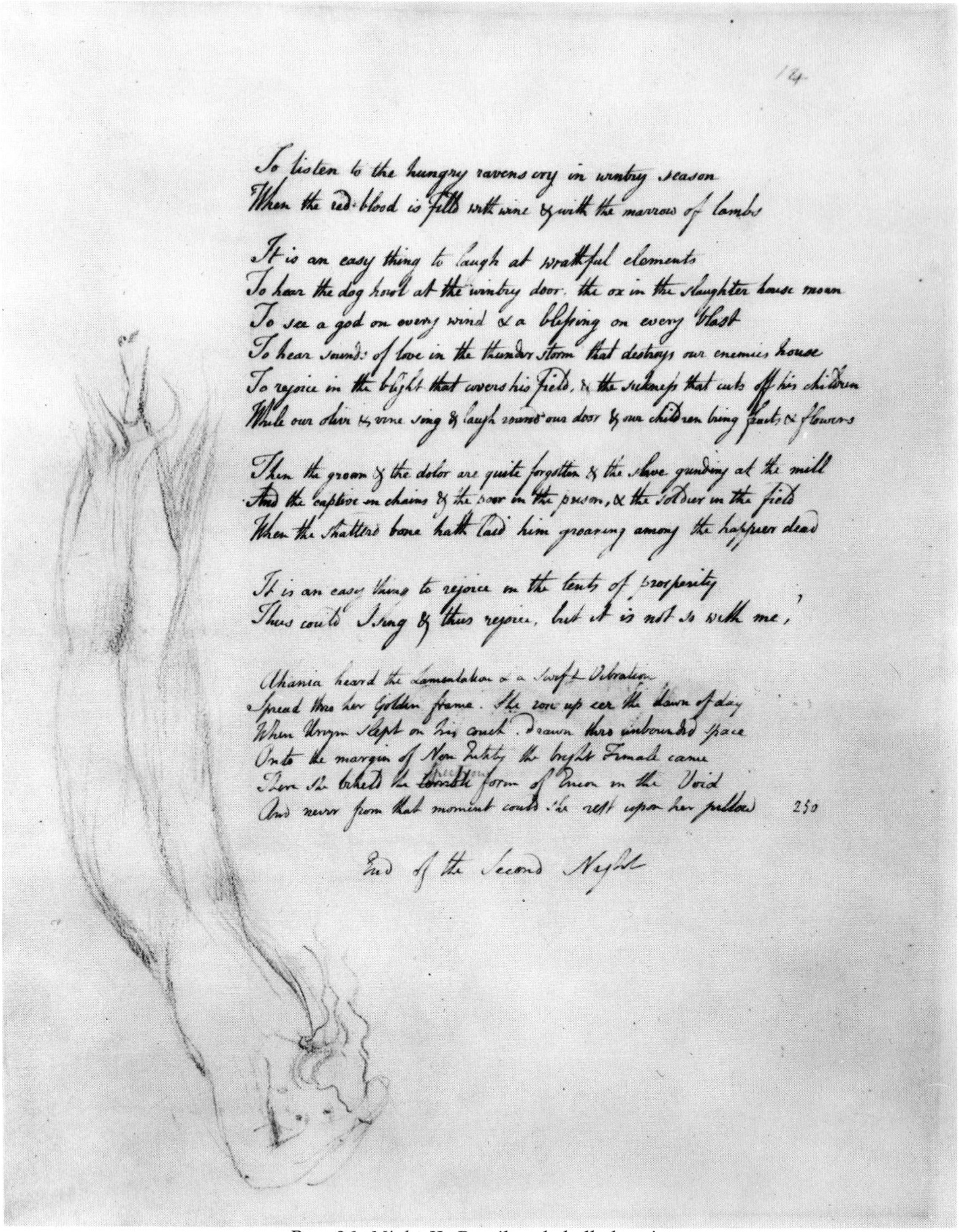

To listen to the hungry ravens cry in wintry season
When the red-blood is fill'd with wine & with the marrow of lambs

It is an easy thing to laugh at wrathful elements
To hear the dog howl at the wintry door. the ox in the slaughter house moan
To see a god on every wind & a blessing on every blast
To hear sounds of love in the thunder storm that destroys our enemies house
To rejoice in the blight that covers his field, & the sickness that cuts off his children
While our olive & vine sing & laugh round our door & our children bring fruits & flowers

Then the groan & the dolor are quite forgotten & the slave grinding at the mill
And the captive in chains & the poor in the prison, & the soldier in the field
When the shatter'd bone hath laid him groaning among the happier dead

It is an easy thing to rejoice in the tents of prosperity
Thus could I sing & thus rejoice, but it is not so with me,

Ahania heard the Lamentation & a swift Vibration
Spread thro her Golden frame. She rose up eer the dawn of day
When Urizen slept on his couch. drawn thro unbounded space
Onto the margin of Non Entity the bright Female came
There she beheld the terrible form of Orion in the Void
And never from that moment could she rest upon her pillow   250

End of the Second Night

Page 36. Night II. Pencil and chalk drawing.

150

VALA

Night the Third.

Now sat the King of Light on high upon his starry throne
And bright Ahania bowd herself before his splendid feet

O Urizen look on Me *that like a mournful stream*
Embraces round thy knees & wets my bright hair with her tears:
Why sighs my Lord! are not the morning stars thy obedient Sons
Do they not bow their bright heads at thy voice; at thy command
Do they not fly into their stations & return their light to thee
The immortal Atmospheres are thine, there thou art seen in glory
Surrounded by the ever changing Daughters of the Light
Thou exist in harmony for God hath set thee over all
Why wilt thou look up of futurity darkning present joy

She ceas'd the Prince his light obscurd by the splendors of his crown

Ingolbee

Page 37. Night III. Chalk drawing.

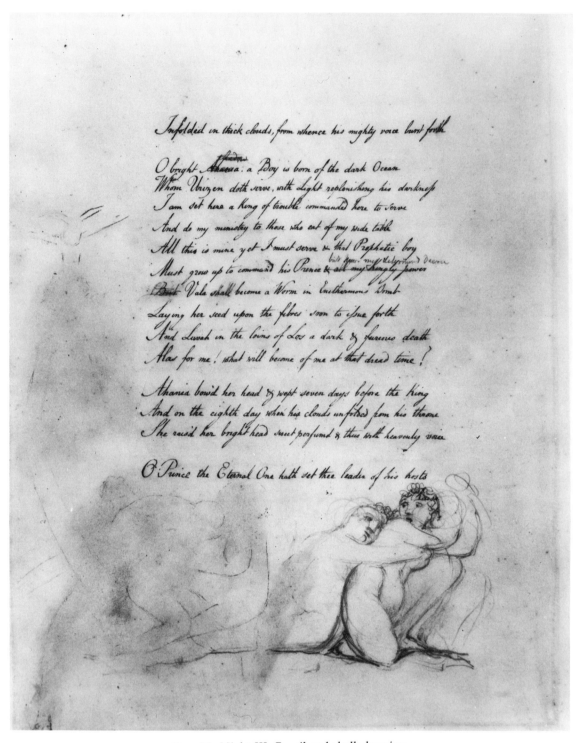

Infolded in thick clouds, from whence his mighty voice burst forth

O bright Ahania: a Boy is born of the dark Ocean
Whom Urizen doth serve, with Light replenishing his darkness
I am set here a King of trouble commanded here to serve
And do my ministry to those who eat of my wide table
All this is mine yet I must serve & that Prophetic boy
Must grow up to command his Prince & all my kingly power

Vala shall become a Worm in Enitharmons Womb
Laying her seed upon the fibres soon to issue forth
And Luvah in the loins of Los a dark & furious death
Alas for me! what will become of me at that dread time?

Ahania bow'd her head & wept seven days before the King
And on the eighth day when his clouds unfolded from his throne
She rais'd her bright head sweet perfumd & thus with heavenly voice

O Prince the Eternal One hath set thee leader of his hosts

Page 38. Night III. Pencil and chalk drawing.

Raise then thy radiant eyes to him raise thy obedient hands

And comforts shall descend from heaven into thy darkning clouds
Why lead all futurity toft him assume thy field of light
Why didst thou listen to the voice of Luvah that dread morn
To give the immortal Steeds of light to his deceitful hands
No longer now obedient to thy will thou art compell'd
To forge the curbs of iron & brass to build the iron mangers
To feed them with intoxication from the wine presses of Luvah
Till the Divine Vision & Fruition is quite obliterated
They call thy lions to the fields of blood, they rouze thy tygers
Out of the halls of justice, till these dens thy wisdom framd
Golden & beautiful but O how unlike those sweet fields of bliss
Where liberty was justice & eternal science was mercy
Then O my dear lord listen to Ahania, listen to the vision
The vision of Ahania in the slumbers of Urizen
When Urizen slept in the porch & the Ancient Man was smitten

The Darkning Man walkd on the steps of fire before his halls
And Vala walkd with him in dreams of soft deluding slumber
He looked up & saw thee Prince of light thy splendor faded
But saw not Los nor Enitharmon for Luvah hid them in shadow

Page 39. Night III. Pencil drawing.

153

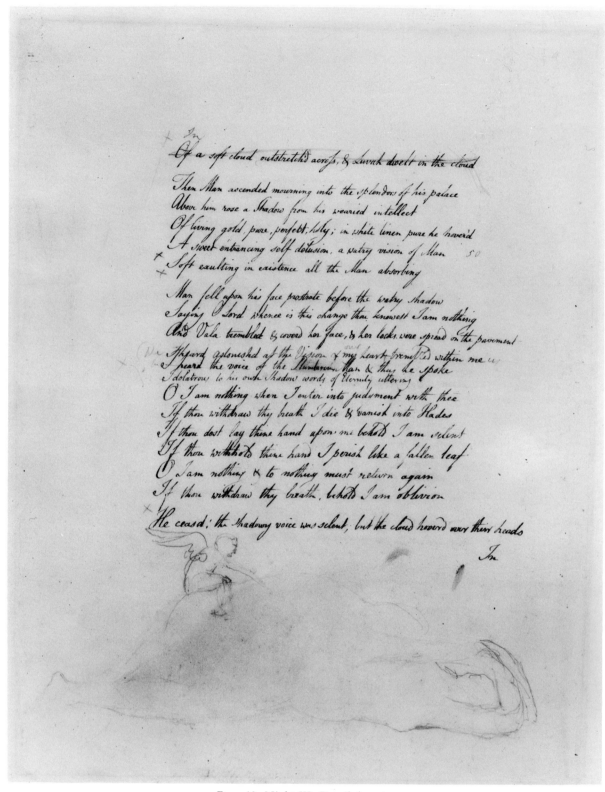

Of a soft cloud outstretch'd across, & Luvah dwelt in the cloud

Then Man ascended mourning into the splendors of his palace
Above him rose a Shadow from his wearied intellect
Of living gold, pure, perfect, holy; in white linen pure he hover'd
A sweet entrancing self delusion, a watry vision of Man 50
Soft exulting in existence all the Man absorbing

Man fell upon his face prostrate before the watry shadow
Saying O Lord whence is this change thou knowest I am nothing
And Vala trembled & coverd her face, & her locks were spread on the pavement
We heard astonishd at the Vision & my heart trembled within me us
I heard the voice of the Slumbrous Man & thus he spoke
Idolatrous to his own Shadow words of Eternity uttering
O I am nothing when I enter into judgment with thee
If thou withdraw thy breath I die & vanish into Hades
If thou dost lay thine hand upon me behold I am silent
If thou withhold thine hand I perish like a fallen leaf
O I am nothing & to nothing must return again
If thou withdraw thy breath. behold I am oblivion

He ceasd: the Shadowy voice was silent, but the cloud hoverd over their heads

Page 40. Night III. Pencil drawing.

154

In golden wreathes, the sorrow of Man & the balmy drops fell down
And Lo that Son of Man, that shadowy Spirit of the ~~Fallen~~ Once Albion
Luvah, descended from the cloud; In ~~terror~~ Man arose
Indignant rose the ~~Fallen~~ Man & turnd his back on Vala

Why roll thy clouds in sickning mists. I can no longer hide
The dismal vision of mine eyes, O love & life & light!
Prophetic dreads urge me to speak. futurity is before me
Like a dark lamp. Eternal death haunts all my expectation
Rent from Eternal Brotherhood we die & are no more

Wes I heard the Voice of the ~~fallen~~ starting from his sleep

Whence is this voice crying Enion that soundeth in my ears
O cruel pity! O dark deceit, can Love seek for dominion

And Luvah strove to gain dominion over the mighty Albion
They strove together above the Body where Vala was inclosd
And the dark Body of Man left prostrate upon the crystal pavement
Coverd with boils from head to foot. the terrible smitings of Luvah

Then frownd the ~~Fallen~~ Man & put forth Luvah from his presence
(I heard him: frown not Urizen: but listen to my Vision)

Page 41. Night III. Pencil drawing.

155

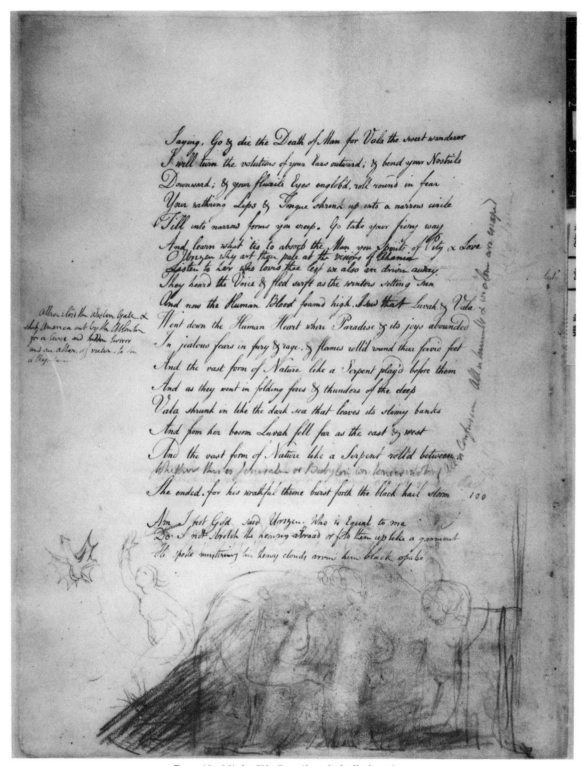

Saying, Go & die the Death of Man for Vala the sweet wanderer

I will turn the volutions of your ears outward; & bend your Nostrils

Downward; & your fluxile Eyes englob'd, roll round in fear

Your withring Lips & Tongue shrunk up into a narrow circle

Till into narrow forms you creep. Go take your fiery way

And learn what 'tis to absorb the Man you Spirits of Pity & Love

O Urizen why art thou pale at the visions of Ahania

Listen to her who loves thee lest we also are driven away

They heard the Voice & fled swift as the winters setting Sun

And now the Human Blood foamd high, I saw that Luvah & Vala

Went down the Human Heart where Paradise & its joys abounded

In jealous fears in fury & rage, & flames rolld round their fervid feet

And the vast form of Nature like a Serpent playd before them

And as they went in folding fires & thunders of the deep

Vala shrunk in like the dark sea that leaves its slimy banks

And from her bosom Luvah fell far as the east & west

And the vast form of Nature like a Serpent rolld between

Whether this is Jerusalem or Babylon we know not

She ended, for his wrathful throne burst forth the black hail storm   100

Am I not God said Urizen. Who is Equal to me

Do I not stretch the heavens abroad or fold them up like a garment

He spoke mustering his heavy clouds around him black opake

Page 42. Night III. Pencil and chalk drawing.

Page 43. Night III. Proof: NT 108:30E.

As when the thunder bolt down falleth on the appointed place
Fell down down rushing ruining thundering darting shuddering
Into the Caverns of the Grave & places of Human seed
Where the impressions of Despair & Hope enroll for ever
A world of darkness. Ahania fell far into Non Entity

She continued falling. Loud the Crash continued loud & hoarse
From the Crash roared a flame of blue sulphureous fire from the flame
A dolorous groan that struck with dumbness all confusion
Swallowing up the horrible din in agony on agony
Thro the Confusion like a crack across from immense to immense
Loud strong a universal groan of death louder
Than all the wracking elements deafend & rended worse
Than Urizen & all his hosts in curst despair down rushing
But from the Dolorous Groan one like a shadow of smoke appeard
And human bones rattling together in the smoke & stamping
The nether Abyss & gnashing in fierce despair. panting in sobs
Thick short incessant bursting sobbing. deep despairing stamping struggling
Struggling to utter the voice of Man struggling to take the features of Man Struggling
To take the limbs of Man at length emerging from the smoke   180
Of Urizen dashed in pieces from his precipitant fall
Tharmas reard up his hands & stood on the affrighted Ocean
The dead reard up his Voice & stood on the resounding shore

Crying fury in my limbs. destruction in my bones & marrow
My skull riven into filaments. my eyes into sea jellies
Floating upon the tide wander bubbling & bubbling
Uttering my lamentations & begetting little monsters
Who sit mocking upon the little pebbles of the tide
In all my rivers & on dried shells that the fish

Page 44. Night III. Pencil and chalk drawing.

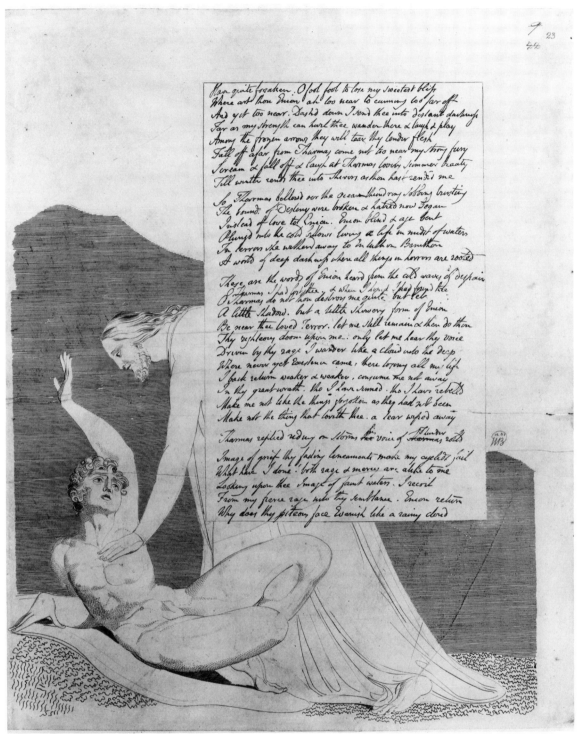

Page 45. Night III. Proof: NT 148 : 40E, first state.

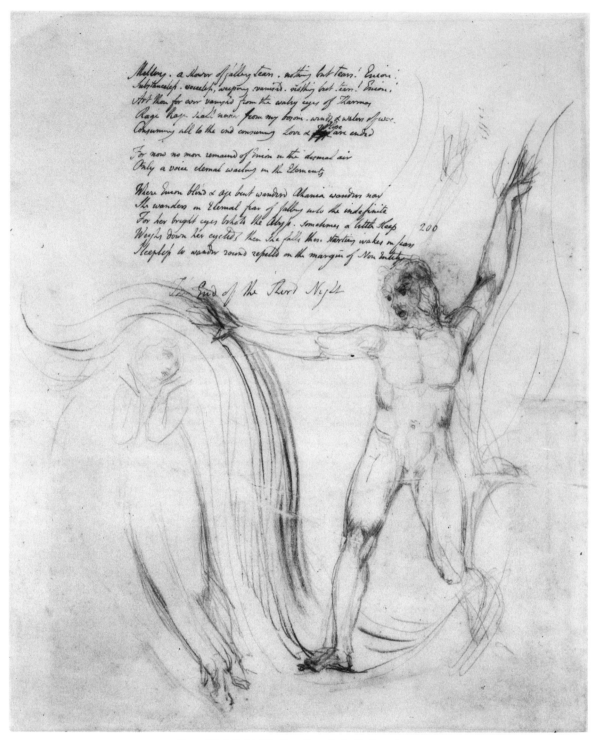

Page 46. Night III. Pencil and chalk drawing.

Page 47. Night IV. Proof: NT 87:26E.

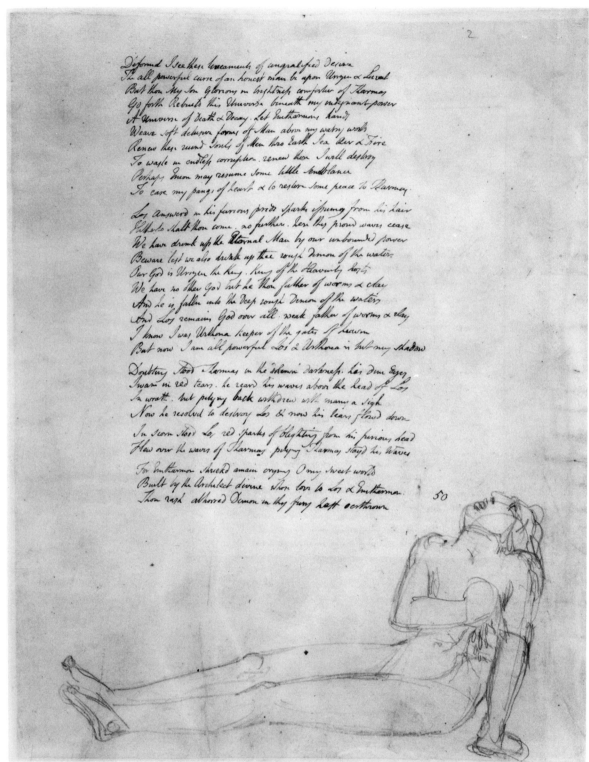

Deformd I see these lineaments of ungratified desire
The all powerful curse of an honest man be upon Urizen & Luvah
But thou My Son Glorious in brightness comforter of Tharmas
Go forth Rebuild this Universe beneath my indignant power
A Universe of death & decay. Let Enitharmons hands
Weave soft delusive forms of Man above my watry world
Renew these ruind Souls of Men thro Earth Sea Air & Fire
To waste in endless corruption. renew thou I will destroy
Perhaps Enion may resume some little semblance
To ease my pangs of heart & to restore some peace to Tharmas.

Los answerd in his furious pride sparks issuing from his hair
Hitherto shalt thou come. no further. here thy proud waves cease
We have drunk up the Eternal Man by our unbounded power
Beware lest we also drink up thee rough Demon of the waters
Our God is Urizen the King. King of the Heavenly hosts
We have no other God but he thou father of worms & clay
And he is fallen into the Deep rough Demon of the waters
And Los remains God over all. weak father of worms & clay
I know I was Urthona keeper of the gates of heaven
But now I am all powerful Los & Urthona is but my shadow

Doubting stood Tharmas in the solemn darkness. his dim Eyes
Swam in red tears. he reard his waves above the head of Los
In wrath. but pitying back withdrew with many a sigh
Now he resolved to destroy Los & now his tears flowd down

In scorn stood Los. red sparks of blighting from his furious head
Flew over the waves of Tharmas pitying Tharmas stayd his Waves

For Enitharmon shriekd amain crying O my sweet world
Built by the Architect divine whose love to Los & Enitharmon.
Thou rash abhorred Demon in thy fury hast oerthrown

50

Page 48. Night IV. Pencil drawings, one erased.

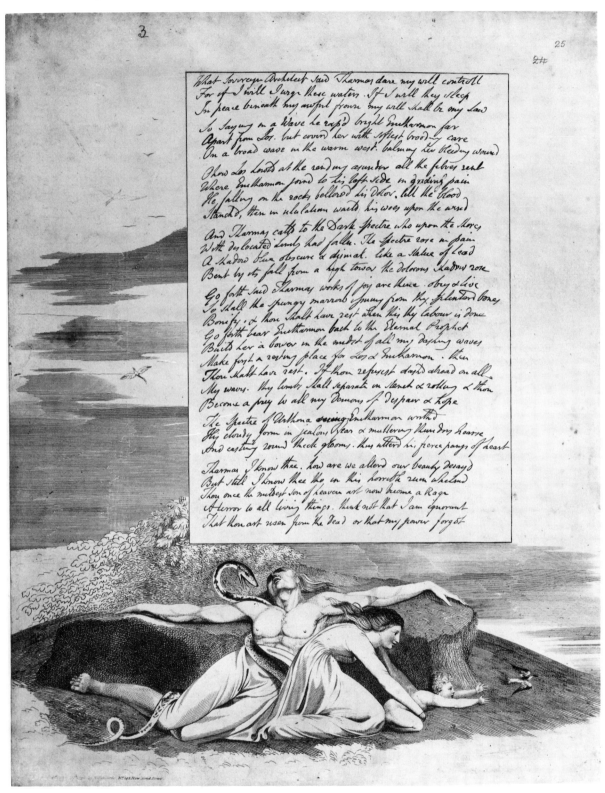

That Sovreign Architect said Tharmas dare my will controll
For if I will I urge these waters. If I will they sleep
In peace beneath my awful frown my will shall be my law

So saying on a Wave he rapd bright Enitharmon far
Apart from Los. but coverd her with softest brooding care
On a broad wave in the warm west. balming her bleeding wound

O how Los howld at the rending asunder all the fibres rent
Where Enitharmon joind to his left side in griding pain
He falling on the rocks bellowd his Dolor. till the blood
Stanchd, then in ululation waild his woes upon the wind

And Tharmas calld to the Dark Spectre who upon the Shores,
With dislocated Limbs had fallen. The Spectre rose in pain
A Shadow blue obscure & dismal. like a statue of lead
Bent by its fall from a high tower the dolorous shadow rose

Go forth said Tharmas works of joy are thine. obey & live
So shall the spungy marrow issuing from thy splinterd bones
Bonify. & thou shalt have rest when this thy labour is done
Go forth bear Enitharmon back to the Eternal Prophet
Build her a bower in the midst of all my dashing waves
Make first a resting place for Los & Enitharmon. then
Thou shalt have rest. If thou refusest dashd abroad on all
My waves. thy limbs shall separate in stench & rotting & thou
Become a prey to all my Demons of despair & hope

The Spectre of Urthona seeing Enitharmon writhd
His cloudy form in jealous fear & muttering thunders hoarse
And casting round thick glooms. thus utterd his fierce pangs of heart

Tharmas I know thee. how are we alterd our beauty decayd
But still I know thee tho in this horrible ruin whelmd
Thou once the mildest son of heaven art now become a Rage
A terror to all living things. think not that I am ignorant
That thou art risen from the dead or that my power forgot

I slumber here in weak repose: I will remember the Day
The day of terror & abhorrence
When fleeing from the battle thou fleeing like the raven
Of dawn outstretching an expanse where neer expanse had been
Drewst all the Sons of Beulah into thy dread vortex following
Thy Eddying spirit down the hills of Beulah. All my sons
Stood round me at the anvil where new heated the wedge
Of iron glowd furious prepard for spades & mattocks
Hearing the symphonies of war loud sounding All my sons
Fled from my side then pangs smote me unknown before. I saw
My loins begin to break forth into veiny pipes & writhe
Before me in the wind englobing trembling with strong vibrations
The bloody mass began to animate. I bending over
Wept bitter tears incessant. Still beholding how the piteous form
Dividing & dividing from my loins a weak & piteous
Soft cloud of snow a female pale & weak I soft embracd
My counter part & calld it Love I namd her Enitharmon
But found myself & her together issuing down the tide
Which now our rivers were become delving thro caverns huge
Of goary blood struggling to be delivered from our bonds
She strove in vain not so Urthona strove for breaking forth
A shadow blue obscure & dismal from the breathing Nostrils
Of Enion I issued into the air divided from Enitharmon
I howld in sorrow I beheld thee rotting upon the Rocks
I pitying hoverd over thee I protected thy ghastly corse
From Vultures of the deep then wherefore shouldst thou rage
Against me who thee guarded in the night of death from harm

Tharmas replied. Art thou Urthona My friend my old companion
With whom I livd in happiness before that deadly night
When Urizen gave the horses of Light into the hands of Luvah
Thou knowest not what Tharmas knows. O I could tell thee tales
That would enrage thee as it has enraged me even
From death in wrath & fury. But now come bear back
Thy loved Enitharmon. For thou hast her here before thine eyes

100

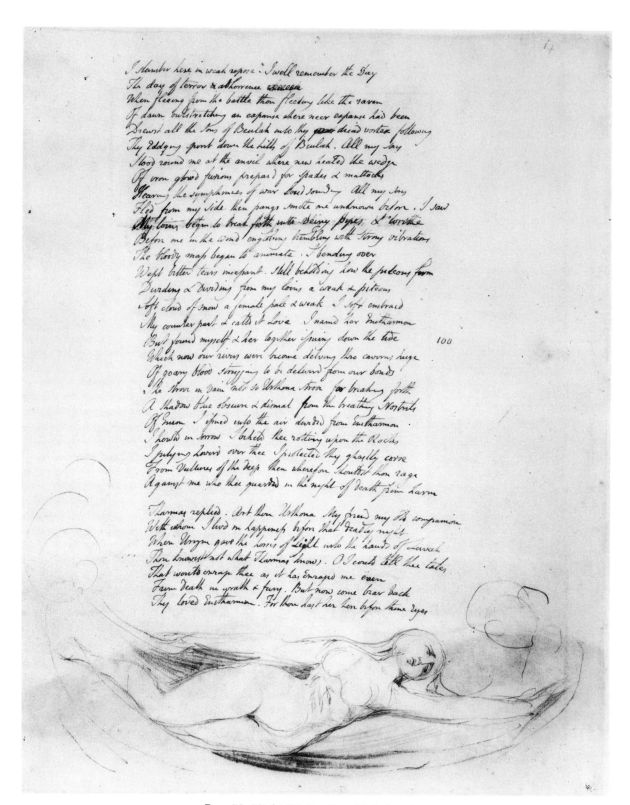

Page 50. Night IV. Pencil and ink drawing.

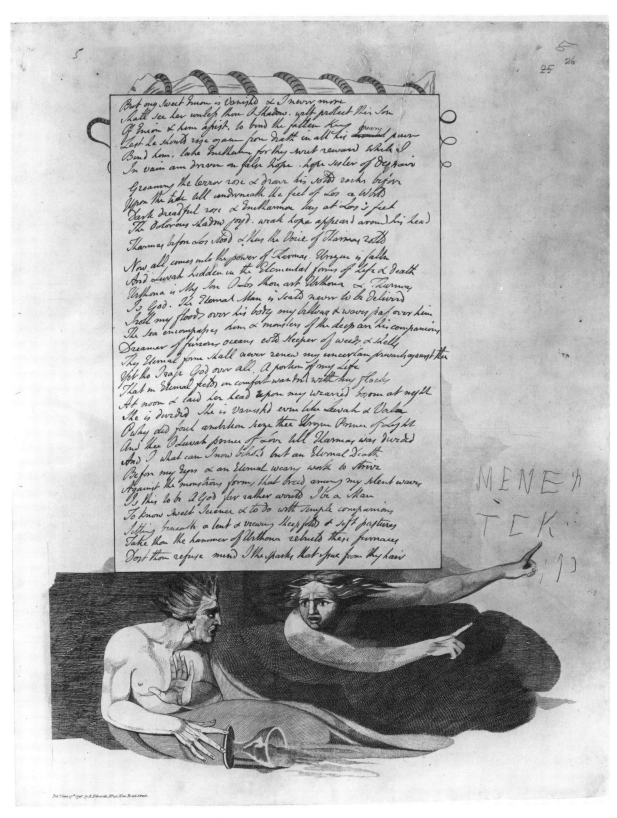

Page 51. Night IV. Proof: NT 60:19E.

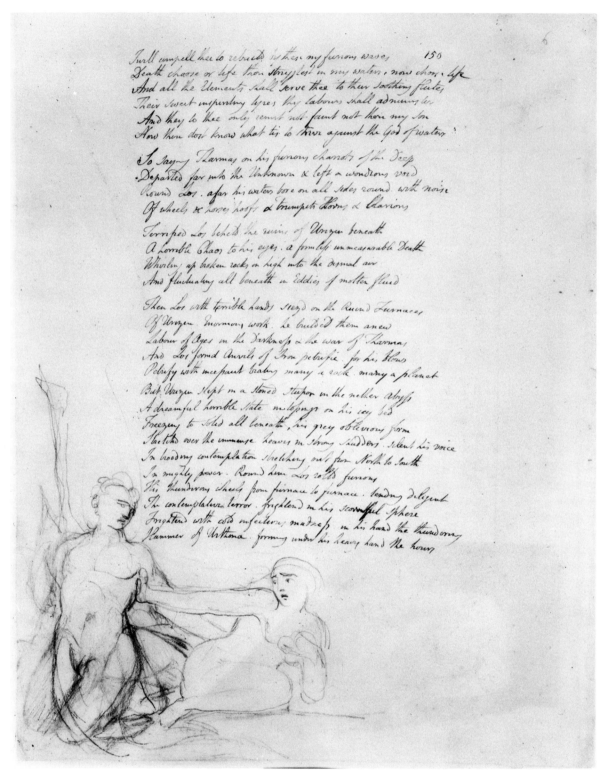

I'll compell thee to rebuild by these my furious waves,   150
Death choose or life thou strugglest in my waters. now choose. Life
And all the Elements shall serve thee to their soothing flutes,
Their sweet inspiring lyres thy labours shall administer
And they to thee only remit not faint not thou my Son
Now thou dost know what tis to strive against the God of waters

So saying Tharmas on his furious chariots of the Deep
Departed far into the Unknown & left a wondrous void
Round Los. afar his waters bore on all sides round. with noise
Of wheels & horses hoofs & trumpets Horns & Clarions

Terrified Los beheld the ruins of Urizen beneath
A horrible Chaos to his eyes. a formless unmeasurable Death
Whirling up broken rocks on high into the dismal air
And fluctuating all beneath in Eddies of molten fluid

Then Los with terrible hands siezd on the Ruind Furnaces
Of Urizen. Enormous work. he builded them anew
Labour of Ages in the Darkness & the war of Tharmas
And Los formd Anvils of Iron petrific. for his blows
Petrify with incessant beating many a rock. many a planet
But Urizen slept in a stoned stupor in the nether abyss
A dreamful horrible State in tossings on his icy bed
Freezing to solid all beneath, his grey oblivious form
Stretchd over the immense heaves in strong shudders. silent his voice
In brooding contemplation stretching out from North to South
In mighty power. Round him Los rolld furious
His thundrous wheels from furnace to furnace. tending diligent
The contemplative terror. frightend in his scornful sphere
Frightend with cold infectious madness. in his hand the thundrous
Hammer of Urthona. forming under his heavy hand the hours

Page 52. Night IV. Pencil and chalk drawing.

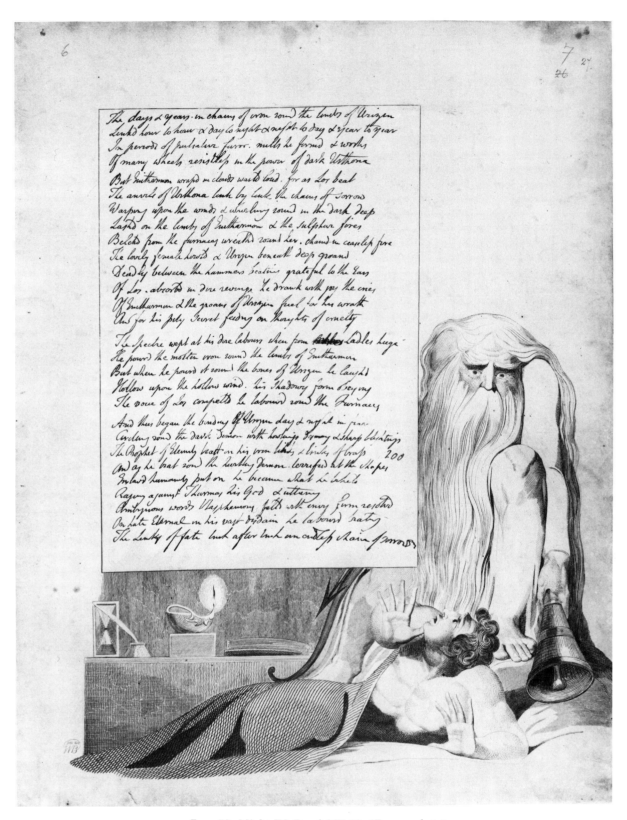

The days & years. in chains of iron round the limbs of Urizen
Linkd hour to hour & day to night & night to day & year to year
In periods of pulsative furor. mills he formd & workd
Of many wheels resistless in the power of dark Urthona
But Enitharmon wrapd in clouds waild loud. for as Los beat
The anvils of Urthona link by link the chains of sorrow
Warping upon the winds & whirling round in the dark deep
Lashd on the limbs of Enitharmon & the sulphur fires
Belch'd from the furnaces wreathd round her. chaind in ceaseless fire
The lovely female howld & Urizen beneath deep groand
Deadly between the hammers beating grateful to the Ears
Of Los. absorbd in dire revenge he drank with joy the cries
Of Enitharmon & the groans of Urizen fuel for his wrath
And for his pity Secret feeding on thoughts of cruelty

The Spectre wept at his dire labours when from Ladles huge
He pourd the molten iron round the limbs of Enitharmon
But when he pourd it round the bones of Urizen he laughd
Hollow upon the hollow wind. his Shadowy form obeying
The voice of Los compelld he labourd round the Furnaces

And thus began the binding of Urizen day & night in fear
Circling round the dark Demon with howlings dismay & sharp blightings
The Prophet of Eternity beat on his iron links & links of brass   200
And as he beat round the hurtling Demon. terrified at the shapes
Enslavd humanity put on he became what he beheld
Raging against Tharmas his God & uttering
Ambiguous words blasphemous fill'd with envy firm resolved
On hate Eternal in his vast disdain he labourd beating
The Links of fate link after link an endless chain of sorrows

Page 53. Night IV. Proof: NT 18:4E, second state.

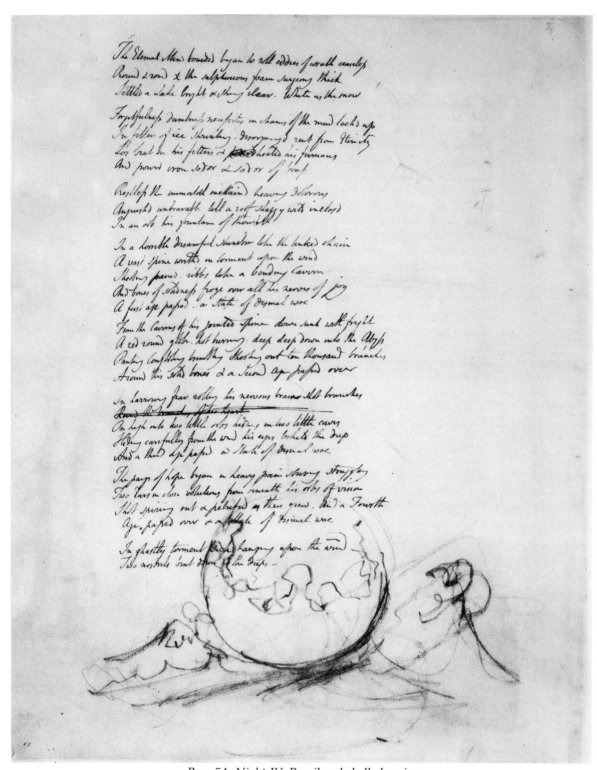

Page 54. Night IV. Pencil and chalk drawing.

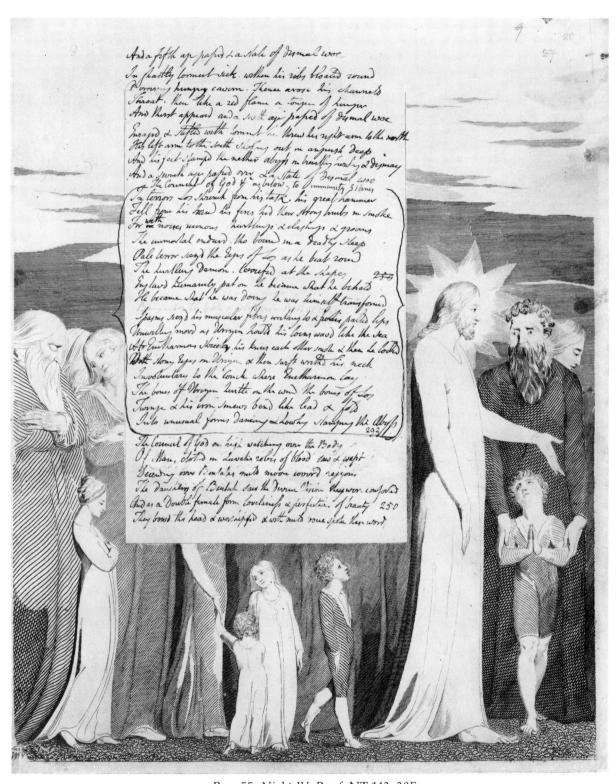

Page 55. Night IV. Proof: NT 143 : 38E.

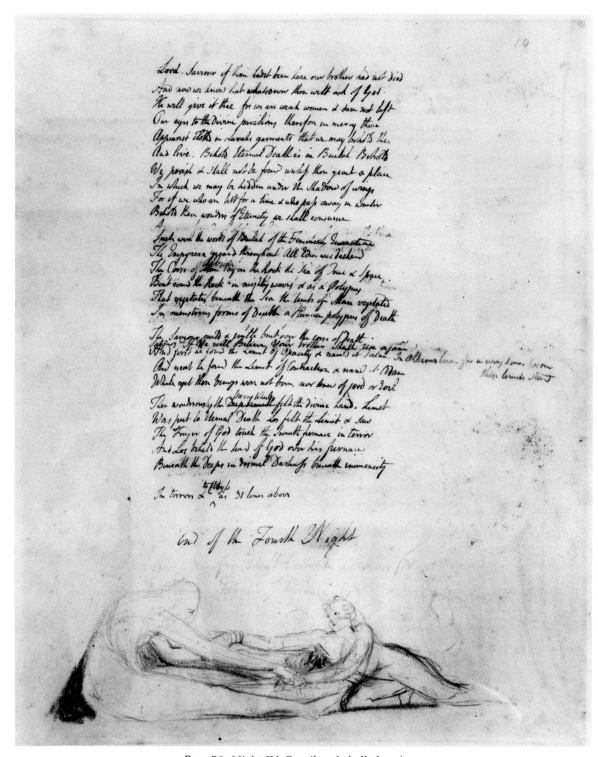

Page 56. Night IV. Pencil and chalk drawing.

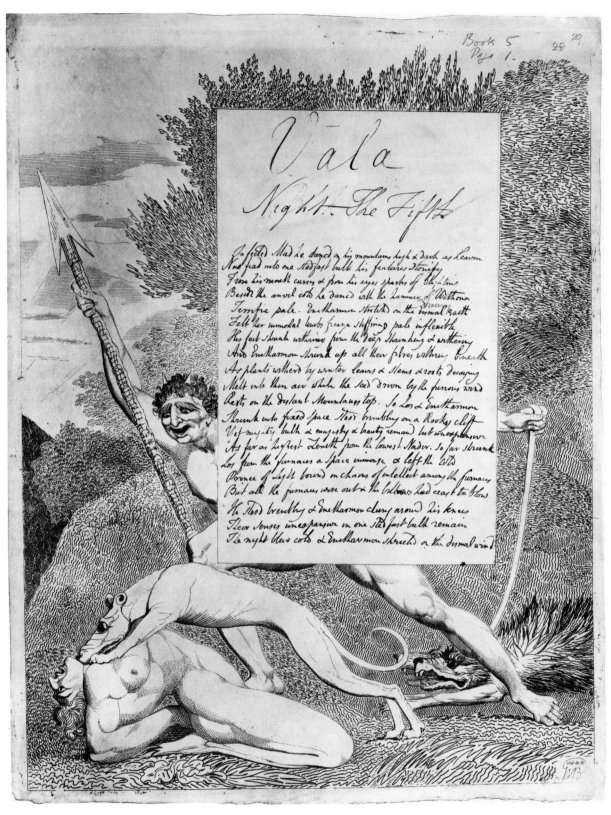

Page 57. Night V. Proof: NT 117 : 32E.

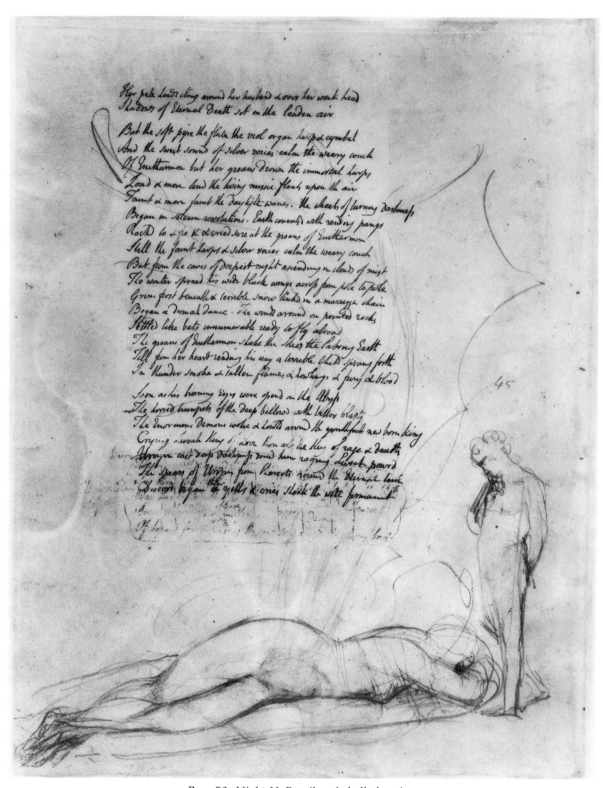

Page 58. Night V. Pencil and chalk drawing.

Where is sweet Vala gloomy prophet where the lovely form
That drew the body of Man from heaven into this dark Abyss
Soft tears & sighs where are you come forth shout on bloody fields
Shew thy soul Vala shew thy bow & quiver of secret fires

Draw thy bow Vala from the depths of hell thy black bow draw 50
And twang the bow string to our howlings let thine arrows black
Sing in the Sky as once they sang upon the hills of Light
When dark Urthona wept in torment of the secret pain
He wept & he divided & he laid his gloomy head
Down on the Rock of Eternity on darkness of the deep
Torn by black storm & ceaseless torrents of consuming fire
Within his breast his fiery sons chained down & filld with cursings

And breathing terrible blood & vengeance gnashing his teeth with pain
Let loose the Enormous spirit in the darkness of the deep
And his dark wife that once fair crystal form divinely clear
Within his ribs producing serpents whose souls are flames of fire
But now the times return upon thee Enitharmons womb
Now holds thee soon to issue forth. Sound Clarions of war
Call Vala from her close recess in all her dark deceit
Then rage on rage shall fierce redound out of her crystal quiver

So sung the Demons round red Orc & round faint Enitharmon
Sweat & blood stood on the limbs of Los in globes his fiery Eyelids
Faded. he rouzd he siezd the wonder in his hands & went
Shuddering & weeping thro the Gloom & down into the deeps

Enitharmon nursd her fiery child in the dark deeps
Sitting in darkness. over her Los mournd in anguish fierce
Coverd with gloom. the fiery boy grew fed by the milk
Of Enitharmon. Los around her builded pillars of iron

Page 59. Night V. Proof: NT 131:34E, second state.

And brass & silver & gold fourfold in dark prophetic fear
For now he feard Eternal Death & uttermost Extinction
He builded Golgonooza on the Lake of Udan Adan
Upon the Limit of Translucence then he builded Luban
Tharmas laid the Foundation & Los finishd it in howling woe

But when fourteen summers & winters had revolved over
Their solemn habitation Los beheld the ruddy boy
Embracing his bright mother & beheld malignant fires
In his young eyes discerning plain that Orc plotted his death
Grief rose upon his ruddy brows. a lightning girdle grew
Around his bosom like a bloody cord. in secret sobs
He burst it, but next morn another girdle succeeds
Around his bosom. Every day he viewd the fiery youth
With silent fear & his immortal cheeks grew deadly pale
Till many a morn & many a night passed over in dire woe
Forming a girdle in the day & bursting it at night
The girdle was formd by day by night was burst in twain
Falling down on the rock an iron chain link by link lockd

Enitharmon beheld the bloody chain of nights & days
Depending from the bosom of Los & how with griding pain
He went each morning to his labours with the spectre dark
Calld it the chain of Jealousy. Now Los began to speak
His woes aloud to Enitharmon. since he could not hide
His uncouth plague. He siezd the boy in his immortal hands
While Enitharmon followd him weeping in dismal woe
Up to the iron mountains top & there the jealous chain
Fell from his bosom on the mountain. The spectre dark
Held the fierce boy Los naild him down binding around his limbs
The accursed chain O how bright Enitharmon howld & cried
Over her Son. Obdurate Los bound down her loved Joy

Page 60. Night V. Ink and chalk drawing with chalk shading.

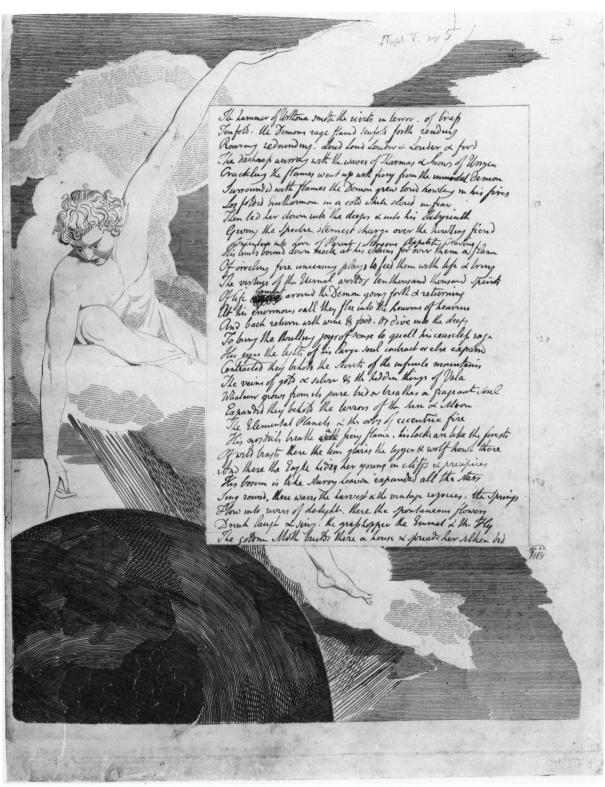

The hammer of Urthona smote the rivets in terror. of brass
Tenfold. the Demons rage flam'd tenfold forth rending
Roaring redounding. loud loud louder & louder & fierce
The dark fires warring with the waves of Tharmas & snows of Urizen
Crackling the flames went up with fury from the immortal Demon
Surrounded with flames the Demon grew loud howling in his fires
Los folded Enitharmon in a cold white cloud in fear
Then led her down into the deeps & into his labyrinth
Giving the Spectre sternest charge over the howling fiend
Concentring into love of Parent Storgous Appetite craving
His limbs bound down mock at his chains for over them a flame
Of circling fire unceasing plays to feed them with life & bring
The virtues of the Eternal worlds ten thousand thousand spirits
Of life lament around the Demon going forth & returning
At his enormous call they flee into the heavens of heavens
And back return with wine & food. Or dive into the deeps
To bring the thrilling joys of sense to quell his ceaseless rage
His eyes the lights of his large soul contract or else expand
Contracted they behold the secrets of the infinite mountains
The veins of gold & silver & the hidden things of Vala
Whatever grows from its pure bud or breathes a fragrant soul
Expanded they behold the terrors of the Sun & Moon
The Elemental Planets & the orbs of eccentric fire
His nostrils breathe a fiery flame. his locks are like the forests
Of wild beasts there the lion glares the tyger & wolf howl there
And there the Eagle hides her young in cliffs & precipices
His bosom is like starry heaven expanded all the stars
Sing round. there waves the harvest & the vintage rejoices. the springs
Flow into rivers of delight. there the spontaneous flowers
Drink laugh & sing. the grasshopper the Emmet & the Fly
The golden Moth builds there a house & spreads her silken bed

Page 61. Night V. Proof: NT 141:37E, first state.

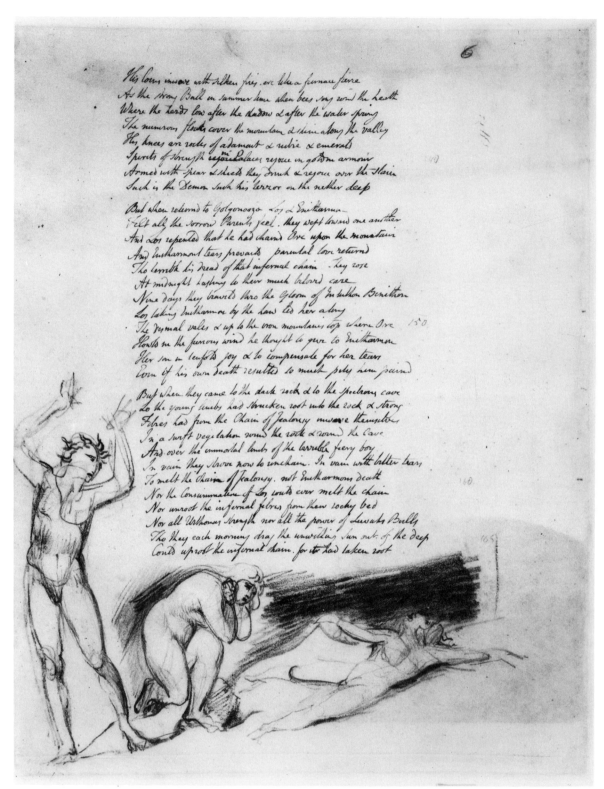

His loins inwove with silken fires, are like a furnace fierce
As the iron Ball in summer time when bees sing round the heath
Where the herds low after the shadow & after the water spring
The numerous flocks cover the mountain & shine along the valley
His knees are rocks of adamant & ruby & emerald
Spirits of strength in palaces rejoice in golden armour
Armed with spear & shield they drink & rejoice over the slain
Such is the Demon such his terror on the nether deep

But when returnd to Golgonooza Los & Enitharmon
Felt all the sorrow Parents feel, they wept toward one another
And Los repented that he had chaind Orc upon the mountain
And Enitharmons tears prevaild parental love returnd
Tho terrible his dread of that infernal chain They rose
At midnight hasting to their much belovd care
Nine days they traveld thro the Gloom of Entuthon Benithon
Los taking Enitharmon by the hand led her along
The dismal vales & up to the iron mountains top where Orc
Howld in the furious wind he thought to give to Enitharmon
Her son in tenfold joy & to compensate for her tears
Even if his own death resulted so much pity him paind

But when they came to the dark rock & to the spectrous cave
Lo the young limbs had strucken root into the rock & strong
Fibres had from the Chain of Jealousy inwove themselves
In a swift vegetation round the rock & round the Cave
And over the immortal limbs of the terrible fiery boy
In vain they strove now to unchain. In vain with bitter tears
To melt the Chain of Jealousy. not Enitharmons death
Nor the Consummation of Los could ever melt the chain
Nor unroot the infernal fibres from their rocky bed
Nor all Urthonas strength nor all the power of Luvahs Bulls
Tho they each morning drag the unwilling Sun out of the deep
Could uproot the infernal chain. for it had taken root

Page 62. Night V. Pencil and chalk drawing with chalk shading.

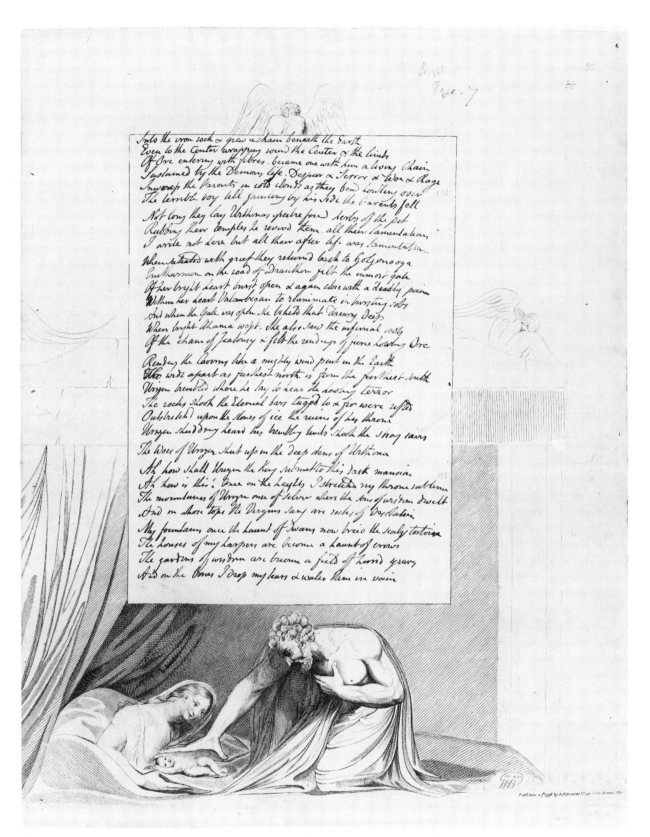

Into the iron rock & grew a chain beneath the earth
Even to the Center wrapping round the Center & the limbs
Of Orc entering with fibres. became one with him a living Chain
Sustained by the Demons life. Despair & Terror & Woe & Rage
Inwrap the Parents in cold clouds as they bend howling over
The terrible boy till fainting by his Side the Parents fell

Not long they lay Urthonas spectre found herbs of the pit
Rubbing their temples he revivd them. all their lamentations
I write not here but all their after life was lamentation

When satiated with grief they returnd back to Golgonooza
Enitharmon on the road of Drauthon felt the inmost gate
Of her bright heart burst open & again close with a deadly pain
Within her heart Vala began to reanimate in bursting sobs
And when the Gate was open she beheld that dreary deep
When bright Ahania wept. She also saw the infernal roots
Of the chain of Jealousy & felt the rendings of fierce howling Orc

Rending the Caverns like a mighty wind pent in the Earth
Tho wide apart as furthest north is from the furthest south
Urizen trembled where he lay to hear the howling terror
The rocks shook the Eternal bars tuggd to & fro were rifted
Outstretchd upon the stones of ice the ruins of his throne
Urizen shuddring heard his trembling limbs shook the strong caves

The Woes of Urizen shut up in the deep dens of Urthona

Ah how shall Urizen the King submit to this dark mansion
Ah how is this! Once on the heights I stretchd my throne sublime
The mountains of Urizen once of silver where the sons of wisdom dwelt
And on whose tops the Virgins sang are rocks of Desolation

My fountains once the haunt of Swans now breed the scaly tortoise
The houses of my harpers are become a haunt of crows
The gardens of wisdom are become a field of horrid graves
And on the bones I drop my tears & water them in vain

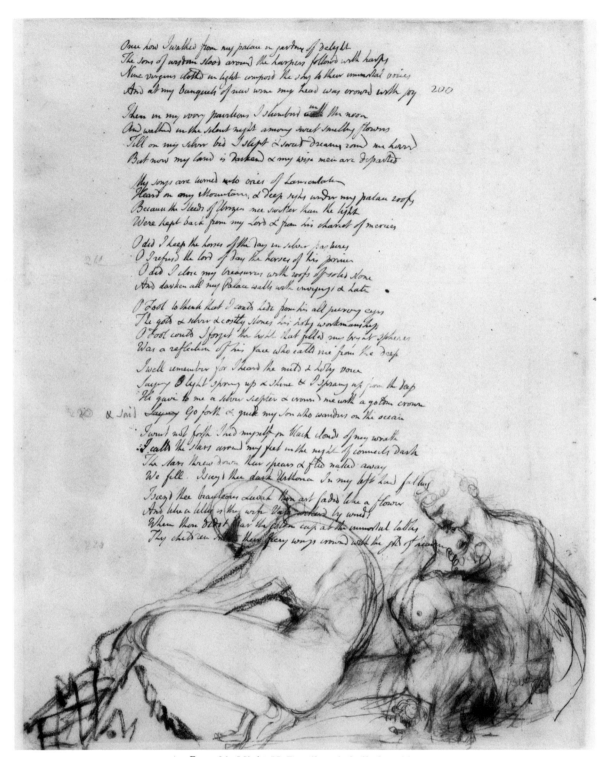

Once how I walked from my palace in gardens of delight
The sons of wisdom stood around the harpers followd with harps
Nine virgins clothd in light compard the day to their immortal voices
And at my banquets of new wine my head was crownd with joy   200

Then in my ivory pavilions I slumberd in the noon
And walked in the silent night among sweet smelling flowers
Till on my silver bed I slept & sweet dreams round me hoverd
But now my land is darkend & my wise men are departed

My songs are turned into cries of Lamentation
Heard on my mountains & deep sighs under my palace roofs
Because the Steeds of Urizen were swifter than the light
Were kept back from my Lord & from his chariot of mercies

O did I keep the horses of the day in silver pastures
O I refusd the lord of day the horses of his prince
O did I close my treasuries with roofs of solid stone
And darken all my Palace walls with envyings & hate

O Fool to think that I could hide from his all piercing eyes
The gold & silver & costly stones his holy workmanship
O Fool could I forget the light that filld my bright spheres
Was a reflection of his face who calls me from the deep

I well remember for I heard the mild & holy voice
Saying O light spring up & shine & I sprang up from the deep
He gave to me a silver scepter & crownd me with a golden crown
& said Saying Go forth & guide my Son who wanders on the ocean

I went not forth I hid myself in black clouds of my wrath
I calld the stars around my feet in the night of councils dark
The stars threw down their spears & fled naked away
We fell. I seizd thee dark Urthona In my left hand falling

I seizd thee beauteous Luvah thou art faded like a flower
And like a lily is thy wife Vala witherd by winds
When thou didst bear the golden cup at the immortal tables
Thy children smote their fiery wings crownd with the gold of heaven

Page 64. Night V. Pencil and chalk drawing.

Page 65. Night V. Proof: NT 133:36E.

Page 66. Night V. Pencil and chalk drawing.

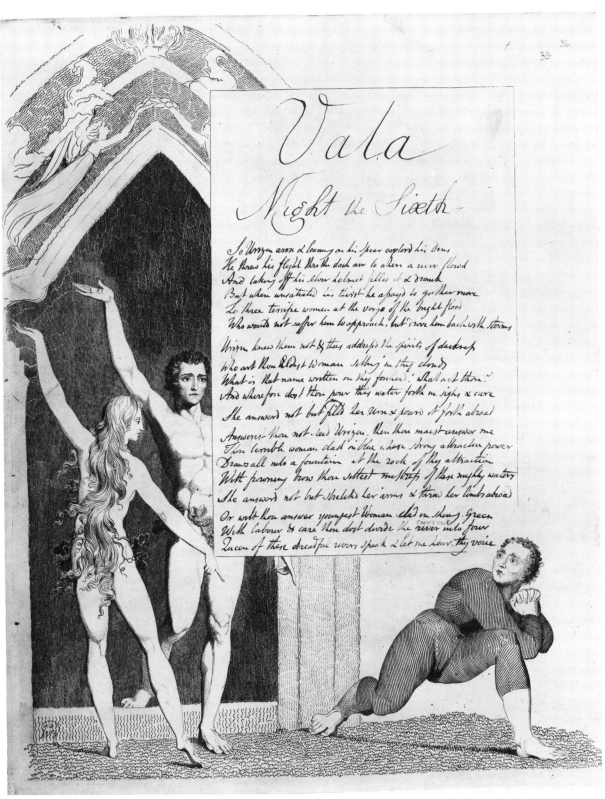

Page 67. Night VI. Proof: NT 119:33E.

Then Urizen raisd his spear. but they reard up a wall of rocks
They gave a Scream, they knew their father Urizen knew his daughters
They shrunk into their channels. dry the rocky strand beneath his feet
Hiding themselves in rocky forms from the Eyes of Urizen

Then Urizen Wept & thus his lamentation poured forth

O horrible O dreadful state! those whom I loved best
On whom I pourd the beauties of my light adorning them
With jewels & precious ornament labourd with art divine
Vests of the radiant colours of heaven & crowns of golden fire
I gave sweet lillies to their breath & roses to their hair
I taught them songs of sweet delight I gave their tender voices
Into the blue expanse & I invented with laborious art
Sweet instruments of sound. in pride encompassing my knees
They poured their radiance above all. the daughters of Luvah envied
At their exceeding brightness & the sons of eternity sent them gifts
Now will I pour my fury on them & I will reverse
The precious benediction. for their colours of loveliness
I will give blackness for jewels hoarse croak for ornament deformity
For crowns wreathd Serpents for sweet odors stinking corruptibility
For voices of delight hoarse croakings inarticulate thro frost
For labourd fatherly care & sweet instruction. I will give
Chains of dark ignorance & cords of twisted self conceit
And whips of stern repentance & food of stubborn obstinacy
That they may curse Tharmas their God & Los his adopted Son
That they may curse & worship the obscure demon of destruction
That they may worship terrors & obey the violent
Go forth sons of my curse Go forth daughters of my abhorrence

Tharmas heard the deadly scream across his watry world
And Urizens loud sounding voice lamenting on the wind
And he came riding in his fury. froze to solid were his waves.

Page 68. Night VI. Pencil and chalk drawing with chalk shading.

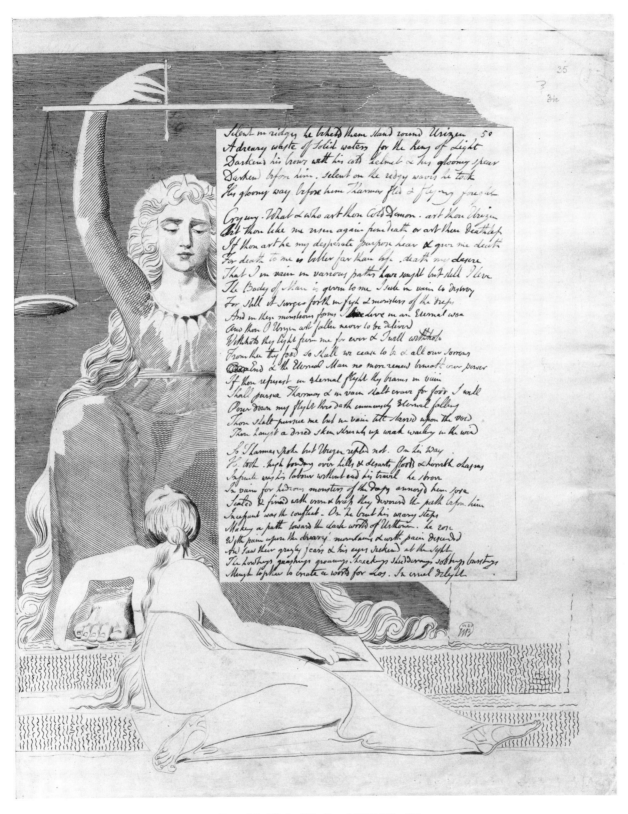

Silent in ridgy he beheld them stand round Urizen 50
A dreary waste of solid waters for the king of Light
Darkend his brows with his cold helmet & his gloomy spear
Darken before him. silent on the ridgy waves he took
His gloomy way before him Tharmas fled & flying fought

Crying. What & who art thou Cold Demon. art thou Urizen
Art thou like me risen again from death or art thou deathless
If thou art he my desperate purpose hear & give me death
For death to me is better far than life . death my desire
That I in vain in various paths have sought but still I live
The Body of Man is given to me I seek in vain to destroy
For still it surges forth in fish & monsters of the deeps
And in their monstrous forms I live in an Eternal woe
And thou O Urizen art fallen never to be deliverd
Withhold thy light from me for ever & I will withhold
From thee thy food so shall we cease to be & all our sorrows
End & the Eternal Man no more renew beneath our power
If thou refusest in eternal flight thy beams in vain
Shall pursue Tharmas & in vain shalt crave for food I will
Pour down my flight thro dark immensity Eternal falling
Thou shalt pursue me but in vain till starvd upon the void
Thou hangst a dried skin shrunk up weak wailing in the wind

So Tharmas spoke but Urizen replied not. On his way
He took . high bounding over hills & desarts floods & horrible chasms
Infinite was his labour without end his travel he strove
In vain for hideous monsters of the deeps annoyd him sore
Scaled & finnd with iron & brass they devoured the path before him
Incessant was the conflict. On he bent his weary steps
Making a path toward the dark world of Urthona. he rose
With pain upon the dreary mountains & with pain descended
And saw their grisly fears & his eyes sickend at the sight
The howlings gnashings groanings shriekings shudderings sobbings burstings
Mingle together to create a world for Los. In cruel delight

Page 69. Night VI. Proof: NT 151:41E.

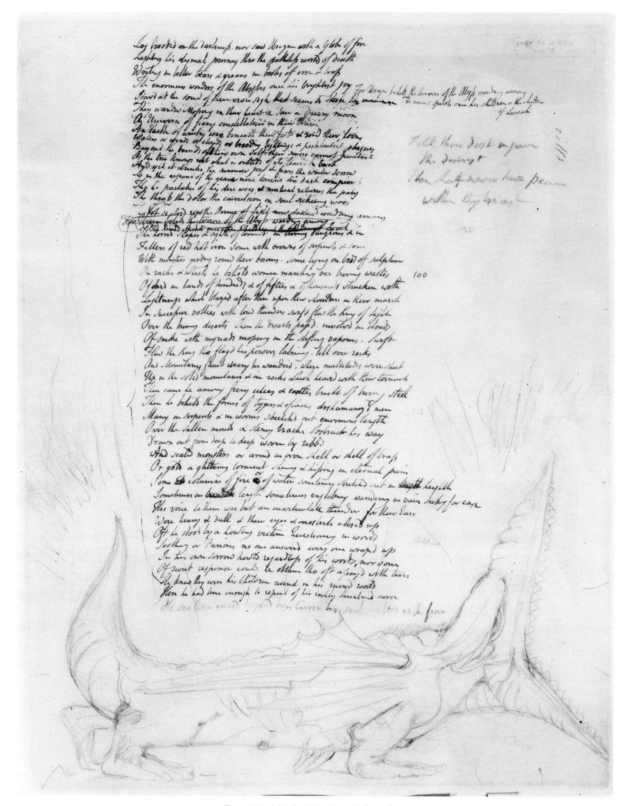

Page 70. Night VI. Pencil drawing.

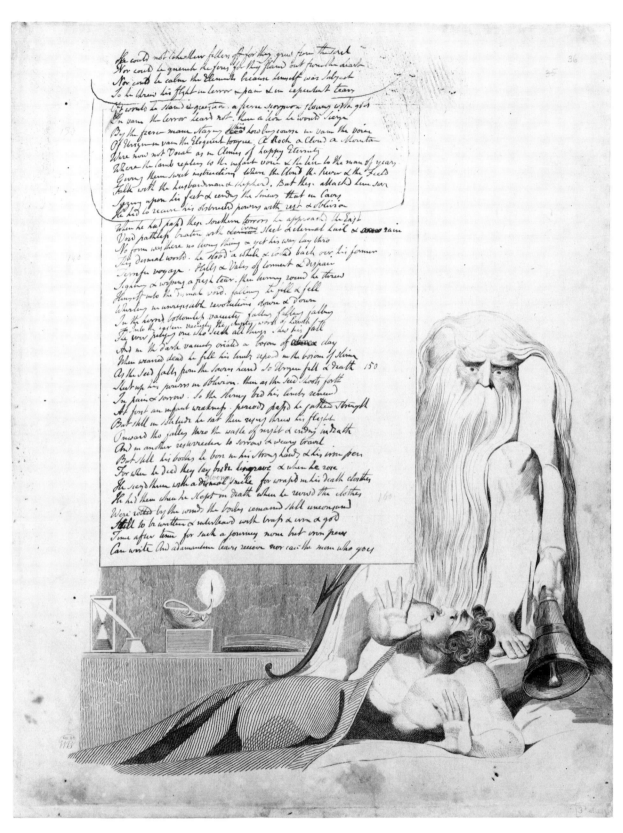

Page 71. Night VI. Proof: NT 18 : 4E, first state.

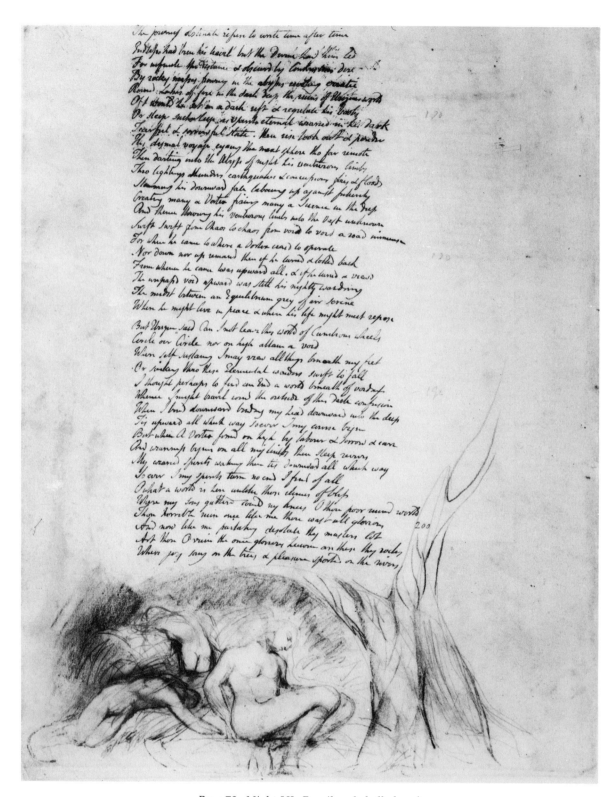

Page 72. Night VI. Pencil and chalk drawing.

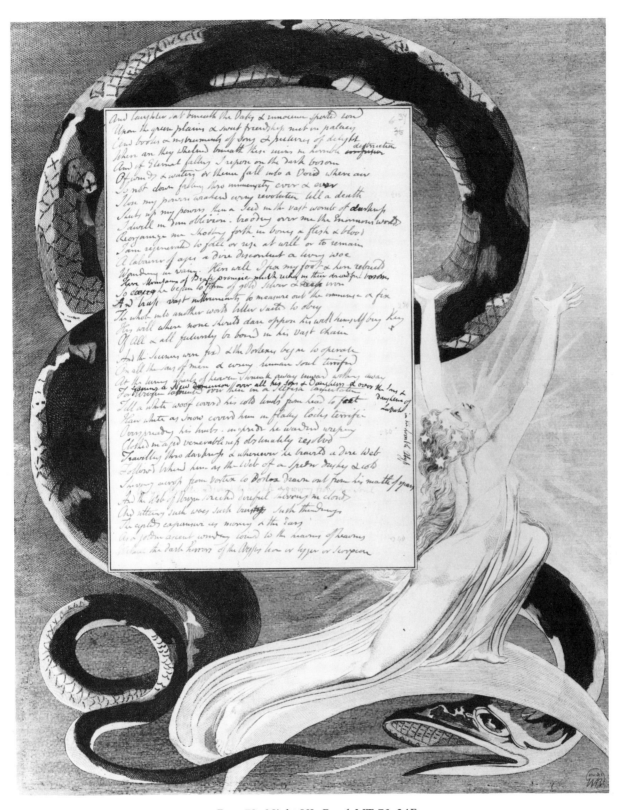

Page 73. Night VI. Proof: NT 78:24E.

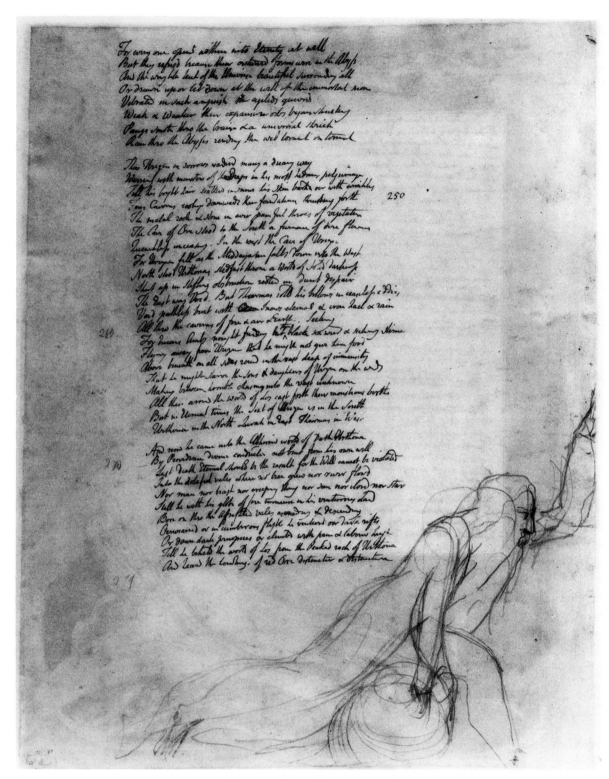

Page 74. Night VI. Pencil and chalk drawing.

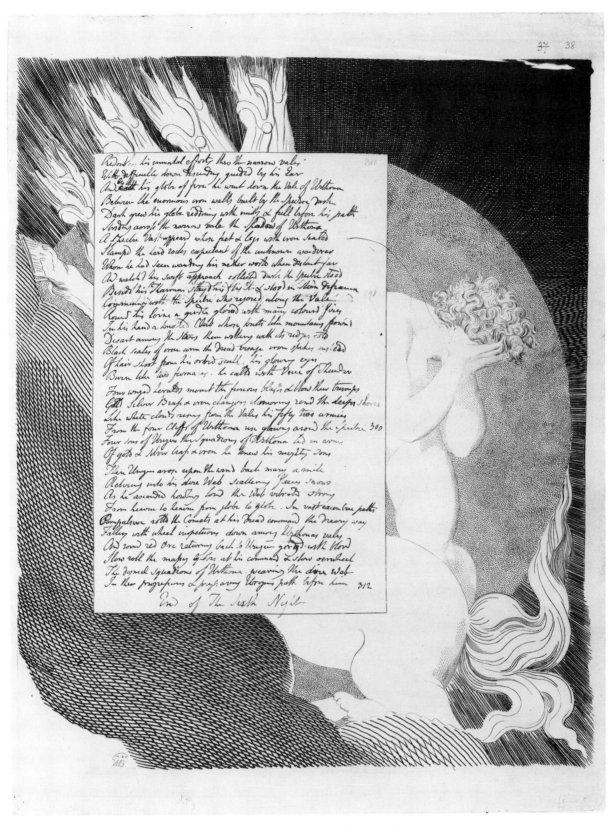

Page 75. Night VI. Proof: NT 27:35E.

Page 76. Night VI. Pencil and chalk drawing.

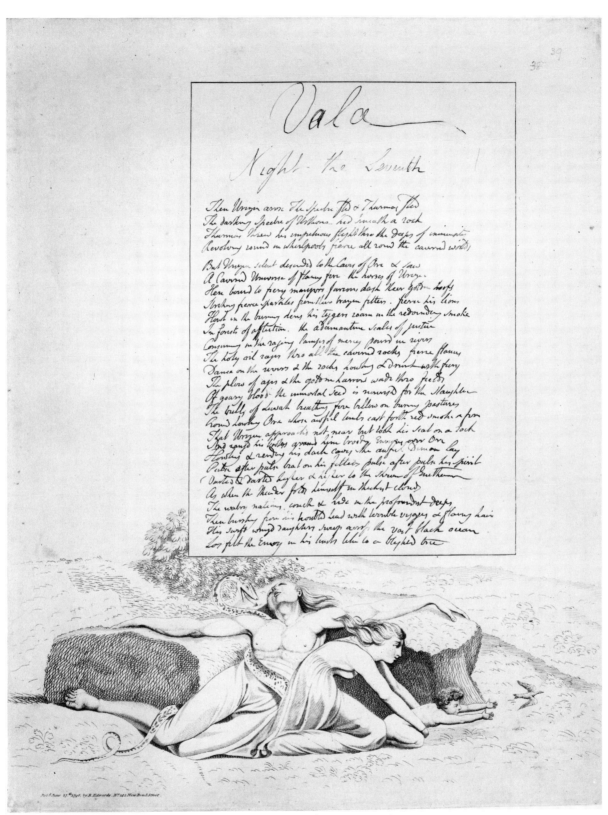

Page 77. Night VII. Proof: NT 27:7E, first state.

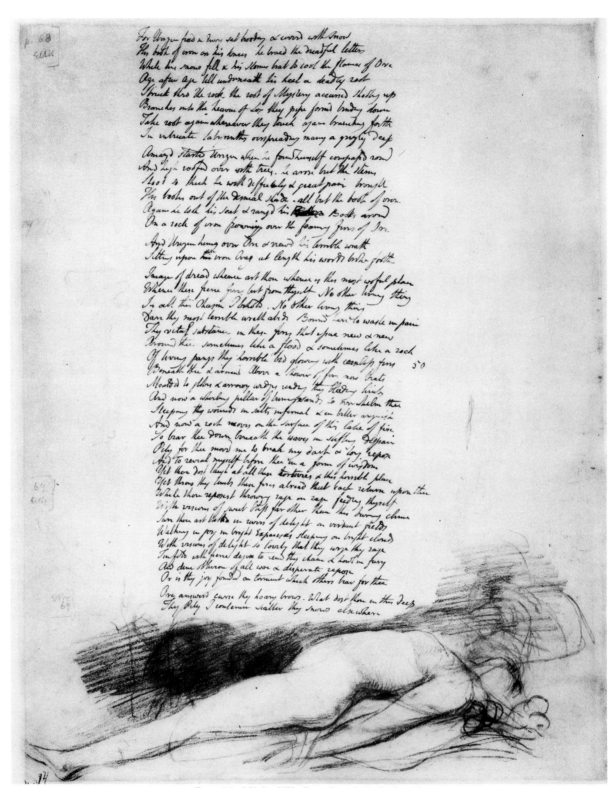

Page 78. Night VII. Pencil and chalk drawing.

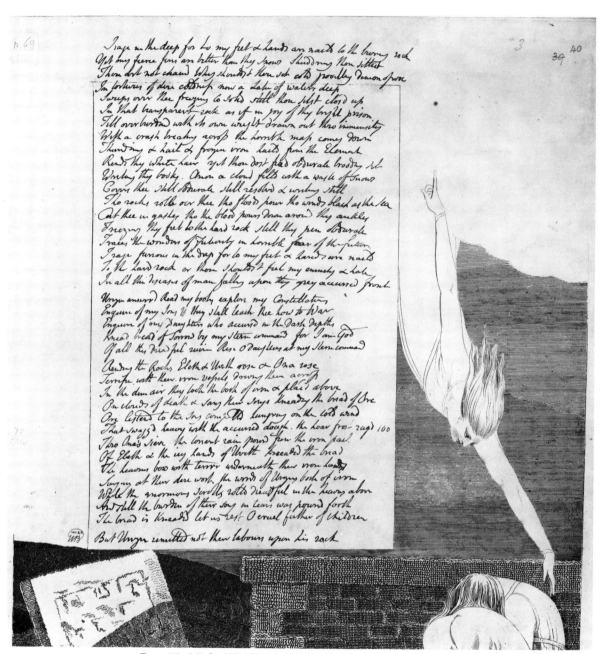

Rage in the deep for lo my feet & hands are naild to th burning rock
Yet my fierce fires are better than thy snows Shuddring thou sittest
Thou dost not chaunt Why shouldst thou sit cold Grovelling demon of woe
In tortures of dire coldness now a Lake of waters deep
Sweeps over thee freezing to solid still thou sittst closd up
In that transparent rock as if in joy of thy bright prison
Till overburdend with its own weight drawn out thro immensity
With a crash breaking across the horrible mass comes down
Thundring & hail & frozen iron haild from the Element
Rends thy white hair yet thou dost fixd obdurate brooding sit
Writing thy books. Anon a cloud filld with a waste of snows
Covers thee still obdurate still resolvd & writing still
Tho rocks roll oer thee tho floods pour tho winds black as the sea
Cut thee in gashes tho the blood pours down around thy ankles
Freezing thy feet to the hard rock still thy pen obdurate
Traces the wonders of futurity in horrible fear of the future
I rage furious in the deep for lo my feet & hands are naild
To the hard rock or thou shouldst feel my enmity & hate
In all the diseases of man falling upon thy grey accursed front

Urizen answerd Read my books explore my Constellations
Enquire of my Suns & they shall teach thee how to War
Enquire of my Daughters who accursd in the Dark depths
Knead bread of Sorrow by my stern command for I am God
Of all this dreadful ruin Rise O daughters at my Stern command

Rending the Rocks Eleth & Uveth rose & Ona rose
Terrific with their iron vessels driving them across
In the dim air they took the book of iron & placd above
On clouds of death & sang their songs kneading the bread of Orc
Orc listend to the Song compelld hungring on the cold wind
That swagd heavy with the accursed dough. the hoar frost ragd
Thro Onas sieve the torrent rain pourd from the iron pail
Of Eleth & the icy hands of Uveth kneaded the bread
The heavens bow with terror underneath their iron hands
Singing at their dire work the words of Urizens book of iron
While the enormous scrolls rolld dreadful in the heavens above
And still the burden of their song in tears was pourd forth
The bread is kneaded let us rest O cruel father of children

But Urizen remitted not their labours upon his rock

Page 79. Night VII. Proof: NT 96:28E, trimmed at bottom.

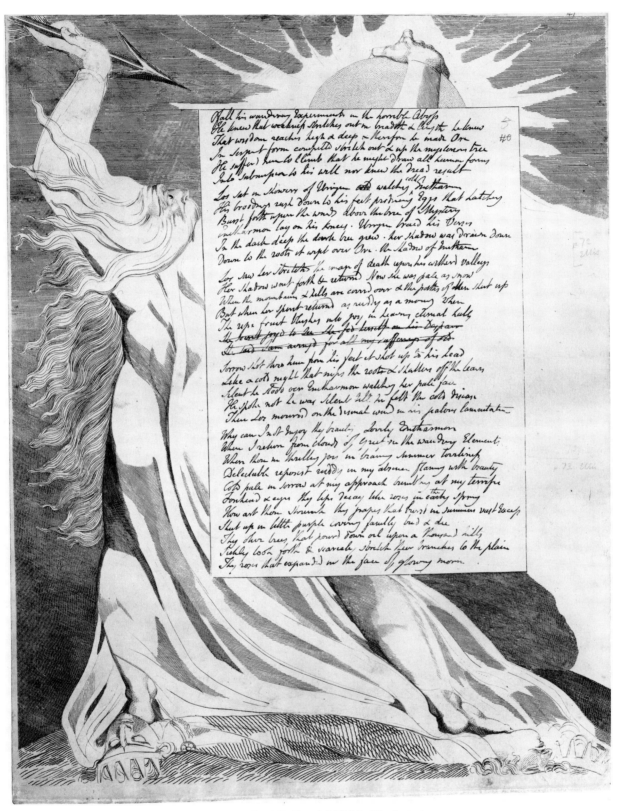

Page 81. Night VII. Proof: NT 20:5E, first state.

His in a little silken veil scarce breathe & faintly shine
Thy lillies that gave light what time the morning looked forth
Hid in the vales faintly lament & no one hears their voice
All things beside the woful Los enjoy the delights of beauty
Once how I sang & called the beasts & birds to their delights
Nor knew that I alone exempted from the joys of love
Must war with secret monsters of the animating worlds
O that I had not seen the day then should I be at rest
Nor felt the stingings of desire nor longings after life
For life is sweet to Los the wretched to his weeping eyes
Is given a crawling cry that they may eat at night on barren rocks
And what their breath & taste the air & watch the opening dawn
And stretch till at the mells of blood they stretch their boney wings
And eat the worms like arrows shot by troops of Destiny

Thus Los lamented in the night unheard by Enitharmon
For the shadow of Enitharmon descended down the tree of Mystery
The Spectre saw the Shade shivering over his gloomy rocks
Beneath the tree of Mystery which in the dismal Abyss
Began to blossom in fierce pain shooting its writhing buds
In throes of birth & now the blossoms falling shining fruit
Appeard of many colours & of various poisonous qualities
Of Plagues hidden in shining globes that grew on the woven tree

The Spectre of Urthona saw the Shadow of Enitharmon
Beneath the tree of Mystery among the leaves & fruit
Reddning the demon strong prepard the poison of Sweet Love
He turnd from side to side in tears he wept & he embraced
The fleeting image & in whispers mild wood the faint shade

Loveliest delight of Men. Enitharmon shady hiding
In secret places where no eye can trace thy watry way
Have I found thee have I found thee tremblest thou in fear
Because of Orc because he rent his discordant way
From thy sweet loves of Bliss. red flowd thy blood
Pale grew thy face the lightnings playd around thee thunders hoverd
Over thee, & the terrible Orc rent his discordant way
But the next joy of thine shall be in sweet delusion
And its birth in fainting & sleep & sweet delusions of Vala

The Shadow of Enitharmon answerd Art thou terrible Shade
Set over this sweet boy of mine to guard him lest he rend

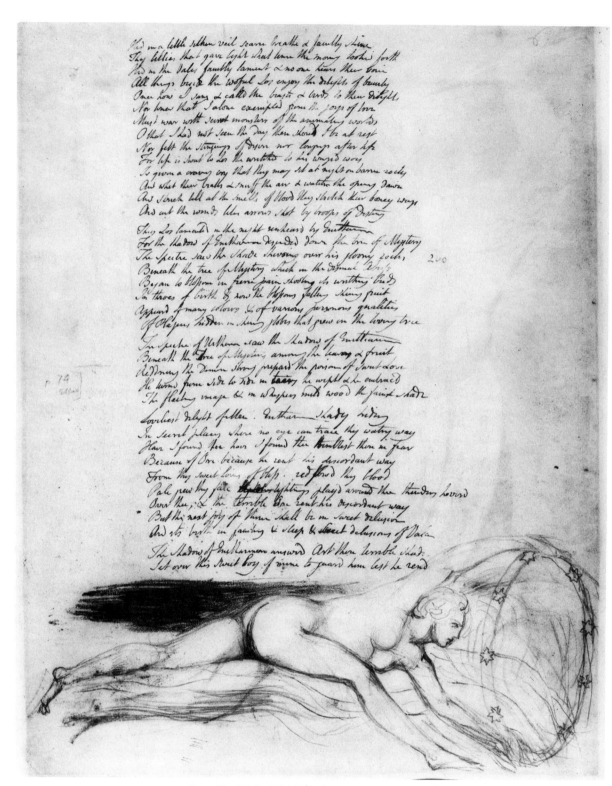

Page 82. Night VII. Pencil and chalk drawing.

Page 83. Night VII. Proof: NT 94:27E.

Page 84. Night VII. Pencil drawing.

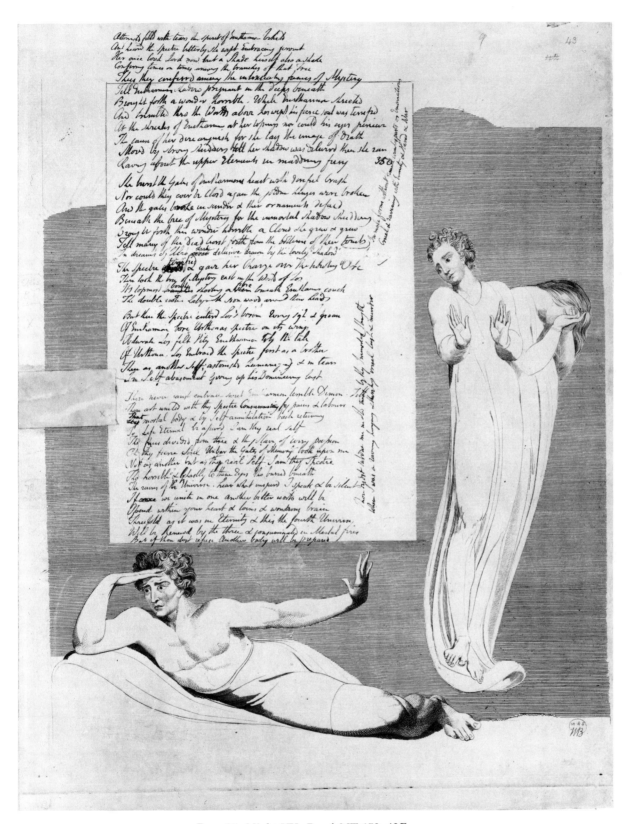

Page 85. Night VII. Proof: NT 153:42E.

Page 86. Night VII. Pencil and chalk drawing with chalk shading.

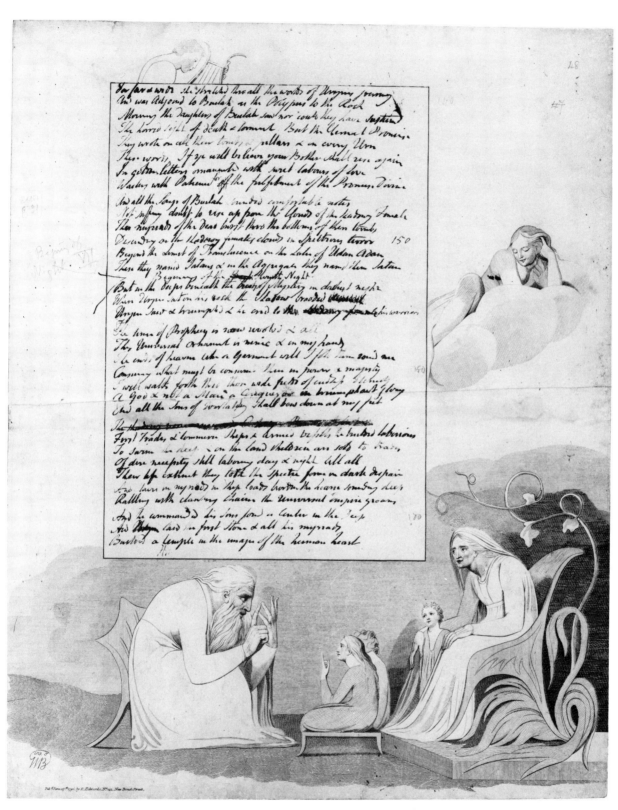

Page 87[95]. Night VII. Proof: NT 64:20E.

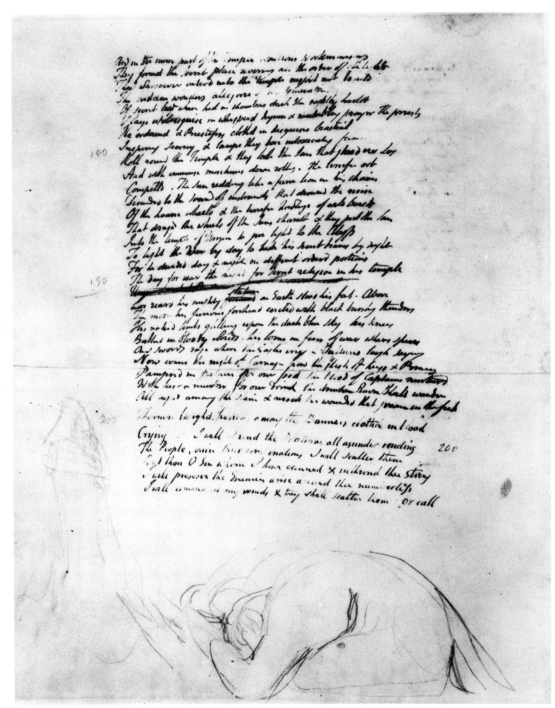

Page 88[96]. Night VII. Pencil drawing.

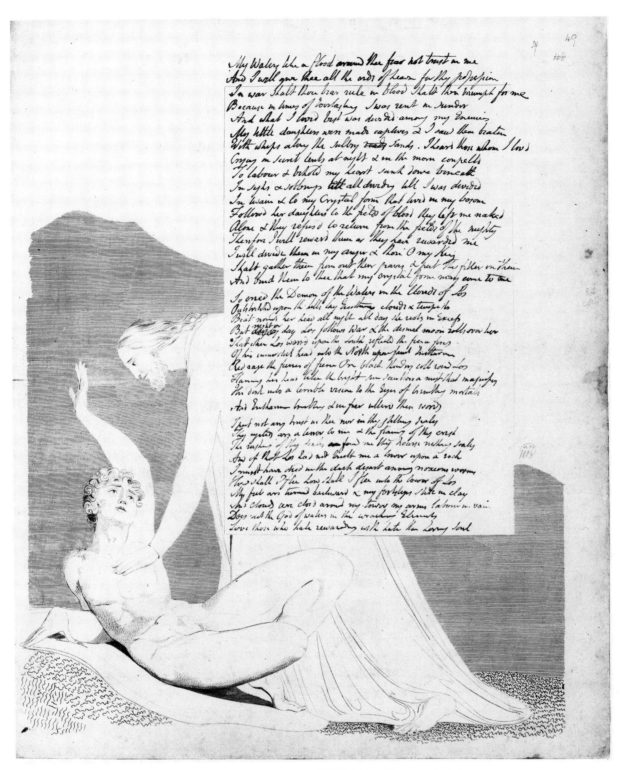

My Waters like a flood around thee fear not trust in me
And I will give thee all the orbs of heaven for thy possession
In war shalt thou bear rule in blood shalt thou triumph for me
Because in times of Everlasting I was rent in sunder
And that I loved best was divided among my Enemies
My little daughters were made captives & I saw them beaten
With whips along the sultry sands. I heard those whom I lovd
Crying in secret tents at night & in the morn compelld
To labour & behold my heart sunk down beneath
In sighs & sobbings all distracted till I was divided
In twain & to my Crystal form that livd in my bosom
Followd her daughters to the fields of blood they left me naked
Alone & they refusd to return from the fields of the mighty
Therefore I will reward them as they have rewarded me
I will divide them in my anger & thou O my King
Shalt gather them from out their graves & put the fetter on them
And bind them to thee that my crystal form may come to me

So cried the Demon of the Waters in the Clouds of Los
Outstretchd upon the hills lay Enitharmon clouds & tempests
Beat round her head all night all day she rests in sleep
But morning day Los follows War & the dismal moon rolls over her
That when Los wound upon the South refulx the fierce fires
Of his immortal head into the North upon faint Enitharmon
Red rage the furies of fierce Orc black thundring roll round Los
Flaming his head like the bright sun seen thro a mist that magnifies
Her dark into a terrible vision to the Eyes of trembling mortals
And Enitharmon trembling & in fear utterd these words

I put not any trust in thee nor in thy glittering scales
Thy eyelids are a terror to me & the flaming of thy crest
The rushing of thy scales confound me thy hoarse nostrils scaly
Son of Roth Los had not trust me a terror upon a rock
I must have died in the dark desert among noxious worms
How shall I flee how shall I flee into the towers of Los
My feet are turned backward & my footsteps slide in clay
And clouds are closd around my towers my arms labour in vain
Does not the God of waters in the wrackish Eternity
Love those who hate rewarding with hate the loving soul

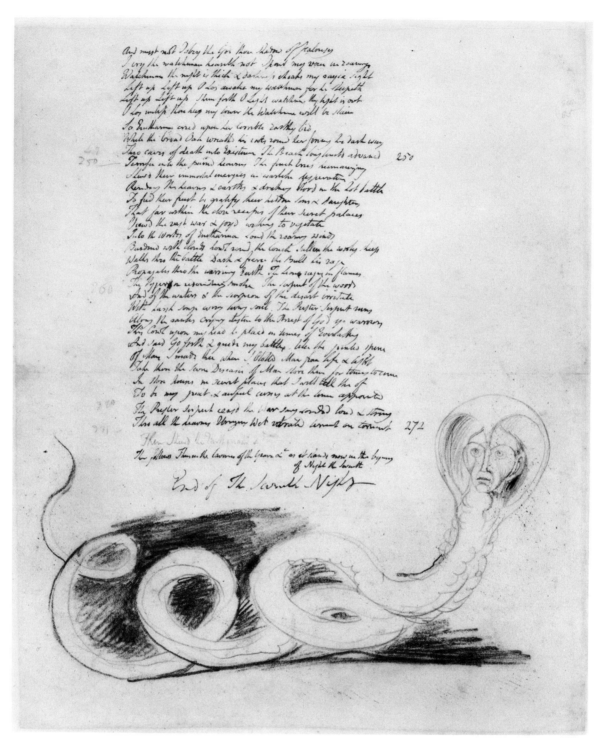

Page 90[98]. Night VII. Pencil and chalk drawing with chalk shading.

Page 91. Night VII. Proof: NT 34:9E.

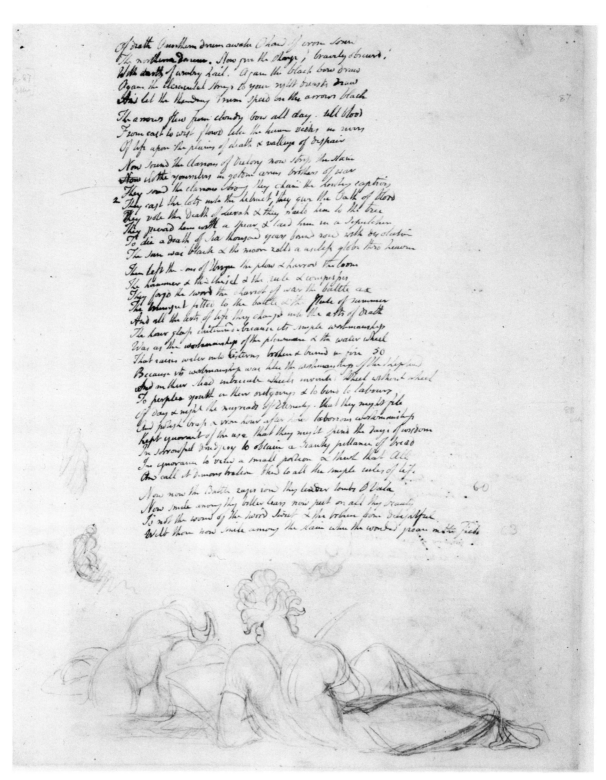

Page 92. Night VII. Pencil and chalk drawing.

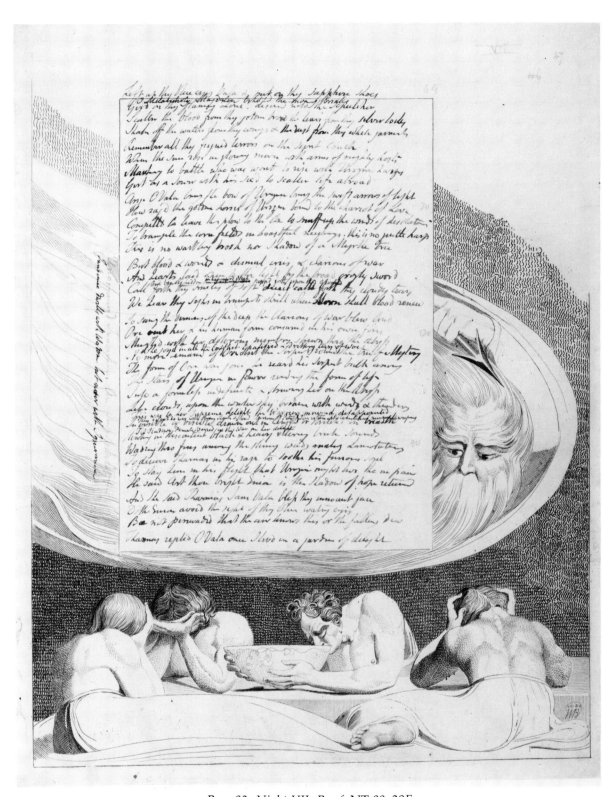

Page 93. Night VII. Proof: NT 99:29E.

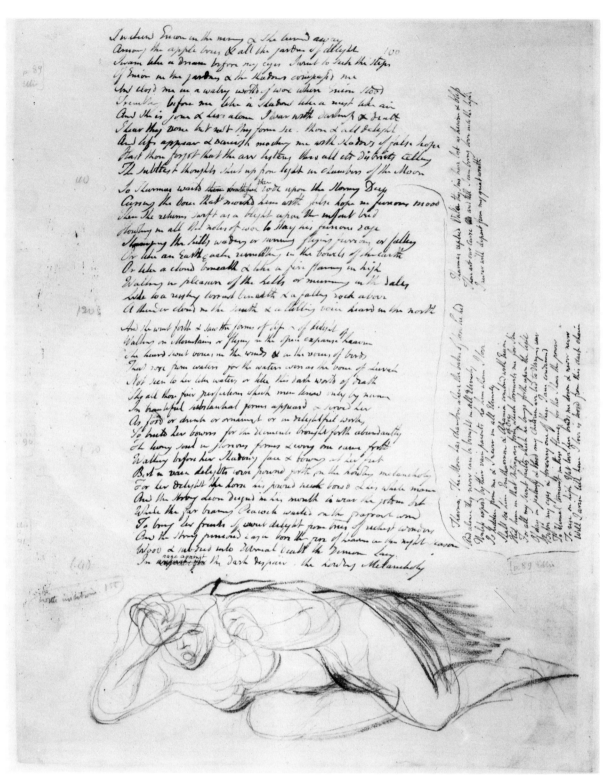

Page 94. Night VII. Pencil and chalk drawing.

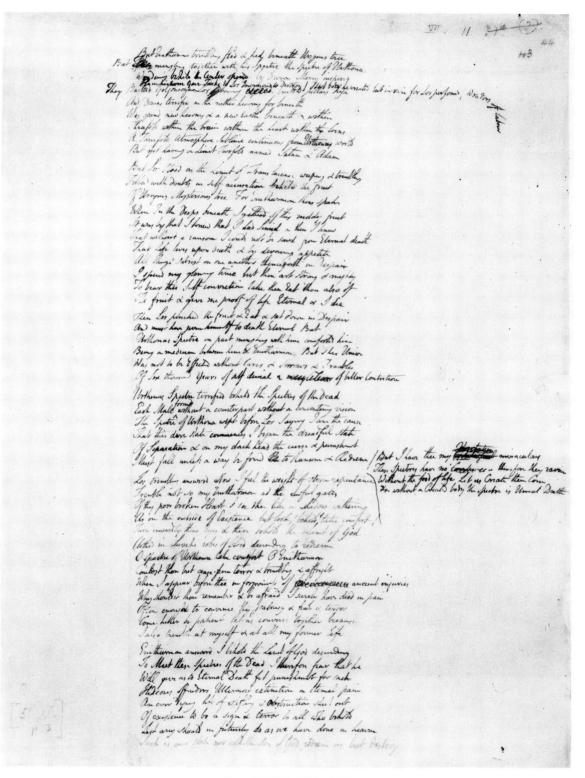

Page 95[87]. Night VII.

Page 96[88]. Edward and Elenor *print, right-hand segment.*

Page 97[89]. Left-hand segment; pencil drawing in margin.

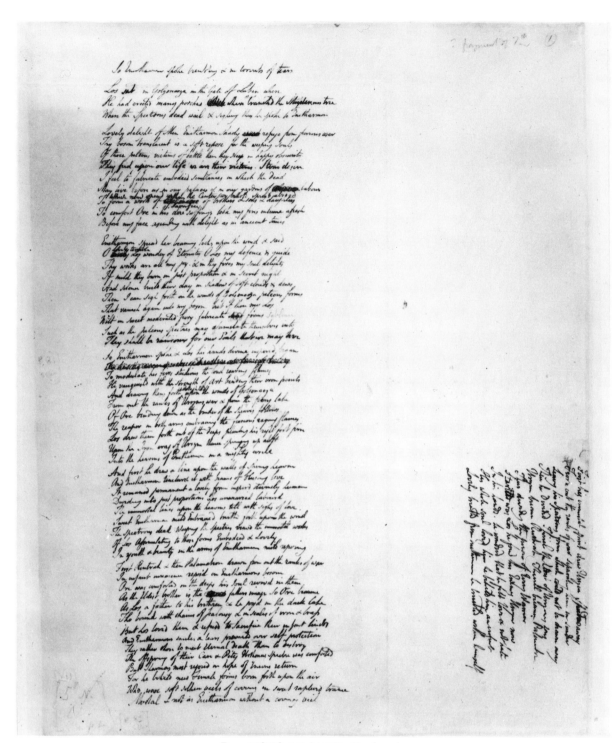

Page 98[90]. Night VII. No drawings.

Page 99. Night VIII. Proof: NT 45:14E, early state with pencil revisions.

Page 100. Night VIII. Pencil and chalk drawing with chalk
shading.

Page 101. Night VIII. Proof: NT 31:8E.

215

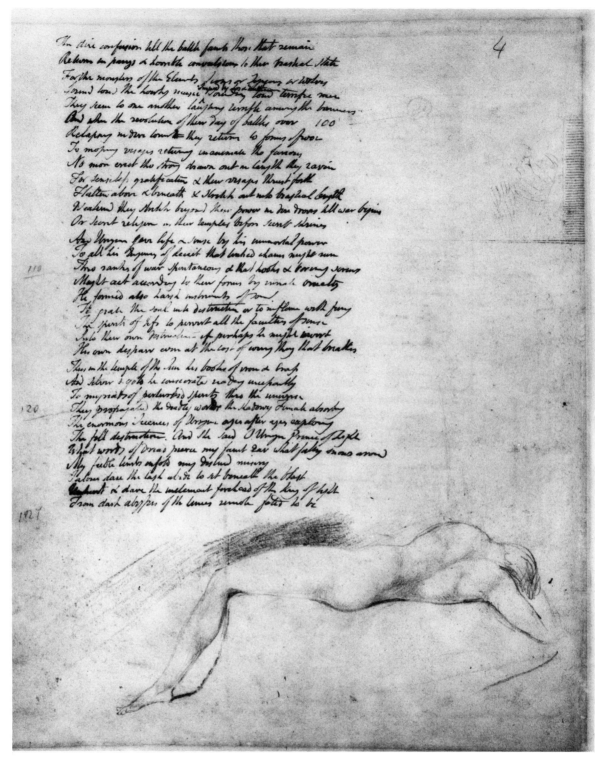

Page 102. Night VIII. Pencil and chalk drawing with chalk shading.

Page 103. Night VIII. Proof: NT 52:17E.

And furthermore name the Female prasure the body
Wondering she saw the Lamb of God within Jerusalems Veil
The divine Vision seen within the inmost deep recess
Of fair Jerusalems bosom in a gently beaming fire

Then sang the Sons of Eden round the Lamb of God & said
Glory Glory Glory to the holy Lamb of God
Who now beginneth to put off the dark Satanic body
Now we behold redemption Now we know that life Eternal
Depends alone upon the Universal hand & not in us
Is aught but death In individual weakness sorrow & pain
We now behold the ends of Beulah & we now behold
Where death eternal is put off Eternally
Assume the dark Satanic body in the Virgins womb
O Lamb Divine it cannot thee annoy O pitying one
Thy pity is from the foundation of the World & thy Redemption
Begun Already in Eternity Come then O Lamb of God
Come Lord Jesus come quickly

So sang they in Eternity looking down into Beulah
The war roard round Jerusalems Gates it took a hideous form
Seen in the aggregate a Vast Hermaphroditic form
Heavd like an Earthquake labring with convulsive groans
Intolerable at length an awful wonder burst
From the Hermaphroditic bosom Satan he was named
Son of Perdition terrible his form dishumanizd monstrous
A male without a female counterpart a howling fiend
Forlorn of Eden & repugnant to the forms of life
Absord according into Orulro an eternal death

Being multitudes of tyrant Men in union blasphemous
Against the divine image. Congregated assemblies of wicked men 195.

Saying the Lamb of God descended thro Jerusalems gates
To put off Mystery time after time & as a Man
Is born on Earth So was he born of Fair Jerusalem
In mysterys woven mantle & in the Robes of Luvah

He stood in fair Jerusalem to awake up into Eden 200.
The fallen Man but first to give his vegetated body
To be cut off & separated that the Spiritual body may be Reveald

Page 104. Night VIII. Pencil drawing with chalk shading.

Page 105[113]. Night VIII. No drawings.

Page 106[114]. Night VIII. Proof: NT 1:31E, second state.

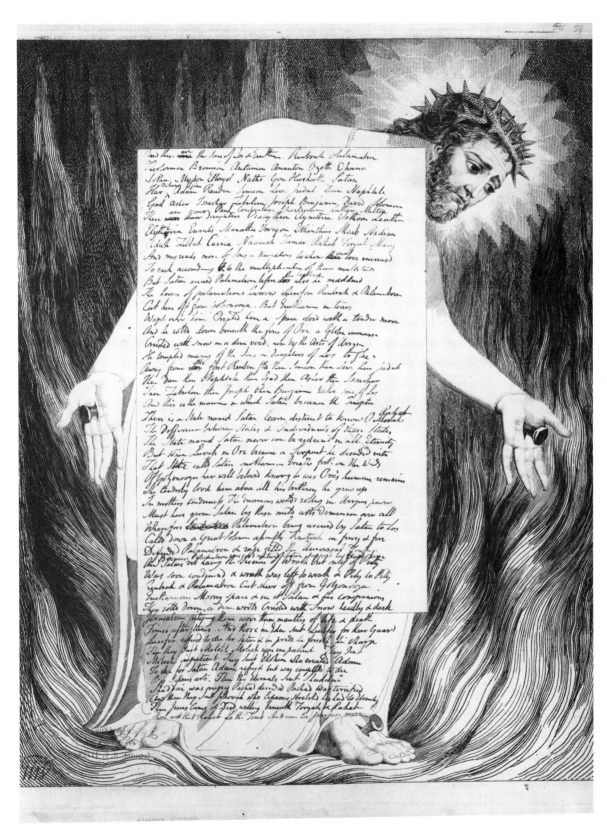

Page 107[115]. Night VIII. Proof: NT 121:34E, third state.

Page 108[116]. Night VIII. Pencil and chalk drawing.

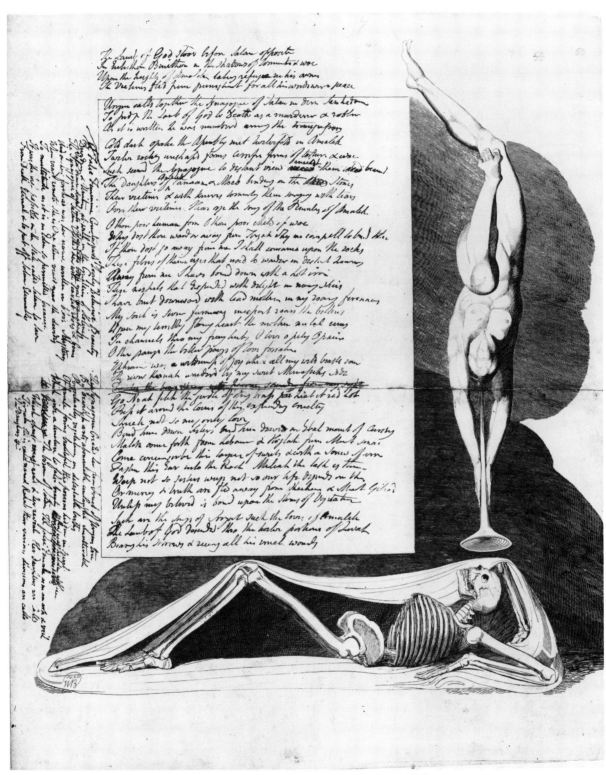

The Lamb of God stood before Satan opposite
In Entuthon Benithon in the Shadows of torments & woe
Upon the heights of Amalek taking refuge in his arms
The victims fled from punishment for all his wonderous peace

Urizen calls together the Synagogue of Satan in dire Sanhedrim
To judge the Lamb of God to Death as a murderer & robber
As it is written he was numberd among the transgressors

Cold dark opake the Assembly met twelvefold in Amalek
Twelve rocky unshapd forms terrific forms of torture & woe
Such seemd the Synagogue to distant view amidst them came
The daughters of Canaan & Moab binding on the Stones
Their victims & with knives tormenting them singing with tears
Over their victims Hear ye the song of the females of Amalek

O thou poor human form O thou poor child of woe
Why dost thou wander away from Tirzah why me compell to bind thee
If thou dost go away from me I shall consume upon the rocks
These fibres of thine eyes that used to wander in distant heavens
Away from me I have bound down with a hot iron
These nostrils that Expanded with delight in morning skies
I have bent downward with lead molten in my roaring furnace
My soul is seven furnaces incessant roars the bellows
Upon my terribly flaming heart the molten metal runs
In channels thro my fiery limbs O love O pity O pain
O the pangs the bitter pangs of love forsaken
Ephraim was a wilderness of joy where all my wild beasts ran
The river Kanah wanderd by my sweet Manassehs side
Go Noah fetch the girdle of strong brass heat it red hot
Press it around the loins of this expanding cruelty
Shriek not so my only love
Bind him down Sisters bind him down on Ebal mount of cursing
Malah come forth from Lebanon & Hoglah from Mount Sinai
Come circumscribe this tongue of sweets & with a screw of iron
Fasten this Ear into the Rock Milcah the task is thine
Weep not so Sisters weep not so our life depends on this
Or mercy & truth are fled away from Shechem & Mount Gilead
Unless my beloved is bound upon the Stems of Vegetation

Such are the songs of Tirzah such the loves of Amalek
The Lamb of God descended thro the twelve portions of Israel
Bearing his sorrows & recieving all his cruel wounds

Page 109[105]. Night VIII. Proof: NT 38:12E.

223

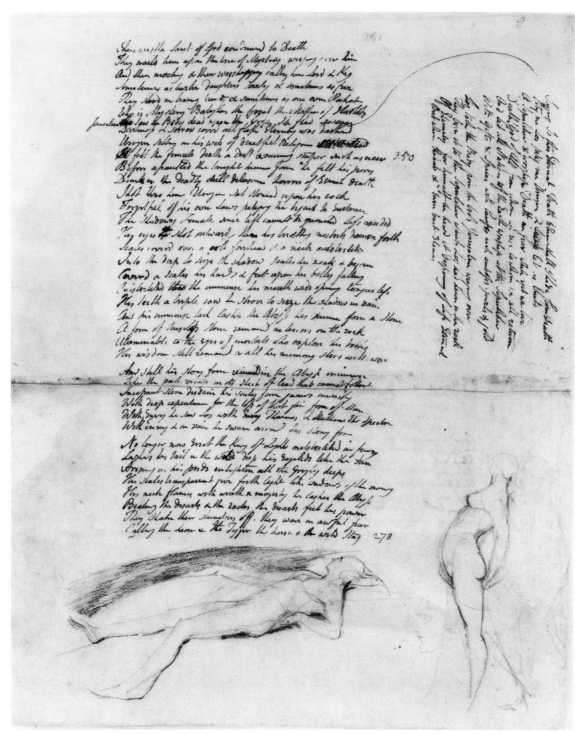

Page 110[106]. Night VIII. Pencil and chalk drawing with chalk shading.

Page 111[107]. Night VIII. Proof: NT 14:3E, second state.

Page 112[108]. Night VIII. Pencil and chalk drawing with chalk shading.

Page 113[109]. Night VIII. Proof: NT 156:43E.

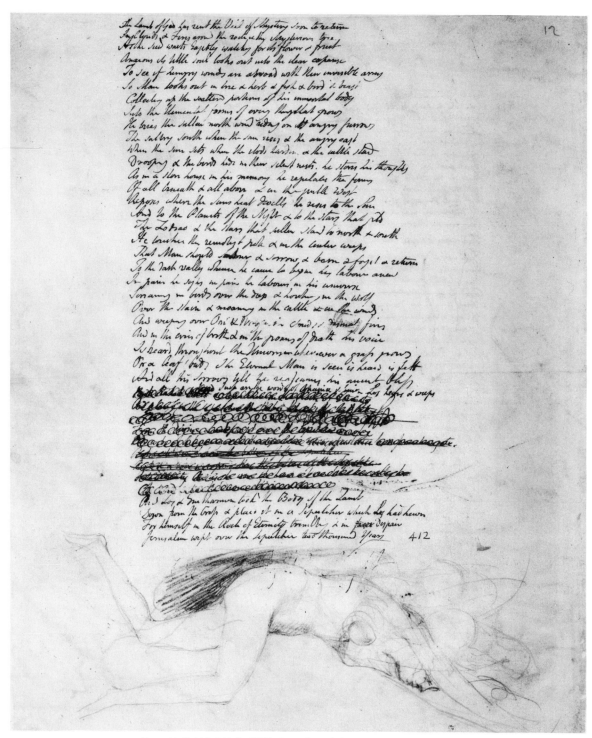

The Lamb of God has rent the Veil of Mystery soon to return
In Clouds & Fires around the rock & the Mysterious tree
As the Seed waits Eagerly watches for its flower & fruit
Anxious its little soul looks out into the clear expanse
To see if hungry winds are abroad with their invisible army
So Man looks out in tree & herb & fish & bird & beast
Collecting up the scattered portions of his immortal body
Into the Elemental forms of every thing that grows
He tries the sullen north wind riding on its angry furrows
The sultry south when the sun rises & the angry east
When the sun sets when the clods harden & the cattle stand
Drooping & the birds hide in their silent nests. he stores his thoughts
As in a store house in his memory he regulates the forms
Of all beneath & all above & in the gentle west
Reposes where the Suns heat dwells he rises to the Sun
And to the Planets of the Night & to the Stars that gild
The Zodiac & the Stars that sullen Stand to north & south
He touches the remotest pole & in the center weeps
That Man should Labour & sorrow & learn & forget & return
To the dark valley whence he came to begin his labours anew
In pain he sighs in pain he labours in his universe
Sorrowing in birds over the deep & howling in the Wolf
Over the slain & moaning in the cattle & in the winds
And weeping over Orc & Urizen in clouds & flaming fires
And in the cries of birth & in the groans of death his voice
Is heard throughout the Universe wherever a grass grows
Or a leaf buds The Eternal Man is seen is heard is felt
And all his Sorrows till he reassumes his ancient bliss

And Joseph of Arimathea took the Body of the Lamb
Down from the Cross & placed it in a Sepulcher which he had hewn
For himself in the Rock of Eternity trembling & in fear despair
Jerusalem wept over the Sepulcher two thousand Years

Page 114[110]. Night VIII. Pencil and chalk drawing with chalk shading.

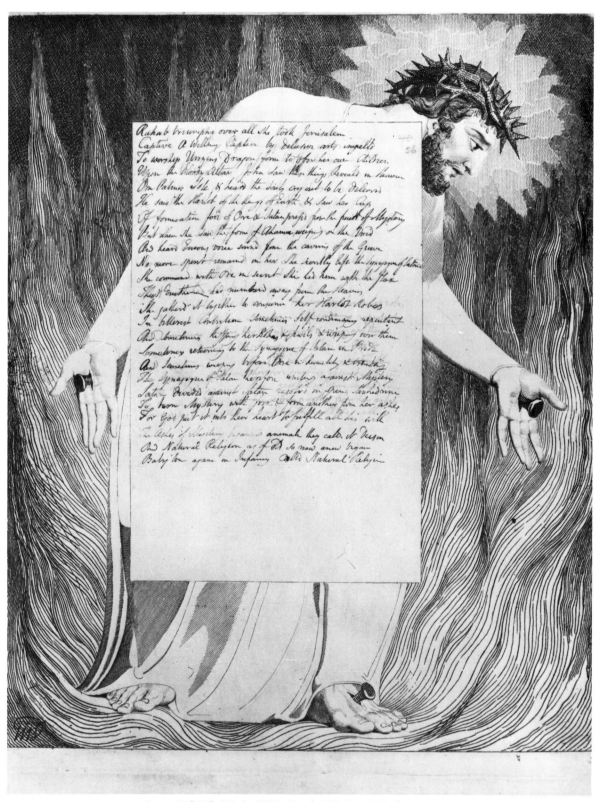

Page 115[111]. Night VIII. Proof: NT 121:34E, first state.

Page 116[112]. Night VIII. Pencil drawing.

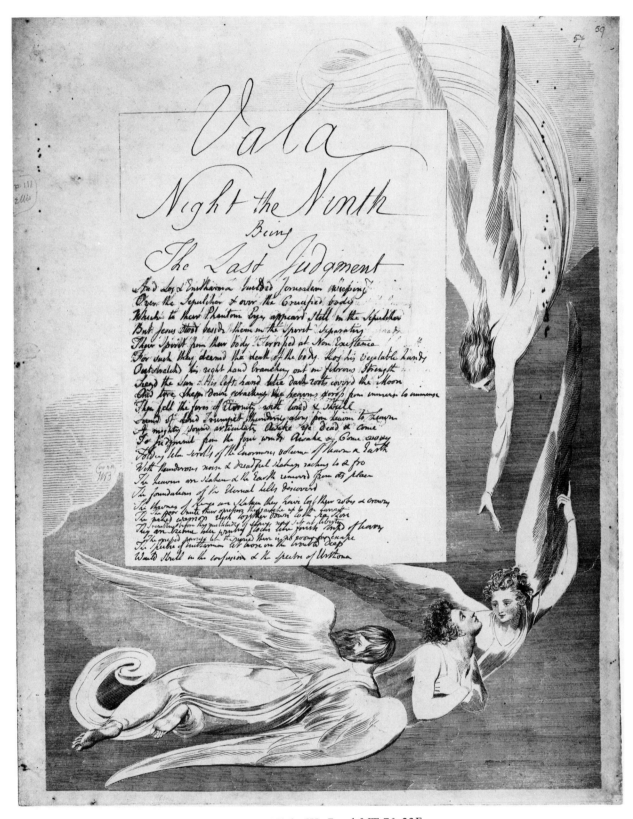

Page 117. Night IX. Proof: NT 76:23E.

Page 118. Night IX. Pencil and chalk drawing with chalk shading.

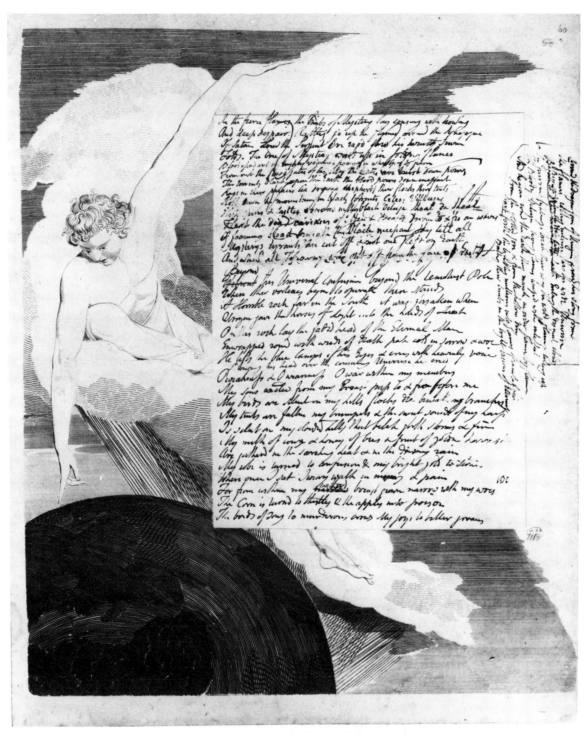

Page 119. Night IX. Proof: NT 141:37E, second state.

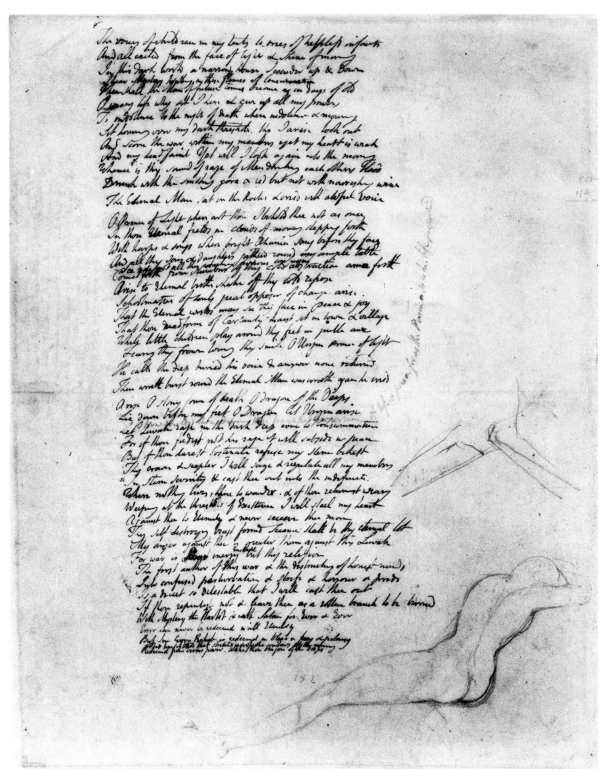

Page 120. Night IX. Pencil and chalk drawing.

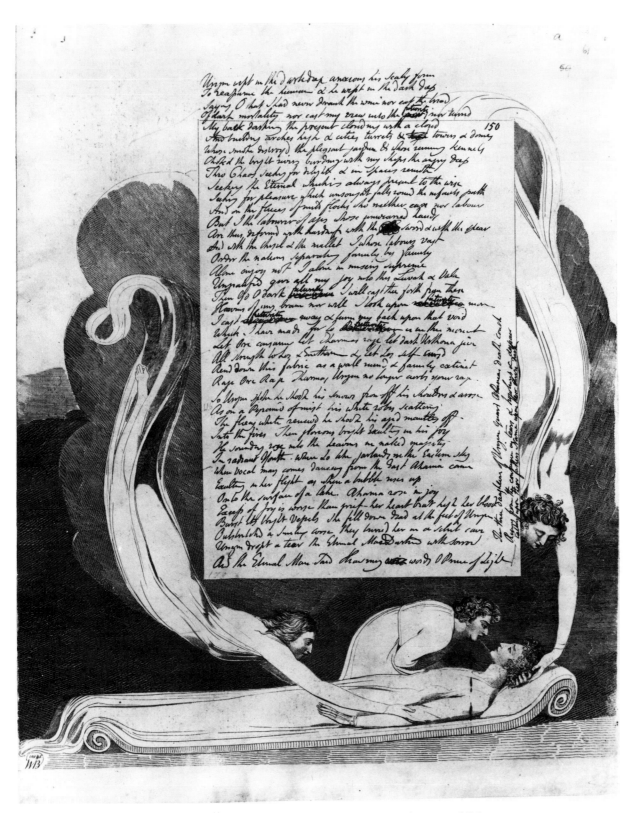

Page 121. Night IX. Proof: NT 71:22E, second state; reddish brown streak across chest of reclining figure.

Blake Jerusalem in whose bosom the Lamb of God is seen
Is seen thro Slain before her Gates he self renewd remains
Eternal & I thro him awake to life from deaths dark vale
The times revolve the time is coming when all these Delights
Shall be renewd & all these Elements that now consume
Shall reflourish. Then bright Ahania shall awake from death
A glorious Vision to thine Eyes a Self renewing Vision
The spring. the summer to be thine then sleep the wintry days
In silken garments spun by her own hands against her funeral
The winter thou shalt plow & lay thy stores into thy barns
Expecting to receive Ahania in the spring with joy
Immortal thou Regenerate she & all the lovely sex
From her shall learn obedience & prepare for a wintry grave
That spring may see them rise in tenfold joy & sweet delight
Thus shall the male & female live the life of Eternity
Because the Lamb of God Creates himself a bride & wife
That we his Children evermore may live in Jerusalem
Which now descendeth out of heaven a City yet a Woman
Mother of myriads redeemd & born in her spiritual palaces
By a New Spiritual birth Regenerated from Death   200

Urizen said. I have Erred & my Error remains with me
What Chain encompasses in what Lock is the river of light confind
That issues forth in the morning by measure & the evening by carefulness
Where shall we take our stand to view the infinite & unbounded
Or where are human feet for lo our eyes are in the heavens
He ceasd for won luck from back he turning Universe explodes
All things reversd flew from their centers rattling bones
To bones join. Making converted the shivering clay breathes
Each speck of dust to the Earths center nestles round & round
In pangs of an Eternal Birth in torment — awe & fear
All spirits deceased let loose from reptile prisons come in shoals
Wild furies from the lepers brain & from the doms Eyes
And from the ox & ass come moping terrors. from the Eagle
And raven numerous as the leaves of autumn every species
Flock to the trumpet muttering over the sides of the grave & crying
In the fierce and round heavens rocky & mountains pilld with groans
In ruffled rocks suspended in the air by inward fires
Many a woful company & many on clouds & waters
Fathers & friends Mothers & Infants Kings & Warriors
Priests & chaind Captives met together in a horrible fear
And every one of the dead appears as he had livd before

Page 122. Night IX. Pencil and chalk drawing with chalk shading.

Page 123. Night IX. Proof: NT 35:10E.

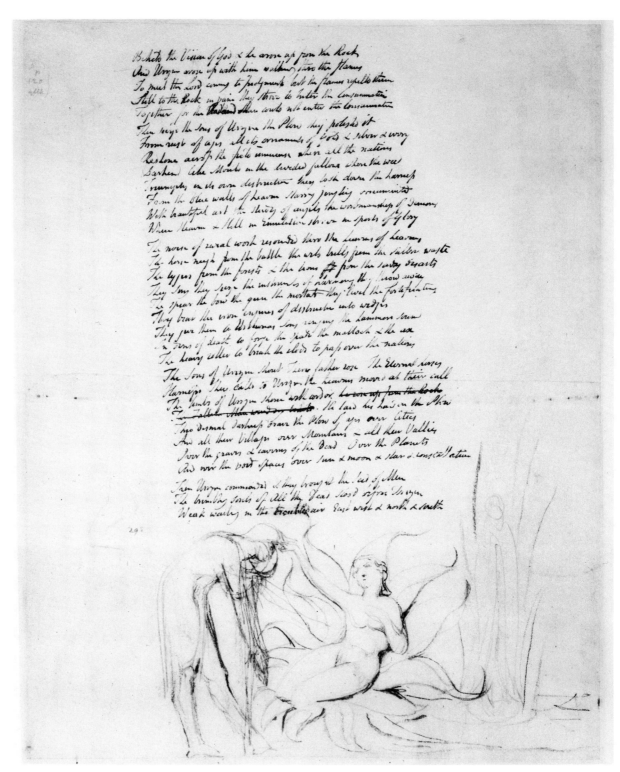

Page 124. Night IX. Pencil and chalk drawing.

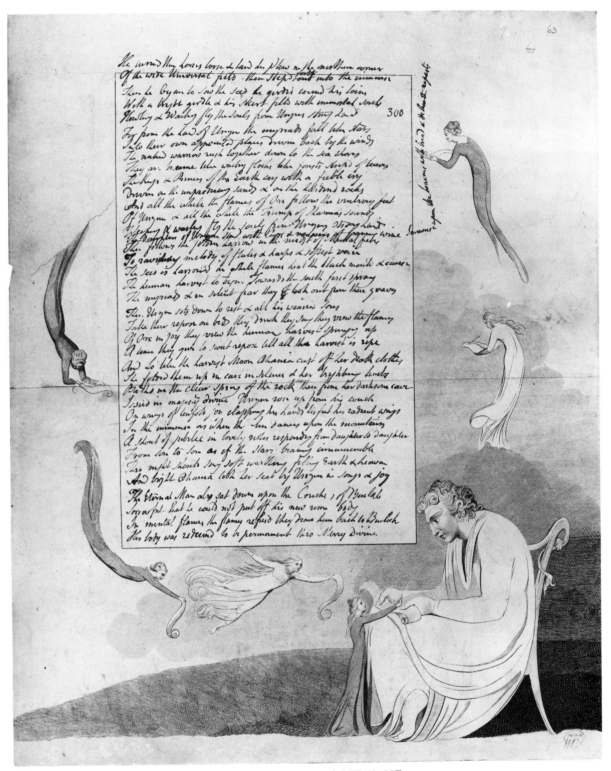

He wound them loose & laid the plow in the northern corner
Of the wide Universal field then stepd forth into the immense

Then he began to sow the seed he girded round his loins
With a bright girdle & his skirt filld with immortal souls
Howling & wailing fly the souls from Urizens stony Law   300

Fly from the land of Urizen the myriads fall like Stars
Into their own appointed places drawn back by the wrath
The naked warriors rush together down to the sea shores
They are become like wintry flocks like forests stripd of leaves
The Kings & Princes of the Earth cry with a feeble cry
Driven on the unproducing sands & on the hardend rocks
And all the while the flames of Orc follow the venturous feet
Of Urizen & all the while the Trump of Hamas sounded
Sweeping & wailing fly the souls from Urizens stony hard
The Bellows of Urizen stand with bows & weapons of agony woven Immense
Then follows the golden harrow in the midst of Mental fires
To ravishing melody of flutes & harps & softest voice
The seed is harrowd in while flames heat the black mould & cause
The human harvest to begin Towards the south first sprang
The myriads & in silent fear they look out from their graves

Then Urizen sits down to rest & all his weaned Sons
Take their repose on beds they drink they sing they view the flames
Of Orc in joy they view the human harvest springing up
A time they give to sweet repose till all the harvest is ripe
And Lo like the harvest Moon Ahania cast off her death clothes
She folded them up in care in silence & her brightning limbs
Bathd in the clear spring of the rock then from her darksome cave
Issued in majesty divine Urizen rose up from his couch
On wings of tenfold joy clapping his hands his feet his radiant wings
In the immense as when the sun dances upon the mountains
A shout of jubilee in lovely notes responds from daughter to daughter
From son to son as if the stars beaming innumerable
Thro night should sing soft warbling filling Earth & heaven
And bright Ahania took her seat by Urizen in songs & joy

The Eternal Man also sat down upon the Couches of Beulah
Sorrowful that he could not put off his new risen body
In mental flames the flames refused they drove him back to Beulah
His body was redeemd to be permanent thro Mercy divine

Page 125. Night IX. Proof: NT 58:18E.

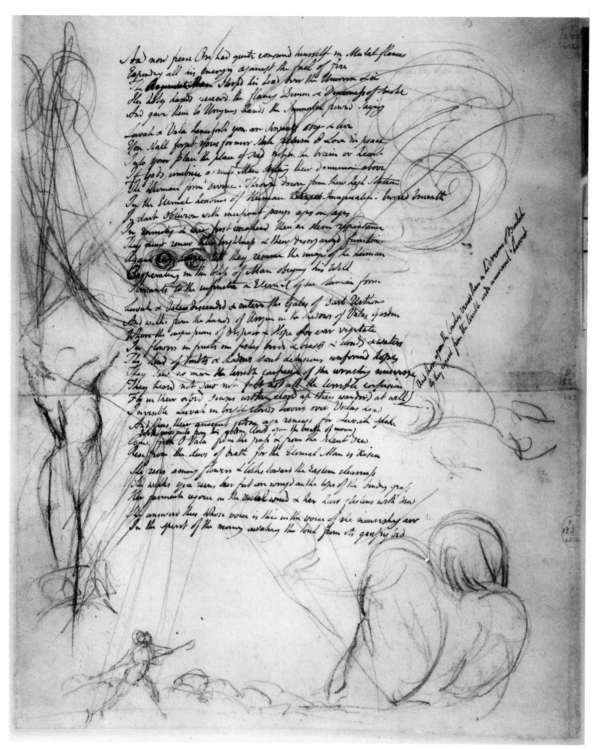

Page 126. Night IX. Pencil and chalk drawing.

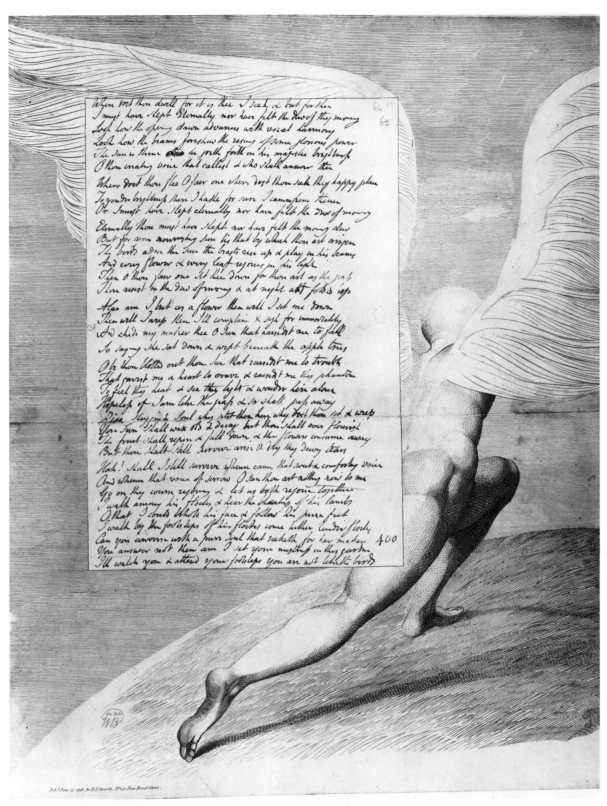

Page 127. Night IX. Proof: NT 46 :15E.

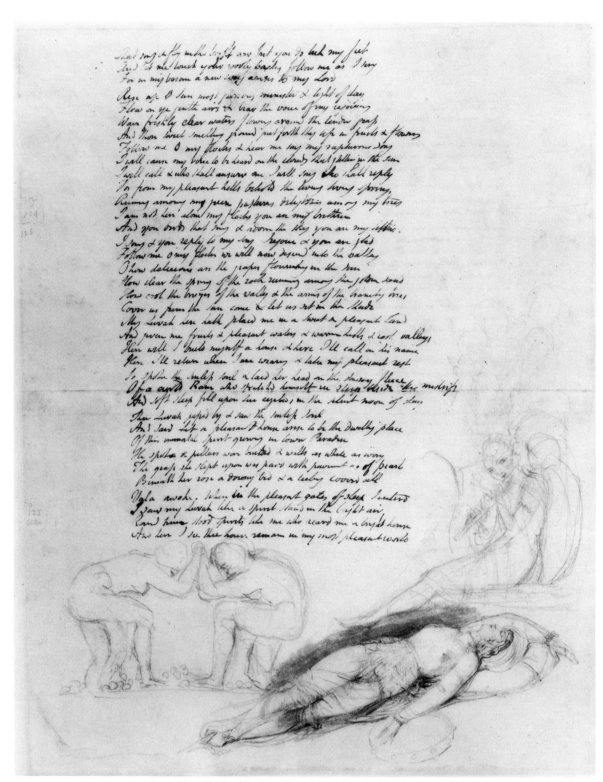

Page 128. Night IX. Pencil and ink drawing with blue, pink-purple, and brown washes. (See color plate below.)

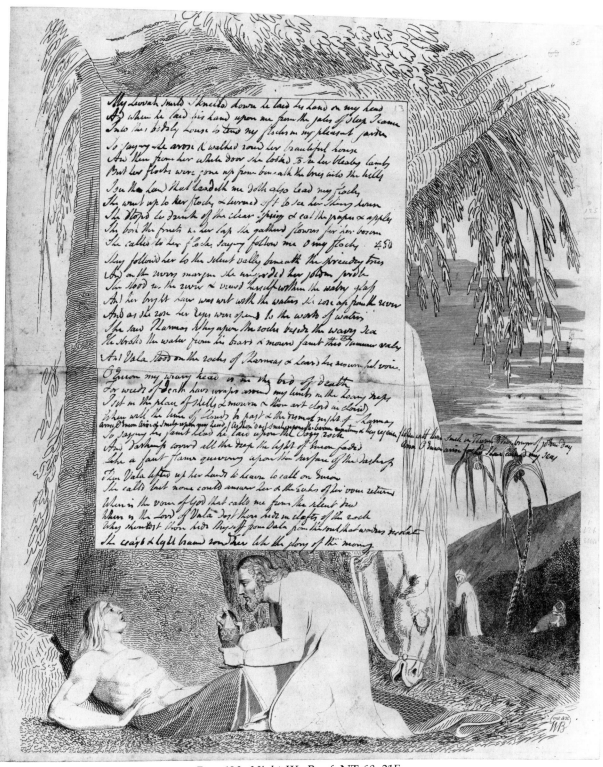

Page 129. Night IX. Proof: NT 68:21E.

Page 130. Night IX. Pencil drawing with chalk shading.

Page 131. Night IX. Proof: NT 71:22E, first state.

Page 132. Night IX. Pencil drawing.

Page 133. Night IX. Proof: NT 20:5E, second state.

247

Page 134. Night IX. Pencil and chalk drawing.

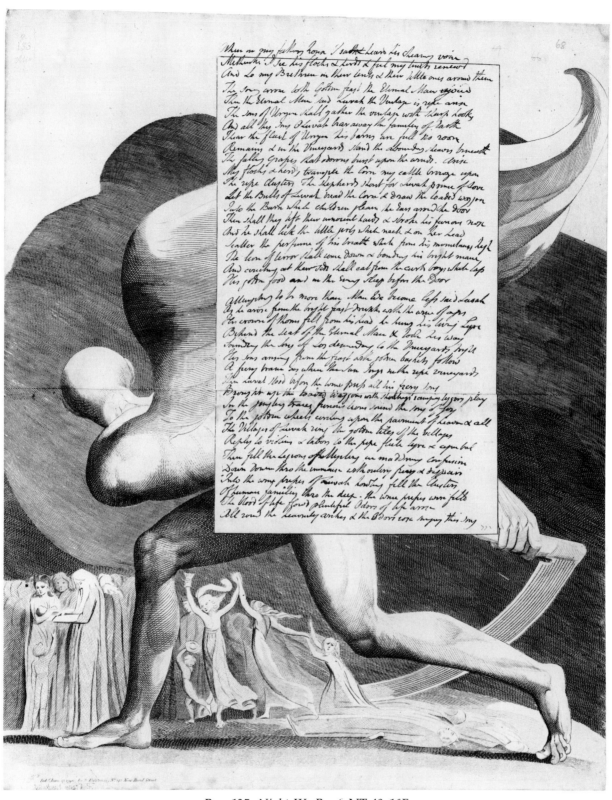

Page 135. Night IX. Proof: NT 49:16E.

Horrible were pangs of Luvahs Caverns of the grave

How lovely the delights of those risen again from death

O trembling joy excess of joy is like Excess of grief

So sang the human Odors round the wine presses of Luvah

But in the Wine presses is wailing terror & despair

Forsaken of their Elements they vanish & are no more

No more but a desire of Being a distracted ravening desire

Desiring like the hungry worm & like the gaping grave

They plunge into the Elements the Elements cast them forth

Or else consume their shadowy semblance Yet they sustenate

The pained to distraction Cry O let us Exist for

This dreadful Non Existence is worse than pains of Eternal Birth

Eternal Death who can endure. let us consume in fires

In waters stifling or on air corroding or on earth shut up

The Pangs of Eternal birth are better than the Pangs of Eternal death

How red the Sons & daughters of Luvah how they tread the Grapes

Laughing & shouting drunk with odors many fall ocrwearied

Drownd in the wine is many a youth & maiden those around

Lay them on skins of Tygers & the spotted Leopard & wild Ass

Till they revive or bury them in cool Grots making lamentation

But in the Wine Presses the Human Grapes Sing not nor dance

They howl & writhe in shoals of torment in fierce flames consuming

In chains of iron & in dungeons circled with ceaseless fires

In pits & dens & shades of death in shapes of torment & woe

The plates the screws & racks & saws & cords & fires & floods

The cruel joy of Luvahs daughters lacerates with knives

And whips their Victims & the deadly sport of Luvahs sons

Timbrels & Violins sport round the Wine Presses The little Seed

The sportive root the Earthworm the small beetle the wise Emmet

Dance round the Wine Presses of Luvah the Centipede is there

The ground Spider with many Eyes the Mole clothed in Velvet

The Earwig armd the tender maggot emblem of immortality

The slow slug the grasshopper that sings & laughs & drinks

The winter comes he folds his slender bones without a murmur

There is the Nettle that stings with soft down & there

The indignant Thistle whose bitterness is bred in his milk

And those who give their lives in the torments of his neighbour then all the idle weeds

That creep about the obscure places shew their various limbs

Naked in all their beauty dancing round the Wine Presses

They Dance around the Dying & they Drink the howl & groan

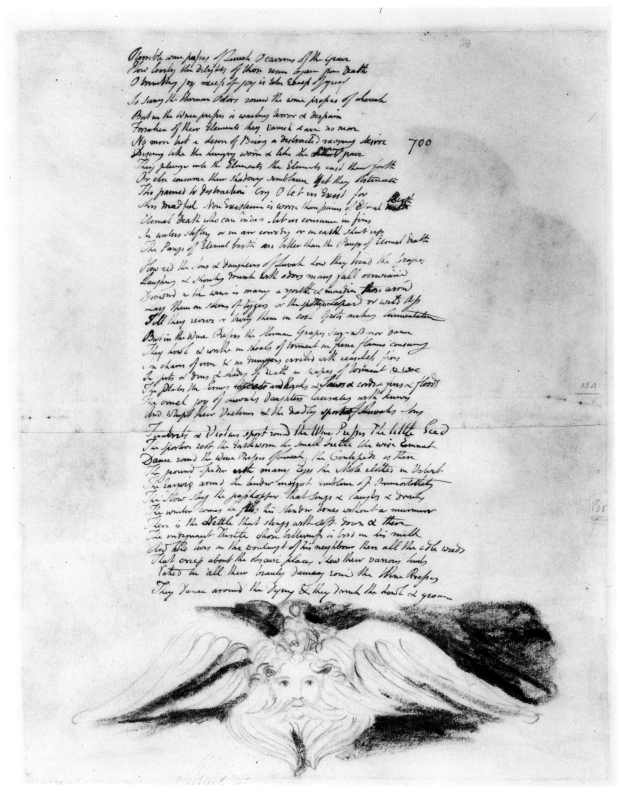

Page 136. Night IX. Pencil and chalk drawing with chalk shading.

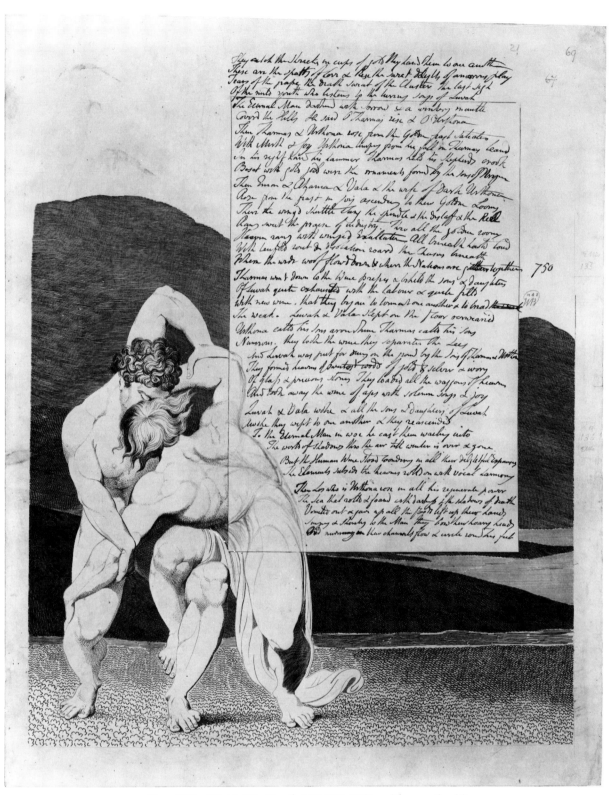

Page 137. Night IX. Proof: NT 145 : 39E, with pencil additions.

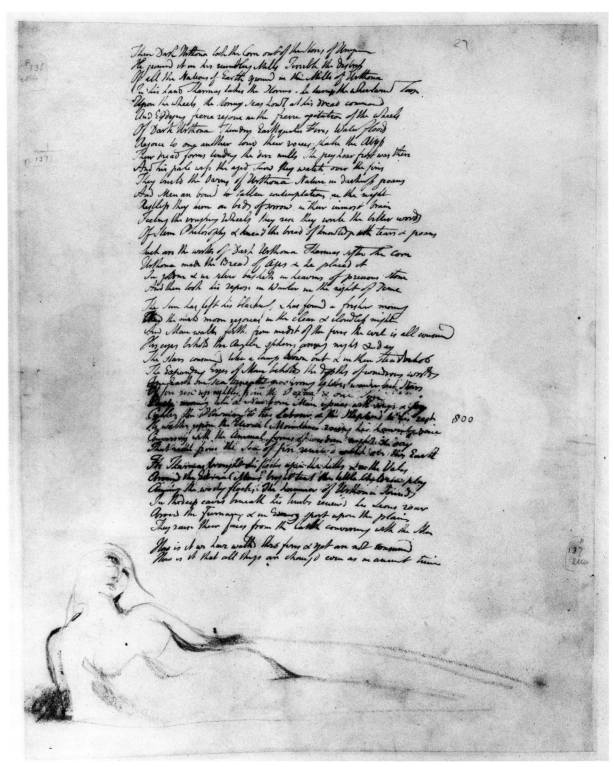

Page 138. Night IX. Pencil and chalk drawing.

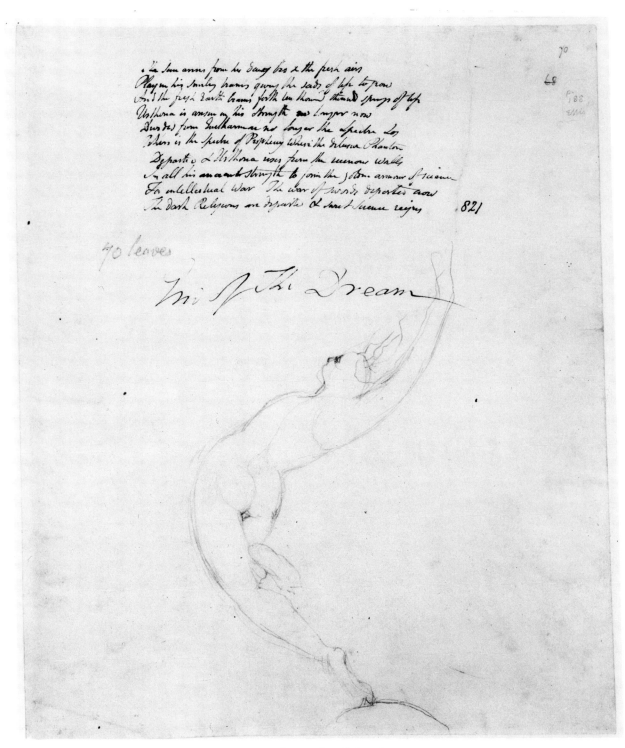

His song arose from his Sweet lips & to the fresh airs
Play on his smiling hands giving the seeds of life to grow
And the fresh Earth beams forth ten thousand thousand springs of life
Urthona is arisen in his strength no longer now
Divided from Enitharmon no longer the Spectre Los
Where is the Spectre of Prophecy where the delusive Phantom
Departed & Urthona rises from the ruinous Walls
In all his ancient strength to form the golden armour of science
For intellectual War The war of swords departed now
The dark Religions are departed & sweet Science reigns

821

40 leaves

End of The Dream

Page 139. Night IX. Pencil drawing.

Page 140. Proof: NT 6:1E, penultimate state.

Vala

Beneath the veil of ~~[deleted]~~ rose Tharmas, from dewy tears

The ancient man bowd his bright head & Urizen prince of light

~~[line heavily deleted]~~

~~[line deleted with loops]~~

Astonishd lookd from his bright portals. Luvah king of love

Awakend Vala. Ariston. ran forth with bright Ahania

And dark Urthona roud his shady bride from her deep den

Pitying they viewd the new born demon. for they could not love

~~[line deleted]~~

Male formd the demon mild athletic force his shoulders spread

And his bright feet firm as a brazen altar. but the parts

To love devoted. female, all astonishd stood the hosts

Of heaven, while Tharmas with wingd speed flew to the sandy shore

He rested on the desart wild & on the raging sea

He stood & stretchd his wings &——

With mantless feet scorring the concave of the joyful sky

Female her form bright as the Summer but the parts of love

Male & her brow radiant as day. darted a lovely scorn

Tharmas beheld from his high rocks &———

Page 141.

255

The ocean calm the clouds fold round & fiery flames of love
Inwrap the immortal limbs struggling in terrific joy
Not long. thunders lightnings swift endings & blushing winds
Sweep oer. the struggling copulation. in fell worthless pangs
They lie in twisting agonies beneath the covering heavens

The womb impressd Enion fled & hid in verdant mountains
Yet here his heavenly orbs be ~

From bosom pours the seed of life & death on all her limbs
Froze. in the womb of Tharmas with the rivers of Enions pain
Trembling he lay swelld with the deluge stifling in the anguish

... mingling their bodies join in burning anguish
Mingling his horrible brightness with her tender limbs then high she soard
Shrieking above the ocean: a bright wonder that nature shudderd at
Half Woman & half Serpent all his lovely changing colours mix
With her fair crystal clearness. in her lips & cheeks his metals rose
In blushes like the morning & his scaly armour softning
A monster lovely in the heavens or wandering on the earth   140
With female voice warbling upon the hills & hollow vales
Beauty all blushing with desire a self enjoying wonder
For Vigion brooded groaning loud the rough seas vegetate. Golden rocks rise from the vast
And they her voice; Glory, delight; & sweet enjoyment born
To mild Eternity shut in a threefold shape delightful
To wander in sweet solitude enraptured at every wind

Page 143.

That I should hide thee with my power &
And now thou darkenest in my presence, never from my sight

Page 144.

257

The Lamb of God stood before, Urizen opposite
In Entuthon Benython in the shadows of torment & woe
Upon the heights of Amalek taking refuge in his arms
The victims fled from punishment for all his words were peace
Urizen calld together all the Synagogue of Satan in dark Sanhedrin
To judge the Lamb of God to death as a murderer & robber
As it is written He was numberd among the transgressors

Cold dark opake the Assembly met twelvefold in Amalek
Twelve rocky unshaped forms terrific forms of torture & woe
Such seemd the Synagogue to distant view around them stood
The daughters of Canaan & Moab binding on the Stones
Their victims & with knives tormenting them singing with tears
Over their victims. Hear was the Lamb of God condemnd to death
They naild him upon the tree of Mystery & weeping over him
And mocking & then worshiping calling him Lord & King
Sometimes as twelve daughters lovely & sometimes as five
They stood in trembling beauty & sometimes as One even Rahab
~~Behold a wonder & a horror~~
Who is Mystery Babylon the Great Mother of Harlots

And Rahab stripd off Luvahs robes from off the Lamb of God
Then first she saw his glory & her Harlot form appeard
In all its purpitude beneath the divine light & of Luvahs robes
She made herself a Mantle
Also the Vegetated bodies which Enitharmon wove in her looms
Opend within the heart & in the loins & in the brain
To Beulah & the dead in Beulah descended thro their gates
And some were woven one fold some two fold & some threefold
In head or heart or reins according to the fittest order
Of most merciful pity & compassion to the spectrous dead
Darkness & sorrow coverd all flesh eternity was darkend
Urizen sitting in his web of deceitful religion was tormented
He felt the female die